TO REV V

BEST WISHE!

FEB. 20, 2017

MW01283954

Our modern world has become a twilight zone of illusions wrapped in a chaos of lies and duplicity. This fine geopolitical analysis of the culture of national and global news and information by author William Eric Cloud, Esq., takes us behind the curtain of Emerald City in its profound explanations, demonstrating how our news organizations boldly distort facts, and echoes Noam Chomsky's famous statement that 'The general public does not know what is happening in the world, neither do they know that they do not know…' Thank you Mr. Cloud for "Deconstructing the News" - and opening a portal out of The Matrix.

~ Tony Regusters, Afrofuturist

Unless otherwise noted, all Scripture quotations are from the NIV Study Bible. 10th Anniversary Edition New International Version Zondervan Publishing House Grand Rapids, Michigan 49530 USA copyright ©1985, 1995, 2002

Published by Black News Examiner, Inc.

Editing, Layout and Cover Design: Karen Bowlding

Includes bibliographical references and index

Library of Congress Control Number: 2014918453
ISBN: 978-0-692-31022-9

Printed in the United States of America 2014

Dedication

To my wonderful, devoted, spiritual, and forgiving wife, Carole, with undying love.

To my grandchildren Cole and Bryce, Jalin, Omar, and Camille. My greatest loves.

Acknowledgements

I want to use this space to acknowledge influences that led to the writing of this book. Above all else, survival takes people in your corner who have your back. I've been blessed with a dedicated group of relatives and friends who have helped to sustain and strengthen me over the years. At the top of the list is my darling daughter and son-in-law, Sharrief and Laurence McGee, my son Evan, my brother Adrian and sister-in-law Patricia, and my nieces, Terrancia, Tovia, and Ebony. This work benefited tremendously from the considerable feedback from my dearest friends Shirley Brookins, Jayna Rivera, and Karen Butler.

The two people who contributed most to my political awareness and development are my longest and best friend, Michael Alexander and my mentor, Rick E.R. Reed.

Mike and I grew up together in Cleveland, Ohio. Unlike most teenagers, we were unusually politically aware for our age. At fifteen years old, we attended services at the Nation of Islam mosque where we were thoroughly indoctrinated; not so much in Islam, but its struggle against white racism through separation and self-determination. We were also drawn by the Nation's Black self-help economic program to fight against poverty and want. Mike and I heard Malcom X speak on three occasions. Although that was more than fifty years ago, I'm still exhilarated by his powerful words. He was and remains the of strongest, articulate, fiery and fearless Black man I have ever heard speak truth to power about the evils of white racism and the oppression of Blacks in America. Those were among the most defining experiences of my life, and I still draw upon Malcolm's words and thinking for inspiration.

I also owe deep gratitude to Rick Reed, my mentor and consummate political activist, for further enhancing my political awareness and education. I met Rick shortly after moving to New York City. Compared to him, I was a country bumpkin, but he took me under his wing. In the summer of 1972, Rick invited me to visit him in Atlanta. Because I was so impressed by the city and its rich Black culture, I moved my family there two months later. With an improbable dream of becoming an attorney, I enrolled in Morris Brown College. My dream became a reality five years later. To Rick I owe a huge debt of gratitude for furthering my political awareness and for giving me inspiration to pursue my dreams. To my deep regret, Rick died in 2002.

I particularly want to dedicate this book to my wife Carole, who I affectionately call Cookie. For a half century she stood by my side for better or worse, even during times when I didn't deserve her dedication. She endured listening and discussing topics that were of little or no interest to her. She dutifully read many of the chapters and always offered constructive feedback. Finally, out of merciful compassion for the hapless individual who made the mistake of expressing as fact something they read or saw on television that I considered propaganda, she often intervened to spare them my lecture that was sure to ensue.

Last but certainly not least, I must acknowledge my appreciation to Karen Bowlding (karenbowlding.net), editor extraordinaire. When the first two editors did not work out, I was referred to Karen; a demure, unassuming, and spiritual lady. Never judge a book by its cover. To my delight, she exceeded my every expectation as an editor. More than that, Karen is a firebrand with a deep understanding of the subject areas I was writing about, and has a burning passion for justice. On many occasions, she offered valuable suggestions and insight that I incorporated in the book. This was a case of divine intervention. Crossing the finish line would not have been possible without you.

In Memory of my brother Terrance…your love and Cleveland-sense of humor will always live on through us.

Preface

Writing this book has been a challenging journey of enlightenment. Before starting, I naively believed I had a fairly good grasp of U.S. domestic and foreign affairs. I soon realized that my understanding of what was going on around the world was actually shallow; if for no other reason than I relied too much on the corporate elite media as my source of information. As I researched, I was shocked by the depth and breadth of lies and disinformation disseminated by the mass media. I learned that my sense of being well informed was terribly misplaced.

This book is the final product of several stages of metamorphoses that started in the Soul Factory, a church pastored by my son, Andre' Deron Eric Cloud, located in Forestville, Maryland. Concerned that his congregation was not abreast of current events, national and world news, he invited me to do a faux Sunday morning news broadcast at the start of service. He called it the *Ninja News*. I spent many hours a week researching news stories I believed would be of interest which were either not being covered, inadequately covered, or spun by the media. In the process of preparing for Sunday broadcasts, I developed a healthy skepticism of the accuracy of news reported in the media. It was difficult to distinguish between the real news and corporate-driven government propaganda. I questioned whether fair and unbiased journalism, to whatever degree it ever existed in the past, had fallen by the wayside. Noam Chomsky and Edward S. Herman accurately described the state of modern journalism in their book,

Manufacturing Consent (Content), The Political Economy of the Mass Media, writing, "the media serve and propagandize on behalf of powerful societal interests that control and finance them. The representatives of these interests have important agendas and principles that they want to advance, and they are well positioned to shape and constrain media policy."[1] My objective was to not parrot the news reported in the mainstream media, but go behind the stories and filter out lies, bias, and propaganda. I sought to *deconstruct* the news.

To make it interesting, the *Ninja News* was presented in a satirical format using irony and deadpan humor, much like the late-night Daily Show on the Comedy Central cable network that focuses on news stories, politics, business and the mainstream media. I chose the Daily Show format because it often focused on the hypocrisy of the media in a humorous vein.

The American public has been programmed to have a short attention span ideally suited to sound bites instead of in-depth coverage. We prefer to be entertained instead of informed. This is "the product of television's increased power over all forms of communication, and that the resulting trend toward short, catchy snippets of information [has] had a significant negative impact on American political discourse."[2] Indeed, during the last 20 years, the length of sound bites has reduced from 20 seconds to 7 or 8 seconds. This constrained the *Ninja News* to adopt the same format, minus propaganda.

The *Ninja News* was well received by the congregation. Church members often told me that they made a point of arriving at church on time to avoid missing it. After Sunday services dismissed, it was not unusual for members to express their appreciation or offer a comment on something that had been reported.

When the *Ninja News's* season ended, I took my son's suggestion to start a blog. *Blacknewsexaminer.com – Deconstructing News from a Black Man's Perspective* was born. This gave me the opportunity to do what I couldn't with the *Ninja News*; more in-depth written coverage of the news. I strove to write thought provoking analysis of national and world news from a perspective rarely presented in the established media. I published more than 40 blog articles.

My friend and accomplished author, Sonsyrea Tate, invited me to join the Capitol Hill Writers Group founded by Brenda Jones, another noted author and intellectual. The group encouraged me to compile the blog articles into a book. This book is the product of their advice. It is a collection of blog articles which have been rewritten and updated to include new developments. It also contains original articles published for the first time. It is important to understand that over time my point of view evolved, making it necessary to revise some of the stories to reflect my new perspective.

It took longer to finalize the book than anticipated because I experienced an information overload. I was overwhelmed by the industrial scale of propaganda in terms of volume, complexity, and direness. I became dismayed by how greed, corruption, and ruthlessness of those at the top have sunk the nature of the world to unbelievable depths of depravity and stupidity. My state of mind reminded me of poet Criss Jami's words in *Venus in Arms*. "In the age of technology there is constant access to vast amounts of information. The basket overflows; people get overwhelmed; the eye of the storm is not so much what goes on in the world, it is the confusion of how to think, feel, digest, and react to what goes on."[3] I shut down and refused to read newspapers, avoided television and radio news broadcasts, and stayed off the internet as much as possible. Three months passed before I recovered enough psychologically to begin writing again.

Many have asked who is the book's target audience. The answer is quite simple. Anyone interested in some of the things going on in the world that has not been filtered through the distorted lens of the corporate controlled media whose sole purpose is to keep the public distracted, misinformed, and uninformed. Everyone should read it! I have no illusions, however, that the book will be widely read. I recognize that not many people are interested in domestic or world events, and don't realize that what goes on in other places does have a direct impact on our lives. The few who are interested get their information from reading newspapers, watching television news or the internet. Americans have been programed to be entertained, not informed, which explains why the country is becoming a post-enlightened wasteland.

But, there is an absolute certainty that this book will be read by analysts in the U.S. intelligence services.

Contents

CHAPTER 1

Mainstream Media Mind Control

If you tell a lie big enough and keep repeating it, people will eventually come to believe it.

~ Joseph Goebbels, Nazi Minister of Propaganda

The focal point of broadcast news is a sweeping overview of the social and/or political big picture of an issue unlikely to feature discussion of the conflict as a whole, or the circumstances surrounding it; avoiding any exploration of social and political tensions that underpin the conflict or event. Problems and potential solutions are often predicated on unscientific opinion polls, spot surveys, and interviews with in-house commentators who are palmed off as uniquely qualified to answer the day's question. An essential part of the formula is to give the report an almost constant sense of urgency, testimonies, rants, and unrepresentative and unreliable polls. Live broadcasts suck in viewers to feel like witnesses to the story, making them less inclined to believe something is being scripted since it's unfolding before their eyes. In place of real news, the corporate media presents nonsense. News broadcasts driven by a quest to distract and gain ratings have evolved in recent years to be more entertaining rather than informational...*infotainment*. Indeed, the media landscape is dominated by programing designed to enhance popularity with audiences and consumers. Infotainment comes in the form of tabloid news, bash-the-guest talk shows, news sit-coms, docu-soap operas, game shows, and mockumentary formats. To broaden appeal, stories incorporate lighthearted human interest angles presented in emotionally-tinged or charged language. The line between traditional hard news and infotainment has been blurred to the point that it's difficult to distinguish between straight news and obvious editorialization.

Every nation has a wealthy aristocratic elite ruling class that dominates its government. The agenda of this powerful group, often referred to as the *Illuminati*, a.k.a., the *one-percenters*, is to bring the earth's inhabitants under the control of a single global state – a New World Order – to subjugate everyone as servants (slaves) to a one world government. Many dismiss the notion that a secret group meddles in world affairs as conspiracy theory nonsense. Anyone who believes otherwise has to be nuts. Since no evidence of its existence has been on television or in the newspapers, the Illuminati has to be a hoax created by delusional people. This view does not square with preeminent historian and Illuminati member, Arthur Schlesinger's prediction that, "We are not going to achieve a new world order without paying for it in blood as well as in words and money."[1] The Illuminati is just another word for power elite; there is no question they are one in the same. Denying the existence of the Illuminati is tantamount to rejecting the fact that a small group of powerful people

William E. Cloud

control the international banks, multinational corporations, influential foundations, and the major communications media, which logically gives them control, albeit hidden, of the levers of political and economic power worldwide.

This book is not so much about the Illuminati, but aims to shed light on its most powerful tool – the media – to define what is normal and acceptable. How it sways public opinion and attitudes to consent to its agenda with minimal pushback. Designed to reach the largest audience possible, the corporate media controls every facet of communications including TV, movies, radio, newspapers, magazines, books, compact discs, video games, and the internet. It secures public consent to domination by keeping us in a maelstrom of confusion. Their insidious and relentless propaganda campaigns are gradually and incrementally striping Americans of their most precious civil liberty…the right to dissent against the government. It has created a culture where facts are interchangeable with opinions, lies become truths, and fantasy is touted as real. The tragedy is that at this point the Illuminati's death grip on the media seems beyond dislodge. Fair, accurate, and balanced journalism is under mortal attack which will inevitably result in the loss of traditional news if not mightily resisted. We will mourn if the battle is lost because it will unmoor us from reality and cast us adrift in a tsunami of lies.

Surrender is not an option, however. This book raises the clarion call being heard around the world to fight corporate propaganda tyranny by, among other things, creating robust alternative sources of information and news.

William E. Cloud

The 1960-70's era of aggressive, in your face, Watergate-style resource-intensive investigative reporting has gone by the way of the dinosaur. In this digital age, news is delivered through sound bites, which over the last couple decades have been shortened from 40 to about five or six seconds to accommodate American's short attention span, particularly for those age 40 and under. Indeed, one poll found that many young people get their news from cable and network TV comedy and political satire shows.

In 1983, when 50 companies delivered the news, Ben Bagdinkian, noted educator and journalist, predicted that by the 1990's, the accelerated pace of media conglomerations would put the dissemination of information in fewer and fewer hands with each corporate merger.[2] His prediction was prophetic. In 2014, ninety percent of American media is owned by only six massive corporations. They are GE, Newscorp, Disney, Viacom, Time-Warner and CBS; controlling what 270 million Americans see, hear, and read.[3] Similarly, just 10 giant corporations virtually control, either directly or indirectly, all consumer products sold in America.

Back in the 1980's there was no network news *business*. The three major TV networks, CBS, NBC and ABC, covered news, but they generally did not expect to earn a profit from news programing. Instead, news programming generated prestige for the network and satisfied their public-service obligations. News programming was subsidized by profits the networks earned from entertainment programming. It is no exaggeration that just about everything has changed since cable networks came on the scene. Viewers were given

William E. Cloud

dozens of channels from which to choose, yet the communication companies were consolidated in a few hands. That created a highly competitive environment that transformed not just TV news, but the entire industry. Today, network owners demand their news operations make money. News programs, particularly in prime time, have become one of the networks' most consistently profitable part of their business. The corporate shareholders' demand for profit ushered in a moral void, though, replacing old-fashioned values of public service that once guided news judgment.

The corporate media abuses its monopoly of the dissemination of news. They have thoroughly programmed Americans through subliminal mind control to accept as fact the published, visual, and sound messages they receive without being consciously aware that they are embracing something they never would have accepted before. Critical analysis and a conscious choice to accept or reject repetitive subliminal messages seen or heard have been circumvented. The media has deliberately diminished Americans' intellectual capacity, and as a consequence we subconsciously react to fabricated stimuli. *We've been dumbed down.*

It is by no means happenstance that the American society's intellectual capacity to critically examine what it is told by the media has been lowered. It's the result of insidious mind control pioneered by Edward Bernays, Sigmund Freud's nephew. Universally considered the father of public relations and propaganda, Bernays relied on his uncle's principles of psychology and mind control to develop and refine techniques that deftly manipulate public perceptions. Bernays aggressively used the modern behavioral sciences to persuade, coerce and manipulate the American public into accepting the corporate-government version of world events as their own. He remains the most skillful and amoral expert of all the experts in mass mind control.

"Bernays got his first taste of the power of propaganda during World War I. He advised US presidents from Woodrow Wilson to Eisenhower and served numerous corporations and business associations."[4] His Jewish heritage did not deter him from proudly acknowledging that Joseph Goebbels, Adolph Hitler's Nazi propaganda chief, used his technique to turn German Jews into a fearsome enemy through a propaganda campaign of half-truths, lies, and manufactured news stories, and then used the created *threat* to justify the Fuhrer's attempt to eradicate them.

He wrote in his 1928 book, *Propaganda*, that, "The conscious and intelligent manipulation of the organized habits and opinions of the masses is an important element in a democratic society. Those who manipulate this unseen mechanism of society constitute an invisible government which is the true ruling power in our country."[5] The genius of Bernays' concept he famously dubbed *engineering of consent*, which was later referred to as *manufactured consent* by Noam Chomsky, is the notion that the masses must never know they are being manipulated. Instead, they must be persuaded to believe that they themselves conceived the ideas or reached the very conclusions the elite wanted them to accept as true. Their aim is to pull the wool over our eyes which neither truth nor the basic values of civilization gets proper consideration. Propaganda renders the public susceptible to slogans, buzzwords, and vulgarly stated half-truths.

"Who, then decides whether the ulterior end to which the public is to be led or driven, with or without its assent, is good? Decision in this all important matter is left to a few people – the very ones who have something to gain by manipulating the public. Furthermore, the identity of these people is seldom disclosed and they are responsible to no one. Propaganda is making these irresponsible and unknown persons the real rulers in American democracy. Thus, by stealth the government through the mass media tells its constituencies what it thinks they need to know. Advertisers use the same techniques. They view the populous as an uneducated, ill-informed mass whose views should be directed rather than allow them to think. Thinking on higher matters was really for managers and rulers who could decide what was best for lesser people."[6]

Not even Machiavelli was that bold.

Bernays' crown achievements were the promotion of President Woodrow Wilson as a democratic visionary and a political force for world harmony to sway American public opinion to join World War I. Equally successful was his campaign to vilify Guatemalan President Jacob Arbenz in the American media as a serious communist threat to the U.S. on behalf of his client, the United Fruit

Company, to influence President Eisenhower to invade Guatemala. The ulterior motive was to stop the democratically elected left-leaning Guatemalan government from implementing its agrarian land reform plan for the compulsory purchase and redistribution of United Fruit's land.

President Wilson pushed for America to intervene in the first World War despite his 1916 election campaign slogan: "He kept us out of war". Isolationist public sentiment was opposed to it. In 1917, Wilson called upon Bernays and his protégé Walter Lippman to reverse negative public opinion of him and accept entering the war. They had their work cut out for them. According to satirical website *Uncyclopedia* "He was considered a complete douchebag during his days in office who made it illegal to call him a douchebag in 1918. He was also a racist douche and a sexist douche."[7]

Because he was such a bad president, there is a ring of truth in its vulgar description of Wilson. For example, he signed into law the Revenue Act of 1913, which created the income tax and made a secret deal with corrupt banksters and Congress to create the Federal Reserve which caused the Great Depression and every other economic crisis since. He also praised the 1915 film, *Birth of a Nation*, which presented a distorted view of the post-Civil War South, glorified the Ku Klux Klan, and falsely portrayed Blacks as rapist of white women and dominating Southern whites during Reconstruction. "It is like writing history with lightning, and my only regret is that it is all so terribly true," remarked Wilson after seeing it.[8] The oppressive racial condition of Blacks in America was just the opposite of what was portrayed in the movie.

Bernays and Lippmann tirelessly worked behind the scenes to improve Wilson's image and gin up Americans into an anti-German frenzy to go "over there" to fight. They succeeded in changing the political landscape when Congress granted Wilson's request to enter the war in 1917 to, "Make the World Safe for Democracy".

Chiquita (United Fruit) was Guatemala's largest landowner, employer, and exporter when Arbenz was elected president by a landslide in 1950. Arbenz's land reforms were perceived by Chiquita as a threat to its corporate interests. On Chiquita's behalf, Bernays launched a propaganda war to convince the American people that Arbenz was a dangerous communist who had to be removed from power. He counseled United Fruit to loudly complain to the U.S. government that the communists had gained a foothold in nearby Guatemala. He got the public's attention by orchestrating a negative media campaign using the most widely circulated magazines in the country, including *Reader's Digest* and the *Saturday Evening Post*. He convinced each magazine to run a slightly different story on some aspect of the Guatemalan *crisis*. His staff wrote some stories in selected cases. "In certain other cases, the magazine might ask us to supply the story, and we, in turn, would engage a most suitable writer to handle the matter."[9] Bernays eventually enlisted the *New York Times* and the *New York Herald Tribune*, among others, to publish articles about the growing influence of Guatemala's communists.

Another part of Bernays' public relations strategy linked consumption of bananas to good health and patriotism.

"With McCarthy-era hysteria in full swing, President Eisenhower secretly ordered the Central Intelligence Agency (CIA) to overthrow Arbenz. The CIA armed and trained an ad-hoc 'Liberation Army' under the command of an exiled Guatemalan army officer, and used them in conjunction with a diplomatic, economic, and propaganda campaign."[10] The Arbenz administration was overthrown in a covert CIA-backed coup in 1954. Sound familiar?

The U.S. used Bernays' tactics to justify fighting in the Second World War, Viet Nam, Afghanistan, Iraq, Libya, and Syria as well as politically interfere and disrupt governments in every corner of the globe. In 2014, ISIS (secretly created by the U.S. CIA, Israeli Mossad, and British M16) in Iraq and Syria took center-stage as the terrorist menace America was obliged to destroy.

If propaganda could be employed in war, it could also be used in peacetime as well reasoned Bernays. He had already successfully convinced women to smoke cigarettes in public by exploiting their aspirations for increased rights during the seminal women's liberation movement in the United States. Cigarettes came to be viewed as symbols of emancipation and equality with men. Bernays cleverly hired women to march under the banner "torches of freedom" while smoking in the New York City Easter Sunday Parade of 1929; a significant, but dubious triumph that lowered social barriers for women smokers…one they would come to regret.

William E. Cloud

Joseph Pulitzer, disparagingly called "Joey the Jew", pioneered *yellow journalism* or fake news...another major innovation in modern journalism. In the late 1800's, the newspaper magnet and creator of the Pulitzer Prize honed to a fine art the use of scary and misleading headlines in bold print, lavish photos, imaginary illustrations, phony experts, fake interviews, and pseudoscience to manipulate peoples' subconscious to conform to advertisers' concept of what is normal. According to a report released by the Center for Media and Democracy in 2006, the use of fake news in TV broadcasting is widespread and undisclosed.[11] The authors documented how commercial propaganda created by public relations experts is extensively presented on TV as video news releases (VNR) by commercial TV news producers. Today's TV news broadcasts are yellow journalism on steroids. In fact, thousands of fake news stories are "produced each year by public relations firms and experts on behalf of corporations and government agencies.

"They appear to be TV news stories, but in fact are biased stories favorable to the corporate or government client who paid for its creation and distribution on TV news. TV journalists commit plagiarism when they take VNRs and disguise them as their own reporting, rather than labeling them so that viewers can see who provided the fake news and on whose behalf. Fake TV news is very widespread but very hidden because it exists as a secret arrangement between PR firms and TV news producers and news editors. The VNRs are very difficult to obtain outside the domain of the commercial TV newsroom."[12]

An amendment was passed in the House of Representatives to bar the White House and federal agencies from contracting with journalists and public relations firms to secretly promote policies through the use of fake news. According to its sponsor, Congressman Maurice Hinchey, "The passage of this amendment is a critical victory for the American people who, as a result of these secret government contracts with writers, broadcasters, and public relations specialists, have been unable to determine whether they are receiving real, objective news or government-sponsored propaganda."[13] The measure died in the Senate.

A recent *Waking Times* article listed six examples of fake news.[14] Two clips were aired on the *Conan O'Brien* comedy talk show involving local news shows provides a revealing truth that what "the media is conveying to a dumbed-down, unsuspecting public differs greatly from what is actually happening behind the scenes...[I]t is easy to see how the mainstream media pushes ulterior motives on the public, and how important it is to be vigilant when consuming consumer info."[15] In one segment, during the Christmas holiday shopping season, 23 local newscasters around the country undoubtedly read from the same script when each recited almost verbatim: "It's okay, you can admit it if you have bought an item or two or maybe ten for yourself."[16] The subliminal suggestion was to go Christmas shopping for yourself. In the second segment, an incredible 51 local newscasters from the East coast to the West coast on the same day gave precisely identical advise to their viewers to: "Don't worry, be happy" when it came to their health.

Likewise, live war coverage is routinely scripted and arranged to create a sense of drama and danger around people where none exists. Correspondents located safely away from any fighting often dub in gunfire sound effects to give the impression they are reporting in the midst of the war zone under heavy fire. The media constantly sends entirely different messages to Americans then it does to the rest of the world. Newspapers and magazines routinely photoshop images of war to influence public opinion. For instance, a photo of someone casually walking on a street with no sign of trouble will be altered with the insertion of a war-torn scene of bombed buildings as the backdrop. This form of propaganda is not unique to the U.S.; all sides of a conflict use it. The takeaway is to use a reasonable degree of skepticism about the authenticity of images published in newspapers, magazines or TV footage. This is going to be difficult because we are indoctrinated at an early age to accept as true what we see on TV or read without questioning the truth therein.

The media is the corporate elite's weapons of mass deception and distraction. The dissemination of domestic propaganda was illegal for decades in the U.S. until as discussed in the chapter on military propaganda, the practice was legalized in 2012 allowing the media unfettered liberty to broadcast and publish government propaganda aimed at Americans with legal impunity. This is a truly troubling development because the government can now *legally deceive the American people.*

News reports are generated by the *political-media complex,* defined as a close, symbiotic-like network "of relationships between a state's political and ruling classes, its media industry, and any interactions with or dependencies upon interest groups with other domains and agencies, such as law... and, particularly, corporations – especially the multinationals."[17] The capitalist media cabal delivers this dribble in sound bites, talking points, and propaganda headline formats full of lies, biased opinion, spin, and jabber. In essence, the news has become paid lying. Sensationalist reporting that distorts, exaggerates or misstates the truth is now the standard fare of journalism. The legalization of propaganda permits the media to lie about vital issues or suppress uncomfortable truths in unqualified support for state and corporate interests. To the public's detriment, the greater good is sacrificed for imperial aims and profits.

It's generally believed that the vast majority of TV and radio news programs have a conservative bias, as does a small minority of liberal news programs. This is a misconception. *All* network, cable TV, radio, and publications regurgitate capitalist lies, disinformation, and omission, and perpetuate the false right-left paradigm that divides people. The corporate media is analogous to professional football which generates enthusiastic fan support for their particular team and disdain for its rivals despite the fact that all the teams are part of the National Football League (NFL) whose rich team owners share in its profits whether their team wins or loses. Likewise, it is of no concern

William E. Cloud

to the power elite whether someone is a conservative Republican, liberal Democrat or something in between; they control the political parties and are going to benefit regardless.

Like sports, Americans increasingly prefer artificial news bias in favor of their side of the argument provided it is pre-packaged in small, entertaining bites delivered with attitude and swag. Instead of having to sift through conflicting, factual relatively dry reports, we have been conditioned to expend as minimal intellectual effort as possible to decipher what's going on in the world. The media accommodates this intellectual deficiency by simplifying news into good guy versus bad guy narratives. It's always presented in black and white terms. Rarely gray. Using half-baked, one-sided news snippets, the media deceives us into believing we are informed and confirmed in our world view by influencing our subconscious to adopt what the ruling elite wants us to believe.

And so nothing is as it seems. Whenever there is truth in a news story, there are lies. Whatever little accurate information is reported is offset by massive misinformation, disinformation, and omission. Wherever there is genuine, there is phony. The mainstream media, therefore, cannot and should not be trusted. Most astonishing is the sheer magnitude of propaganda it shovels out, and the majority of Americans who accept it as true without question or critical analysis. No wonder the constant programing and conditioning by the mass media has made present day society the most manipulated and controlled in history. They've made us stupid!

William E. Cloud

It is crystal clear that the internet is not the bastion of truth either. It's being high-jacked by the same handful of conglomerates that own the mainstream media. In fact, the top twenty most popular internet news outlets are owned by the media cabal and run the same information broadcasted on ABC, CBS, NBC, FOX, CNN, YAHOO, MSNBC, or published in the *Washington Post* or *New York Times*.

It's commonplace to see young people accessing the social media on their cellphones in zombie-like states. They increasingly rely on social media to get their news and information, which is fueling its exploitation as the new frontier for propaganda, fake news, and false advertising.

In June, 2014, Facebook revealed that it carried out a psychological mind-control experiment on hundreds of thousands of its subscribers without their knowledge or consent. Investigating the ways that "news feed" can be manipulated to affect its users' mood, it concluded that when it posted positive information, its users posted more positive comments, and vice-versa; a phenomenon known as *emotional contagion*. A firestorm of outrage erupted on social media when it was revealed a month later that a researcher who authored Facebook's mind-control study, Jeffrey T. Hancock of Cornell University, conducted a similar Department of Defense-funded study on how to quell civil unrest entitled *Modeling Discourse and Social Dynamics in Authoritarian Regimes*. "Hancock's study appeared in 2009, one year before the US Army War College's Strategic Institute warned in a different study, and in the wake of the global financial meltdown, that the United States could experience massive civil unrest from a series of crises it referred to as *"strategic shock."*[18] The studies indicated "that emotions expressed by others on Facebook influence our own emotions, constituting experimental evidence for massive-scale contagion via social networks," according to the researchers who conducted the study.[19] "Given the massive scale of social networks such as Facebook, even small effects can have large aggregated consequences."[20] Using us as lab rats, the Facebook experiment exposes the reality that the corporate media can and does change our emotional response with subliminal messages.

Fake social accounts used to spread propaganda has become a worldwide phenomenon. The Chinese government has long had an online-propaganda program to control and restrict speech by paying people to post upbeat news stories to shape positive public opinion of its policies. Apparently taking a cue from the Chinese, in 2011 the U.S. military awarded a $2.7 million contract to develop software to secretly spread pro-American propaganda on social networks using fake accounts. The software gives U.S. service members and individuals the ability to respond in real-time to online conversations, chatroom posts, messages, blog posts, and other interventions. More recently, the Russian government reportedly used fake Facebook accounts to exaggerate accusations that Ukrainian government protestors were committing atrocities against pro-Russian rebels.

The internet is under attack by the power elite because it does not control it. The internet, the most important source of alternative information, is a direct threat to their corporate media dispensers of propaganda. There is also big money to be made with a corporate dominated internet. Ironically, or probably not, the rule changes proposed for the internet by Obama appointee FCC Chairman Tom Wheeler, a telecommunications executive and industry lobbyist, and approved by other Obama appointees, threatens the internet. Obama's failure to come out in opposition to the proposal is yet another broken campaign promise, that is, his commitment to ensuring equal treatment of all online content over American broadband lines.

The elimination of *net neutrality* will take away the general public's ability to browse the internet at the same speed as big corporations that have the financial resources to pay internet providers (phone/cable companies) a higher fee to ensure their websites run at a faster speed. Those who cannot afford to pay the premium will be left in the so-called "internet slow lane" where the load time for pages will be reminiscent to dial-up internet that seemed to buffer forever. Internet providers will also have the power to deny access to website competitors. Passage of the proposed rules will affect everyone who relies on the internet to deliver products, services or ideas. Fortunately, there appears to be widespread opposition to the rule changes. Time will tell.

One of the most pressing future crisis is with our young people who are increasingly coming from homes where their parents didn't watch TV news or read newspapers every day. They don't associate keeping up with world events as being a worthwhile activity that should be emulated. This makes them particularly susceptible to small, quick sound bites thanks to music videos, texting, tweeting,

William E. Cloud

Facebook and other rapid-fire social media websites on the internet. Consequently, the little news they do get is inadvertent and absorbed almost by osmosis between snippets off the internet, radio play, and surfing TV channels with a remote control. Indeed, "about half of young adults aged 18 to 30 don't have anything that even looks like a news habit, if by the term you mean someone who regularly seeks out and consumes news," observed Thomas Patterson, a professor in Harvard University's School of Government. Even college graduates who were traditionally regular news consumers are now more than likely to have abandoned the habit. Sadly, our growing civilly oblivious young people might not ever learn to be informed citizens in the future.

As previously mentioned, media is controlled by the super-rich whose agenda is to keep us befuddled and bemused with graphic depictions of violence, sex, and consumerism in movies, TV, and music. People, especially young people, are desensitized to real-life violence and encouraged to be sexually promiscuous. The existence of the causal relationship between media violence, sex, and consumerism cannot be creditability denied. The emotional stress and confusion caused by these tensions impairs judgment and increases suggestibility.

CBS's *60 Minutes* Sunday evening news show claims on its website to be "the most successful television broadcast in history, offering investigative reports, interviews, feature segments, episodes." [21] Until recently, this was not a gross exaggeration, but the once highly respected investigative television newsmagazine has been on a downhill slide. It changed its format from hard-hitting journalism to puff pieces that lob softball instead of probing questions to its interviewees. It hit an all-time low in December, 2013 when it aired a National Security Agency (NSA) public relations infomercial masquerading as serious journalism. The interview of its director showed the depths of *60 Minutes'* decline.

The supposedly behind-the-scenes look at the NSA came amid the debate over whether the revelations that it secretly conducted mass surveillance on American citizens and foreign leaders violated information privacy or was warranted by national security. The fact that John Miller conducted the interview of NSA Chief Keith Alexander was the first indication that the propaganda fix was in. Although Miller made the obligatory disclosure before the interview that he was a former official in the office of the director of National Intelligence and the Federal Bureau of Investigation, his affiliation with the intelligence community still raised questions about his objectivity and possible conflict of interest. The ensuing noncontroversial questions Miller asked Alexander during the interview removed all doubt that the viewers were being conned.

The agency's top secret surveillance program gained international attention when Edward Snowden, an NSA contractor, leaked thousands of classified documents to several media outlets revealing that the government was gathering, storing, and analyzing phone calls, emails, and internet traffic of every American citizen. Considered by many to be the most significant leak in U.S. recent history since the Pentagon Papers, the corporate media focused as much attention on Snowden as it did on the constitutionality and illegality of the agency's mass collection of the communications data of American citizens not suspected of being involved in criminal activity. Although Snowden said that he was solely motivated to leak the documents "to inform the public as to that which is done in their name and that which is done against them," media coverage has distinctly tilted in favor of the government's contention that he is a traitor instead of a heroic whistleblower; a strange position for the media to take since it heavily relies on leaks as one of its primary sources of information.

The Justice Department has made it clear that Snowden will be charged with espionage and possibly treason if he returns to the U.S. This is in keeping with Obama's war on leakers which has been the most aggressive since the Nixon administration. Despite promising more transparency, he dramatically stepped up using the Espionage Act to prosecute those accused of leaking classified information. His forceful attempt to control the flow of leaks severely hampers journalists from doing their jobs.

For more than a year, the NSA repeatedly denied that it was collecting data on U.S. citizens. In March 2012, Alexander testified before Congress that his agency didn't even have the ability to collect data on Americans.[22] When questioned about on-the-record interviews with multiple ex-NSA officials who contradicted this, Alexandria categorically denied that the agency collected the domestic data. He unequivocally stated, "No," 14 times when asked questions like: "Does the NSA intercept Americans' cell phone conversations, Google searches, text messages, Amazon.com orders, bank records?" He arrogantly testified that, "Those who would want to weave the story that we have millions or hundreds of millions of dossiers on people is absolutely false…From my perspective, this is absolute nonsense…that would be against the law."[23] Six months later, President Obama also assured us that, "There is no spying on Americans." [24]

After months of denial, the NSA finally fessed-up that there had been violations of its own restrictions on spying on Americans, but that those instances were "very rare on less than 60 people globally who are considered U.S. persons," according to *Bloomberg News*.[25] Glenn Greenwald reported in *The Guardian* newspaper that the NSA wants to "collect it all," meaning it is "attempting to collect, monitor and store all forms of human communication."[26] NSA's repeated denials that it was violating Americans' right to privacy was nary worth mentioning by Miller, nor did he ask Alexander to explain wy he committed perjury in his congressional testimony that his agency was not spying on Americans. Miller even let Alexander sidestep the question about the agency's spying on German Chancellor Angela Merkel and other foreign leaders and organizations; allowing him to pass the buck that the agency was only following orders from other federal departments. He offered Alexander an opportunity to engage in the all-too-typical character assassination of Snowden, complete with unsubstantiated and probably false claims that he cheated on a test and infected NSA computer systems with a virus. The overall impression the interview attempted to convey was that the NSA was

William E. Cloud

the essence of American patriotism that did its job well and occasionally made mistakes, but never intentionally violated citizens' right to privacy. A big fat lie.

Another example of its decline occurred on the evening before Cyber Monday, the biggest online shopping day of the year, when *60 Minutes* coincidently aired a 15-minute primetime segment about Amazon, the largest online retailor in the world. The infamous interview of Amazon founder Jeff Bezos by Charlie Rose amounted to a spectacular public relations bonanza for the company. The suspicious timing of the broadcast on Cyber Monday eve raised questions about the show's journalist integrity. The high or low point of the interview, depending on one's perspective, came when Bezos dramatically revealed that Amazon was developing drone technology which would someday give it the capability to deliver packages directly to customers' homes. Rose gushed and appeared to find it difficult to contain his excitement. Bezos failed to mention that the use of drones as a delivery system in America's crowded airspace is a long way off, if ever. Still, it was a public relations jackpot for Amazon.

Another phony story aired on *60 Minutes* claimed that the Social Security Disability Insurance (SSDI) is dramatically growing out of control and full of fraud and scammers. These claims are Tea Party talking points palmed off as fact. The show's producers obviously did not fact-check the story or consulted an official of the Social Security Administration beforehand. Instead, they interviewed Senator Tom Coburn, an ultra-conservative proponent of fiscal austerity, who cited as authority his own "investigation" and his "commonsense" about the "scalawags" ripping-off Social Security. His obvious bias did not concern *60 Minutes* interviewer Steve Kroft, but *The Nation's* George Zornick ridiculed the "evidence-by-anecdote" focus of the story:

"The report by Steve Kroft made big promises, purporting to reveal a 'secret welfare system' with its own 'disability industrial complex,' and an out-of-control bureaucracy 'ravaged by waste and fraud.' He also said SSDI might be 'the first government benefits program to run out of money.' But when it came time to deliver, Kroft didn't have the goods...."[27]

SSDI is part of the Social Security program that the vast majority of older Americans rely on for retirement benefits. Disability insurance pays "monthly benefits to workers who are no longer able to work due to a significant illness or impairment that is expected to last at least a year or to result in death within a year." To be eligible, a disabled worker must have worked in jobs covered by Social Security and must have paid into the Social Security Trust Fund through payroll taxes. Benefits are based on the disabled worker's past earnings. Thus, the benefits are *earned* as opposed to government entitlements like, say, food stamps. In June, 2014, more than nine million disabled workers received benefits.

The report skimmed over the most salient fact that the aging of the massive baby-boomer population, the millions of long-term unemployed, and the spike in the number of women who recently joined the workforce is responsible for the increased number of people in the program. It's inevitable that there will instances of fraud in a program that large, but the program has very strict requirements and denies far more people than it approves; evidenced by the proliferation of law firm television commercials offering assistance to appeal the denial of benefits. The *60 Minutes* piece was part of the government's propaganda campaign to convince the public that the Disability Insurance program is broken and will become insolvent by 2016, as purported by the Heritage Foundation, a conservative think tank.[28]

Claiming that spending on the program has doubled since 2000, it predicts that when the fund bankrupts, an average 20 percent cut in benefits will lower the dependent retirees' income to below the federal poverty level. It disputes the expansion is due to demographic factors or changes in the labor force. "Rather, as DI benefits have become more accessible and more valuable, individuals have increasingly turned to DI as an early retirement and long-term unemployment program."[29] The *60 Minutes* interview echoed this conservative line of unsubstantiated bull**it in concert with the government's effort to persuade people to accept further restrictions and reductions of disability and Social Security benefits based on government lies and corporate greed. *60 Minutes'* reputation for hard-hitting journalism has faded.

Whereas *60 Minutes* had a reputation for journalistic integrity, the Sunday morning news political interview programs such as CBS's *Face the Nation*, NBC's *Meet the Press*, ABC's *This Week*, and

CNN's *State of the Union*, have always been government propaganda platforms that more conservative Republican guests appear than Democrats, progressives, and independents combined. A 2006 *Media Matters* study examined the political affiliations of 7,000 guests who appeared on the Sunday morning news shows said: "The conclusion is clear: Republicans and conservatives have been offered more opportunities to appear on the Sunday shows – in some cases, dramatically so."[30] Mind you, the ruling class is not concerned one whit which party gets more air time because it controls them and the American political process. Political parties exist to give the illusion of democracy and is a tactic to create dissention among the people.

The same practice prevails on all of the network and cable news programs. For example, when the Islamic State of Iraq and Syria (ISIS) invaded Iraq, CNN gave significant airtime to a group of pro-war pundits, hawkish politicians, and former generals to opine on its emergence and the danger the Jihad group posed to the region. In an eight day span from June 12-19, 2014 CNN featured 30 guests who discussed the situation in either one-on-one interviews or roundtable segments. The guests included eight former military officials, five former Bush administration officials, hawkish politicians, five pundits, eight CNN journalists, including Pentagon reporters and correspondents, a current State Department spokesperson, and a former CIA analyst. The majority of guests were dead wrong when they supported and played a large role in inducing the American people to accept the illegal invasion of Iraq in 2003 even though a fool could have figured out that the Bush administration's justification for going to war with Iraq was based on lies. There is no good reason to believe their opinions are any more reliable or any less militaristic now than they were then.

Senator John McCain, a stalwart warmonger, is on the "A-List" of the Sunday morning government propaganda television broadcasts because he can be counted on to pontificate in favor of U.S. military intervention in most overseas conflicts. Nothing in his background, however, suggests he has the intellectual abilities required of a bono fide expert. McCain's high school academic record was lackluster. Despite his less than outstanding performance in high school, he was accepted to the U.S. Naval Academy on the strength of his father being a retired admiral. McCain graduated in 1965 just four slots from the bottom of his class – 790 out of 795.

Flying a fighter jets requires above average intelligence and skill. McCain possessed neither, but was accepted into the Navel flight school where he was considered a "party man" and a "subpar-flier". A "Top Gun" pilot he was not. In fact, his record as a fighter jet pilot was abysmal. He crashed and damaged *five* jets! The first crash was ruled pilot error. McCain insisted that it was due to engine failure. The investigation of the second crash found that it was caused by engine failure; a rare occurrence. He destroyed a third plane on the deck of USS Forrestal aircraft carrier when he accidently caused the firing of a missile that ignited a disastrous fire…killing 134 sailors. He lost the fourth plane during a bombing mission in Viet Nam over Hanoi. Ace McCain admitted that he was "daredevil clowning" when he flew a fifth jet into power lines.

William E. Cloud

McCain's Rambo attitude is obviously lingering posttraumatic stress emanating from captivity under inhuman conditions as a prisoner in North Viet Nam for five years. He is clearly embittered, and rightly so, by the ill treatment he received. Consequently, he believes that U.S. national interests are always at stake in every overseas conflict, and is unsurprisingly hawkish and gun-ho when it comes to going to war against third world nations that get out of line. In the final analysis, McCain's pedestrian intellect and propensity to favor killing people renders him incapable of offering an objective opinion on matters of war. Dumbness is innate, intelligence cannot be acquired. It is precisely for this reason that the mainstream media routinely seeks his opinion as to how the U.S. should conduct its military foreign policy. It's also important to note that McCain and his wife, Cindy McCain – like many other hawks – are war profiteers. Cindy's leaked tax returns shows that Hensley & Co., her large Anheuser-Busch beer distribution firm, earned millions from military procurement contracts during the Iraq war.[31] McCain, therefore, has a financial incentive to promote war because it fills his pockets with blood-soaked shekels.

Other rabid warmongers like Republican South Carolina Senator Lindsey "Sugar Britches" Graham, and former Vice President and war criminal Dick Cheney are also trusty jingoists the mainstream media counts on to advocate a militaristic American foreign policy.

Nancy Grace is the wicked witch and bottom-feeder of the tabloid television news genre. She is even beneath FOX's dishonest, neo-con clown princes of political spin, Bill O'Reilly and Sean Hannity.

William E. Cloud

Grace is legendary for being a rude, obnoxious know-it-all who is so full of herself that she incredibly believes her opinions actually make a difference. Her current affairs show on Headline News (HLN*)*, CNN's sister network, focuses on scandal, gossip, and human interest features with sensational twists. A former prosecutor, Grace's television career began on *CourtTV* as a co-host with famed defense attorney Johnnie Cochran. Within months after the premiere of *Cochran & Grace* the network decided to split the team up reportedly because the volatile Grace was unable to get along with even-tempered Cochran's resistance to a muckraking format. Nancy's explanation for moving on was that, "Johnnie and I just don't like the crossfire, the arguing back and forth."[32]

Grace describes herself as being "all about crime and justice…my goal has and always will be helping to find missing people, especially children, and helping solve homicides and highlight [criminal] cases I think people should know about." She deludes herself into believing that her nightly mud-raking gabfest solves crimes. This is unlikely since in her view is that everyone accused of a crime is guilty, and proceeds to inundate her fanatical followers with factual distortions, reckless, inflammatory and derogatory comments about defendants, their lawyers, and the criminal justice system. Nancy convicts people accused of a crime in the court of public opinion. This tends to erode public confidence in the American justice system as well as violate the fundamental constitutional guarantee of the right to be presumed innocent until proven guilty in a court of law. The most disturbing and sad aspect of her show is its popularity and that it is still on the air. In today's corporate media world, slime gets high ratings, and profits eclipses journalistic integrity.

Arts and entertainment are also used as mechanisms to deliver propaganda. They are ideal instruments for social engineering because they can influence people's thinking process without them being aware of it. Hence, television's programing departments and newspaper editorial boards transmit and print the oldest form of communication – *story-telling* – about how society works and what's right and wrong. A good story always trumps truth should be the media's motto.

Since perception and reality can be altered by manipulating peoples' minds through entertaining stories, television producers clutter the airways with an avalanche of ridiculous reality shows where film crews follow ordinary people in different situations and professions as they go about their daily lives. While a paltry few shows arguably have some socially redeeming value, most glorify silly antics and obnoxious behavior. All are designed to be entertaining instead of informative. These shows are infinitely more cost efficient. The cost benefit to produce lightly scripted shows about people involved in the paranormal, extraterrestrial sightings, finding Bigfoot, surviving or dating naked, bickering housewives, sex, home improvement, crime, auto repossession, celebrity watching, human melodrama, poor white trash, and ghetto hot messes to name a few outweigh the expense of producing traditional television shows with script writers, directors, actors, film crews, etc.

William E. Cloud

Sports are another elite weapon of mass distraction that keeps Americans in competition with each other and their minds off of what is important. It suckers fans into talking about the game so much that they stop talking about issues that really matter. For instance, instead of concentrating on the trillions of dollars being wasted on the so-called war on terror, neocolonialist military intervention overseas, NSA domestic spying, the bankrupted economy, Federal Reserve and Wall Street bank scams, and the deplorable job situation facing Americans, we are programed to much more likely talk about football, baseball, and car racing statistics; what team will make it to the championship. It's no coincidence that professional sports rake in $4 billion in annual subsidies paid with taxpayer money. The power elite wants to keep sports on the minds of the masses, not only to distract and control them, but to feed the multi-billion dollar illegal betting industry from which they and the government take a cut.

Soccer is the most popular sport in the world, but not in America because it is considered low-scoring and boring. But in the months leading up to the 2014 World Cup games in Brazil, the media tried really, really hard to persuade Americans to love the *other* football. It promoted soccer as though it was as popular as professional football and baseball. Americans were encouraged to stay home from work to watch the games. Television stations looped footage of exuberant crowds huddled together in bars and family rooms in front of TVs across the country cheering for their favorite teams although relatively few understood the rules or recognized the players. The media will undoubtedly intensify its effort in the future to popularize soccer as a major American pastime because huge profits can be made with yet another diversion from reality.

Before proceeding any further, it is imperative to delve into the nefarious war on terror propaganda hoax that even surpasses the Pearl Harbor sneak attack fraud. The Bush lies justifying the Iraqi attack and Obama's eleventh-hour claim before the 2012 election that Osama bin Laden was killed by American forces are runners-ups in audacity. On September 11, 2001, it was reported that Muslim Arabs high-jacked commercial airliners and flew them into the World Trade Center in Manhattan. Two other planes allegedly crashed into the Pentagon in Arlington, Virginia, and a field in Shanksville, Pennsylvania, although there was no evidence of airplane debris at either purported crash scene.

In the chapter accusing Bush of being a war criminal, it is discussed how his Zionist foreign policy advisors developed the plan to expand the U.S.'s neocolonial militaristic adventurism in Iraq *before* Bush was elected president. The implementation of the plan, however, required the war-adverse American populous be persuaded to go along with invading Iraq. Many believe it was also a pretext to execute preexisting plans to wage war worldwide; a page was taken from the warmonger's playbook on false-flagging a horrific attack to justify retaliation. Again, a good story *always* trumps truth. I acknowledge that the claim 9-11 was a hoax is difficult to prove, but that's the beauty of it. After 13 years, there is still no national consensus on this point. There recently has been a perceptible shift in public opinion, however. People who initially expressed doubt were

William E. Cloud

branded conspiracy theory nuts, but as the years have gone by and the people realize how corrupt the government is, increasingly more Americans suspect Bush was directly involved or had prior knowledge of the attack.

In any event, the shocked nation mourned the tragic deaths of nearly 3,000 people, and the immediate public sentiment was that the perpetrators of the atrocity must be punished. Most believed the story the government and official media fed them, that is, arch terrorist and boogieman Osama bin Laden was responsible for the attack, but were unbothered by the fact that less than credible evidence was produced to support the accusation. Indeed, the evidence actually tends to suggest the contrary. In any event, the American public was persuaded that war was the only righteous response to the apparent foreign assault. Unfortunately, it takes only minimal intellectual persuasion to shape contemporary America's public opinion. Based on the good story that America had been attacked by Muslim terrorists was sufficient to kill a million Iraqis, 20,000 – 25,000 Afghans and 5,281 American service men and women in Afghanistan and Iraq wars. Many highly respected journalists such as award-winning reporter Sherman Ross, believed that:

"It's very doubtful that Muslims were behind 9/11. Think about this for one minute: That President Bush's family had done business with the family of the man who allegedly made the terrorist attack, Osama Bin Laden. The Bin Laden family was actually on the board of Bush's oil company. How is it possible that of all the billions of families in the world, the one family that makes the attack on America has done business with the President of America? That sounds more like a favor than anything else. I don't think 9/11 was an Arab conspiracy or a Muslim conspiracy. I think it's an American conspiracy to overthrow the government of the United States and install what is becoming a police state, and also to advance the imperial ambitions of the United States, to swindle the Middle East out of their energy resources."[33]

The corporate media published and broadcast very little that questioned government propaganda that 911 was a terrorist attack or framed it as wild conspiracy theory.

On September 20, 2001, Bush delivered his infamous "War on Terror" speech to rally the nation to prepare for the challenges that lay ahead in fighting a war with an elusive and unidentified enemy. The commander-in-chief vowed to lead the country through one of the darkest chapters of the republic's history, saying, "And in our grief and anger, we have found our mission and our moment." Bush's plans for fighting the war on terror went beyond destroying al Qaida to "pursu[ing] nations that provide aid or safe haven to terrorism. Every nation in every region now has a decision to make: Either you are with us or you are with the terrorists...We will not tire, we will not falter and we will not fail."[34]

Bush also unveiled his plans to create the U.S. Department of Homeland Security. The cost of the war on terror since 2001 ranges

William E. Cloud

from low-end estimates of $1.3 trillion to somewhere between $4.1 to $4.4 trillion! Osama Bin Laden, presuming he was responsible for 9-11, probably never imaged that a single terror attack would cause the U.S. to spend itself into bankruptcy.[35] Assuming for argument sake that 9-11 was committed by terrorists, the government greedily exploited it to achieve preexisting military objectives that went beyond punishing those allegedly responsible for the attack.

The government uses the 9-11 fear of terrorism to manipulate the American public to give up many of their civil liberties. Fear is the primal instinct that has kept man alive since the time of cave dwellers; fearful people are more likely to follow or obey whoever seems to know how to keep them safe. "In times of national crisis, Americans have always been ready to sacrifice civil liberties…Since Sept. 11, Americans have had their civil liberties taken from them. In many cases they don't even know it," according to Barbara Mack, associate professor of journalism and mass communication at Iowa State University.[36]

The array of civil liberties Americans have been stripped of are too numerous to address here, but a short list includes subjecting citizens to arrest for public dissent and peaceful assembly, and domestic spying through the collection and storing of all electronic communications of every American citizen including every telephone call, email, text, social media posts, online purchases, medical, employment, credit, and academic records. American cities across the country have installed extensive video-audio surveillance systems. In fact, Americans are the most spied on in world history.

Local police departments have been militarized with heavy weaponry and armored vehicles and use drones to spy on citizens not suspected of committing a crime. A militaristic police culture now exists in the United States. The government does not spy on citizens to us safe; it's done to keep track of our every interaction to crush dissent and intimidate the people from revealing unflattering information about it. Our right to due process is gradually being stripped away.

As discussed in the chapter on the Defense Authorization Act (DAA) of 2012, puts our civil liberties in greater jeopardy. Under the pretext of national security the government now has the authority to assassinate or indefinitely detain American citizens without criminal charges. It can deny citizens the right to be represented by an attorney or petition a court for habeas corpus release. If a detainee manages to get a court hearing, the government can use *secret evidence* against him that it is not required to disclose. On top of this, the government has secretly interpreted the provisions of the Patriot Act that differs from Congress' intent and what the public believes the law allows. This interpretation that deprives citizens of life, liberty, and property without due process of law is known only to a small group of people.

Eleven years after 9-11, Americans are increasingly unwilling to give up any more personal freedoms in order to reduce the threat of terrorism. Several months before 9-11, thirty-three percent of Americans polled were willing to sacrifice personal freedom to reduce the threat of terrorism. Shortly after 9-11, the public's inclination to give up their rights jumped to 71 percent. In the wake of increased suspicion that 9-11 was an inside job, the Iraq war was based on lies, leaks of NSA ease-dropping, among other revelations of government wrongdoing, in April, 2013 the pendulum swung back to 43 percent in favor of relinquishing civil liberties. "American are more fearful their government will abuse constitutional liberties than fail to keep citizens safe."[37] A January, 2013 Pew Research poll found: "that 53% think that the federal government threatens their own personal rights and freedoms while 43% disagree[d]."[38] This may be an indication that Americans are heeding Benjamin Franklin's admonition that, "They who can give up essential liberty to obtain a little temporary safety, deserve neither liberty nor safety."

Today's newscasters and anchormen are not the Edward R. Murrow's or Walter Cronkite's our parents relied on for at least a semblance of honesty. They were not paragons of truth either, but clearly not blatant liars like Fox's Bill O'Reilly or CNN's Wolf Blitzer who focus on human interest and violent crime stories centering on the actions of small, easily identifiable groups, and certain individuals. Their reporting is totally devoid of accurate public policy components involving major issues, top leaders, or events that significantly impact or disrupt life's daily routine.

During the run-up to the Israel-Palestinian war, for example, CNN dispatched Blitzer, the anchorman of its flagship news show, *The Situation Room*, to Jerusalem for on-the-ground coverage of the conflagration that was about to occur. The show's motto that it "brings yo the latest in political news and international events" omits mentioning that all coverage of Israel is slanted in its favor. It would be difficult to find a journalist, euphemistically speaking, with a more pro-Israel bias than Blitzer. As my mother would say, his background gives him "the can't help its" when it comes to blindly supporting Zionist Israel.

Born to Jewish refugees from Poland, he attended an Israeli university where he became fluent in Hebrew. He got his start in journalism in the Tel Aviv bureau of the *Reuters* news agency, and from there took a position with the Jerusalem Post. By the mid-1970s, Blitzer was the editor of the *Near East Report*, the monthly publication of the American Israel Public Affairs Committee (AIPAC), Israel's all-powerful unregistered foreign agent/lobby organization that holds sway over American politics and foreign policy.

Former congresswoman and Green Party presidential nominee, Cynthia McKinney, revealed that AIPAC requests candidates for both the House and the Senate sign pledges of support for Israel, including promises to vote to provide consistent levels of economic aid to the Zionist state and support Jerusalem as the capital of Israel.

"A candidate that refuses to sign the pledge does so at his or her peril. Every candidate for Congress at that time had a pledge, they were given a pledge to sign..." McKinney said. "If you don't sign the pledge, you don't get money. For example, it was almost like water torture for me. My parents observed this. I would get a call and the person on the other end of the phone would say 'I want to do a fundraiser for you.'

William E. Cloud

And then we would get into the planning. I would get really excited, because of course you have to have money in order to run a campaign. And then two weeks, three weeks into the planning, they would say, 'Did you sign the pledge?' And then I would say, 'No, I didn't sign the pledge.' And then my fundraiser would go kaput."[39]

AIPAC ensures legislators adhere to the pledge throughout legislators throughout their tenure in Congress. This explains why congresspersons and senators rarely voice the slightest criticism of Israel's policies no matter how despicable. Violators of the pledge lose their campaign funding from Jewish sources and the Jewish-controlled media – guardians of Israel's powerful influence on American foreign policy – does its best to tarnish their reputation.

As a former Israeli journalist and mouthpiece for ultra-Zionist AIPAC, Blitzer's opinion on Palestinian rights and statehood are predictably hostile as evidenced in a 1989 college debate on the Middle East conflict. He revealed his extremist pro-Zionist views by demanding the world accept the existence and security of Israel, but refused to concede that the Palestinians also deserved to live in peace in their own state. Wolf's objectivity, especially when it comes to defending Israel, no matter how shamefully it treats the Palestinians, is the same as a wolf guarding a henhouse [Pun intended]. He, like the majority of his mainstream news colleagues, rarely put the conflict in context, which is, Israel is in the process of forcing the

William E. Cloud

Palestinians to leave their land by whatever means necessary, including starving and massacring them out of existence.

To distract the public from this truth, the majority of mainstream newscasters typically start off coverage of the crisis with a condemnation of Hamas for firing rockets from the Gaza Strip into Israeli territory while suggesting that Israel is the innocent victim of a terrorist organization. Israel is falsely portrayed as simply wanting peace and is justified in defending itself from the serious threat to its security. Since 1967, Israel has occupied, blockaded, and isolated the Gaza Strip under siege in deplorable concentration camp conditions described by one observer as the largest prison in the world. Its contention that it no longer *occupies* the Strip because it withdrew its troops and settlers in 2005 is invalid under international law. The withdrawal of troops and settlers did not legally end the Gaza occupation "because (a) Israel continues to exercise 'massive control' over this area, (b) the conflict that produced the occupation has not ended, and (c) an occupying state cannot unilaterally (and without international/diplomatic agreement) transform the international status of occupied territory except, perhaps, if that unilateral action terminates all manner of effective control."[40]

Each day Israel occupies the Gaza Strip violates its duty under international law to protect its citizens; creating unstable and precarious conditions. Another violation of international law is Israel's official policy to keep the Gazan people in a state of food insecurity by limiting food intake to just above starvation levels at 2,100 calories per person daily. Israel also severely restrict their access to fresh water, medical supplies, and the basic necessities of life.

It's no secret that Israel is punishing the Palestinians for refusing to abandon their lands by making their existence unbearably miserable and untenable. A brutally persecuted people can be expected to rebel, even if it appears from the outside observers to be a futile or suicidal exercise. Thus, Israel cannot invoke the often stated specious contention that it has a right to defend itself because "no country would tolerate rocket fire from a neighboring country."[41] This is baseless propaganda to divert attention from the real issue that Israel is guilty of apartheid and genocide.

The media consistently pretends to bemoan the Gazan civilian casualty rate in a way that vilifies Hamas, garners empathy for Israel, and induces resignation in the U.S. and West that civilian deaths and collateral damage is an unavoidable part of war. Collateral damage is the "accidental or unintentional killing or wounding of non-combatants and/or destruction to non-combatant property during attacks on legitimate enemy targets."[42] The mass killing of Palestinians by Israel falls outside the definition of collateral damage.

The media's mild skepticism of the Israeli government's claim that its military scrupulously avoids civilian casualties with precision airstrikes is belied by the horrendously high civilian casualties and the destruction of property that has absolutely no military value. According to news reports, the official Palestinian death toll was over 2,200, mostly innocent men, women, and children. Tens of thousands more were wounded. The media also downplayed the lopsided

Israeli-Palestinian casualty and death tolls. It subtly implied that an Israeli life was worth much more than a Palestinian's. Typically, the reporter would say, "48 Israeli soldiers and 2,000 Palestinians have been killed in the war," as though the 41:1 ratio is comparable.

One of the more absurd contentions often repeated by the corporate media is that the Israeli military gave advance warning to residents of houses it targeted for an airstrike via a telephone call, text message or leaflet. Aside of being a ridiculous claim, it flies in the face of Israel's initial justification for assaulting Gaza in the first place, which was to stop Hamas militants from firing rockets into its territory. If the Israeli military determined that militants were firing rockets from a particular house and targeted for an airstrike, common sense dictates that giving them advance warning the house was about to be bombed would defeat the purpose by giving them the opportunity to escape with rockets in tow. Moreover, if it was true that civilians were warned to leave in advance, why was the death and casualty toll so high? Whoever believed that the murderous, barbaric Israeli military gave advance warning to residents that their home was about to be blown into smithereens is either gullible or stupid.

It is crystal clear that one of Israel's main objectives was the massive destruction of property that had no military value. More than 30,000 homes and hundreds of buildings were demolished. Gaza's only power plant was knocked out, and many underground water pipelines and sewage systems were extensively damaged, causing a severe shortage of clean drinking water and a health hazard. Rocket fire was certainly not coming from 30,000 homes, hospitals, and public utility facilities. The Palestinians cannot rebuild because Israel enforces an embargo on the importation of cement an building materials into the territory. The media gave Israel a pass on explaining the obvious, that is, it intentionally targeted and destroyed non-combatant civilian property in violation of international law, specifically, Article 3 of the Geneva Convention that defines a war crime as the "wanton destruction of cities, towns or villages, or devastation not justified by military necessity."[43]

Woe to journalists who challenge the biased coverage. For example, *NBC News* stopped using Ahmed Mohyeldin, a highly respected foreign correspondent, after his moving first-hand account of an Israeli attack that killed four young Palestinian boys playing soccer on a Gaza beach went viral. His riveting account of the tragedy was aired on NBC's *Today Show*. It generated swift international condemnation of Israel. His story was conspicuously absent from NBC's evening *Nightly News* broadcast, raising suspicion that pressure was put on the network to kill the story. Mohyeldin, an Egyptian-American citizen, was replaced with Richard Engel, a Jewish-American correspondent who curiously reported on the Gaza attack from a safe, remote location in Tel Aviv instead of Gaza, as did Mohyeldin. In response to public outrage, NBC eventually reversed itself and sparingly began using Mohyeldin again.

CNN correspondent Diana Magnay made the mistake of referring to a group of Israelis cheering the bombing of Gaza as *scum* and was banished to Moscow in retaliation. Rula Jebreal, a highly regarded MSNBC reporter experienced the Zionist' ire when she publically criticized the network for the disproportionately greater amount of coverage Israeli government officials and supporters were given compared to a handful of Palestinian representatives who were allowed an opportunity to explain their side of the story. Jebreal, the sole Palestinian contributor to MSNBC, publicly criticized the network's initial sacking of Mohyeldin and excluding Palestinian voices. Speaking on the *Ronan Farrow Daily Show*, she said, "We're ridiculous. We are disgustingly biased when it comes to this issue. Look at how much airtime Netanyahu and his folks have on air on a daily basis, Andrea Mitchell [Jewish wife of notorious financial rapist Alan Greenspan, former chairman of the Federal Reserve] and others. I never see one Palestinian being interviewed on these same issues, not even for…"[44]

Ms. Farrow countered that she has interviewed Palestinians on her show, to which Jebreal responded, "Maybe for 30 seconds, and then you have 25 minutes for Bibi Netanyahu and half an hour for Naftali Bennett [Israel's hardline economy minister who said Israel is at a 'historic crossroads' which demands the war continues until Hamas is beaten] and many others." Jebreal further complained that whenever reporter covers "the Palestinian side, we get upset. It's too pro-Palestinian. We don't like it. We push him back."[45] Finally, Ms. Jebreal objected to being introduced as a Palestinian journalist whereas Jewish reporters were never referred to as such. Retaliation was swift. Immediately after the interview, Jebreal posted on social media, "My forthcoming TV appearances have been cancelled! Is there a link between my expose and the cancellation?" There's no question it was!

The crucial point here is that the media rarely acknowledges that Israeli aggression is collective punishment of 1.8 million Gazan people for their strident refusal to give up their land and Hamas' uncompromising demand for statehood. Why do peace and truce negotiations never directly include Hamas? Israel is not interested in peace with Hamas…it just wants to destroy its military capability to render the Gazan people totally defenseless. This was confirmed by Israel Defense Minister Moshe (Bogie) Ya'alon's statement to the media that even if rocket fire from Gaza stopped, Israel still intended to annihilate Hamas. Israel's *final solution* for the Palestinians, again, is to force them to give up their land by making their lives unbearable or killing them. The media obfuscates this reality.

Meanwhile, the media beats the world over the head *daily* with propaganda that the Nazis tried to exterminate the Jews during the Holocaust, but seem oblivious to the stark contradiction that they are using the same vile propaganda tactics against the Palestinians the Nazis used to demonize and exterminate them. Consequently, international opinion that Israel is a pariah state is intensifying with every war crime it commits.

Truth is the first casualty of war. As discussed in the chapter on chaos in the Middle East, the U.S. and Israel have instigated nasty wars across the region. Truth, more so than ever, now appears to be trapped in a parallel universe. Unfortunately, the corrupt media cannot be trusted to report the truth, especially if it is counter to the power elite's agenda.

No better example of truth being lost is the emergence of the U.S. sponsored Islamic State in Iraq and the Levant, known as ISIS or ISIL. As planned, it has thrown the region into even more chaos.

The Western media describes ISIS as an extremist Sunni militant group that is more hardline and murderous than al Qaeda at the same time Israel was massacring Palestinians. It virtually ignores the fact that in 2012 ISIS was created and trained by U.S. instructors and French and British advisors at a secret base in Jordan to assist American-backed insurgents to fight in Syria against the government of President Bashar al-Assad.[46] ISIS got its funding from American ally Arab Gulf States of Kuwait, Qatar, and Saudi Arabia, and it's no secret that "the money is going through Kuwait and that it's coming from the Arab Gulf," said Andrew Tabler, senior fellow at the Washington Institute for Near East Policy. ISIS seemed to be serving its purpose until the summer of 2014 when it reportedly went rouge, overran Iraqi army forces and captured several major northern Iraqi cities. The corporate media consistently reports that the 4,000 to 34,000 ISIL militants, depending upon the source, were well equipped with American-made high-tech small arms, ammunition, handheld mortar and rocket launchers, jeeps, trucks and tanks they either stole or took after it was abandoned by the Iraq army. One *expert* even claimed that ISIS had fighter jets. "When ISIS invaded northern Iraq from Syria in June, the Iraqi forces deserted or retreated en masse. Many of them abandoned their American equipment. ISIS scooped it up themselves..."[47] The truth is that ISIS was already heavily armed when it advanced into Iraq. It's not clear whether members of the Shite Iraqi military were the ones who cut and ran in fear of the advancing ISIL forces or whether the Sunni Iraqi soldiers deserted and joined ISIS. The corporate media either didn't get this or did not want you to get it; the latter being the most likely. By midsummer, ISIL controlled nearly all of Syria's oil and gas fields and took over Iraq's main oil refinery in Baiji.

The White House now refers to the organization it trained as a fearsome group of terrorists that not only poses a threat to Iraq and Syria, but the entire world. Defense Secretary Chuck Hagel ominously warned that ISIL is "beyond anything that we've seen...The U.S. must 'get ready.'"[48] Further, "ISIL is as sophisticated and well-funded as any group that we have seen...They're beyond just a terrorist group. They marry ideology, a sophistication of strategic and tactical military prowess. They are tremendously well-funded. Oh, this is beyond anything that we've seen. So we must prepare for everything."[49] Again, the U.S. is responsible for ISIS's creation, training, and probably some of its funding, along with several lackey Gulf States. Ironically, the U.S. now considers its creation a Frankenstein monster that must be destroyed.

The Zionist media conceals this from a gullible, easily swayed American public. Only the exceptional talking head on television or newspaper journalist dare reveal these facts. Surely CNN could have called on the some of the many regional experts, activists, politicians, and journalists familiar with ISIL whose opinions differ from the government's talking points instead of calling upon the same warmongering yahoos day in and day out.

The Black Agenda Report blog is one of the most informative sources of propaganda-free news on the internet. Its editor Glen Ford agrees with President Obama and Defense Secretary Hagel, something he does not do often, that ISIL poses a serious threat to U.S. and Zionist national interests. He has a more credible take on ISIL then the mainstream media, however. He argues that it was created to further the U.S.'s proxy war policies in the region, but double-crossed its American, Saudi, Kuwait, Qatar, and Turkish benefactors; a development that threatens the survival of the royal oil states that are essential to American world hegemony. ISIL's message is that, "The legality of all emirates, groups, states and organizations becomes null by the expansion of the caliph's authority and the arrival of its troops to their areas."[50] The same thing happened in Libya when the American and royal Arabian-funded *rebels* overthrew Muammar Gaddafi and then switched up on them when the deed was done, putting a serious roadblock in the U.S. and NATO's empire building plans. According to Ford, bombing ISIL positions in Syria is a subterfuge Obama is using to achieve the ultimate goal of overthrowing Assad. He intends to use ISIL to dupe the war-weary U.S. public to go along with openly joining the fight in Syria against Assad. Ford concluded that, Obama "will tell any lie, or combinations of lies, to somehow turn U.S. bombs on the Syrian government, under the guise of fighting ISIS. You can bet that the CIA is burning the midnight oil, seeking a pretext to turn this strategic U.S. defeat into

William E. Cloud

an excuse to directly attack Syria And that's what makes this moment so dangerous."[51] In September, 2014, the U.S. launched airstrikes in Syria purportedly "to degrade and ultimately destroy" ISIL. By mid-November mission creep in the administration's strategy predictably drifted toward taking out Assad and ISIL. It's too early in the conflict to predict how this is going to turn out, but the constant is that the media will spin it in favor of the elite class.

On another front, the media has slavishly stuck to the government's *party-lie* that the conflict in the Ukraine was started by Russian President Vladimir Putin. Make no mistake. Putin is no more trustworthy than the rest of the bankster-controlled world leaders. It's clear, though, that the U.S. was more of a driving force than Russia in creating the crisis in the Ukrainian conflict. To halt President Viktor Yanuyovch's plan to move Ukraine into Russia's economic sphere, the U.S. conceived and executed the West's plan to remove the democratically elected president. This fact is totally ignored by the mainstream media. The Ukrainian government was caught in a netherworld relationship between Europe and Russia. Yanuyovch wanted to strengthen Ukraine's integration with Europe while maintaining a positive relationship with Russia, instead of choosing one over the other. He was on the horns of a dilemma and was being forced to choose between concluding an association agreement, including a deep and comprehensive free trade arrangement, with the European Union (EU) or join the Russian customs union with Belarus and Kazakhstan. The West and Russia considered this a zero-sum calculation. Each wanted the whole kit and caboodle, and stepped up pressure to force his hand. The IMF offered Ukraine a $1.5 billion loan and an additional $850 million would come from the World Bank if it played ball. In November, 2013, Yanuyovch rejected the offer in favor of joining Russia's Common Union. This proved to be his undoing because the U.S. was not going to tolerate any diminishment of its influence on the world's economy. It was determined to make Ukraine align with the EU, IMF, World Bank, and international financiers despite being the purveyors of staggering suffering to millions around the globe.

To make this happen, the U.S. encouraged opposition groups to stage a coup if Yanukovych refused to step down. In the days leading up to the coup, the U.S. worked behind the scenes, and sometimes openly, to oust him so that a pro-West government could be installed. To back up the threat, well-orchestrated protestors were dispatched to the streets of Kyiv. In December, 2013, Assistant U.S. Secretary of State for Europe and Eurasia Victoria Nuland confirmed that the U.S. had "'invested' more than $5 billion and 'five years worth of work and preparation' in achieving what she called Ukraine's 'European aspirations.'"[52] She reported having a "tough conversation" with Yanukovych during which she made it "absolutely clear" that if he did not immediately accept the EU and the IMF proposals, he would face serious consequences. This was after the State Department announced on its website that while in Kyiv, Nuland planned to "meet with government officials, opposition leaders, civil society and business leaders to encourage agreement on a new government and plan of action."[53]

William E. Cloud

At the eleventh hour, a delegation of EU foreign ministers attempted to persuade Yanukovych to commit the government to installing an interim administration, make constitutional reforms, and schedule new parliamentary and presidential election. Yanukovych's proposed a compromise to step down in three months. His proposal was rejected by the opposition. Within in hours after he refused to step down, the Ukrainian Parliament unconstitutionally voted to oust him and pro-EU forces staged a coup. In fear for his life, Yanukovych fled the country. To reaffirm U.S. support for Ukraine's *territorial integrity*, on March 14, 2014, Vice President Biden congratulated the newly installed Prime Minister Arseniy Yatsenyuk for a job well done.

If the most avid news junky relied on the corporate media for information about the turmoil in the Ukraine, he would find it difficult to glean from it the U.S.'s direct involvement in the coup and the resulting violence and chaos. Coverage of the coup lasted a 48-hour news cycle before disappearing. Indeed, as far as the media is concerned, the coup didn't happen. It pretends that the old government somehow went away and a new government legitimately took its place. News coverage begins after the coup. Following the overthrow, Obama stated, "Countries near Russia have deep concerns and suspicions about this kind of meddling [and] as long as none of us are inside Ukraine trying to meddle and intervene…with decisions that properly belong to Ukrainian people." His comment was both untruthful and hypocritical. In the same breath he accused "Putin of violating international law by sending troops to Crimea," and pledged

$1 billion in aid to the illegal Ukraine government.[54] If any country has deep concerns and suspicions about meddling in their affairs, it should be of the United States. The Ukrainian people who democratically elected their government certainly had nothing to do with the decision to oust it. Most Ukrainians did not realize the key role the U.S. government played in dividing and destabilizing their country. Americans are in the same boat. If all of this is not proof of the U.S.'s involvement in the coup, nothing is.

In conclusion, power elite's propaganda massively produced by the hungry-for-profits media instigates hostility among nations and civilizations. It destroys mutual trust and confidence, and has become the worst enemy of mankind. Their evil world domination agenda can be defeated, however, although it will take an epic David against Goliath battle. A well-organized anti-propaganda campaign involving people around the world communicating with each other to expose their propaganda as a lie and fraud is the best strategy for defeating propaganda. WikiLeaks and Edward Snowden demonstrated that a single leaked e-mail can seriously undermine their propaganda. This can be best accomplished by creating and utilizing alternative sources to the mass media such as e-mails, blogs and social media to get news and information.

Deconstructing the News: Don't Believe the Hype was written to contribute the awakening of the masses to the lies of the elite…the Illuminati who hide behind the shadows of the government. One thing we must *over-stand* is that what's done in darkness can surely be

William E. Cloud

brought into the light. The world's future will be determined by who wins.

William E. Cloud

CHAPTER 2

Military Propaganda Tells Americans That War is Good

We must remember that in time of war what is said on the enemy's side of the front is always propaganda, and what is said on our side of the front is truth and righteousness, the cause of humanity and a crusade for peace.

~ Walter Lippman

Every morning for several years, the cable television Headline News Channel (HLN) broadcasts "Salute to Troops" public interest spots. These segments offer love ones and friends of soldiers serving overseas an opportunity to "shout-out" messages of affection and encouragement. The network's website states, "Whether you're personally connected to the military, or just care about military issues, this is the place for you. Share your thoughts about the military, honor the fallen, and connect with others who are serving their countries."[1] Supporting the troops is a very clever way of persuading the public to also support war or as one writer put it, risk being considered "a selfish, malignant coward who doesn't respect the sacrifice that these amazing men and women apparently give for our freedom.

Unfortunately the average American citizen is so brainwashed by mainstream news that they do not even realize that this is propaganda."

Jeep's "Operation Safe Return Hero at Home" program typifies the corporate public relations commercial. The company gives awards to American civilians in recognition of their "heroism on the home front...for selfless service they have provided to aid our troops and their families...[because] civilians who have never been in the military do not truly comprehend what returning service members and their families have endured."[2] CBS Television's "Operation Gratitude – CBS Cares" is "a non-profit that gives Americans a way to say thank you to the military men and women fighting overseas by shipping out care packages to troops and their families."[3]

In response to a social media call for a *sing-in* at the National Mall in Washington, D.C., on Memorial Day in 2014, hundreds of people showed up to sing patriotic songs. Social media invitations for similar seemingly spontaneous demonstrations of patriotism occurred around the country. As was the case at the National Mall event, television cameras just happened to be on the scene in other cities, and the impromptu affairs were shown on local and national news broadcasts.

These and many other pro-military public interest video spots are televised what seems like a gazillion times a day. They are being used to influence the public to connect on an emotional level with troops waging war and disengage from intellectual reasoning about the legitimacy of the war. The recognition of soldiers making the purported ultimate sacrifice to keep America safe has become as much of a ritual before every amateur and professional sporting event as singing the national anthem. After all, noted Noam Chomsky, "Mobiliz[ing] community opinion in favor of vapid empty concepts like Americanism – who can be against that? Or harmony, who can be against that? Or to bring it up to date, support our troops – who can be against that, or yellow ribbons - who can be against that?"[4]

The public is not told that the support-the-troops refrains in the electronic and print media has little to do with corporate altruism, but is a sophisticated, well-funded propaganda campaign aimed at appealing to hearts and disarming minds of those at home and abroad to accept war.

The Pentagon is the largest media company on earth in terms of size, money, and power. With a $10 billion budget, its Joint Hometown News Service employs 27,000 and in 2013 produced and released 500,000 news products to 14,000 television and radio stations, newspapers, magazines and the internet free of charge.[5]

Not only does the corporate media receive free content, in some cases the government pays them to run pro-war stories. This is a win-win situation for media companies because they also receive lucrative advertising revenue from corporate sponsors that want to be associated with the feel good pieces about American soldiers serving overseas. "As the war has become less popular, they [government] have felt they need to respond to that more," said Sheldon Rampton, research director for the Committee on Media and Democracy that monitors the military's media operations.[6] The military counters that it is obligated to counteract the widespread use of the internet and video dissemination by extremist groups...more propaganda...to inform domestic and overseas audiences of the American side of the story.

In 2006, the Pentagon's inspector general found that the Defense Department "may appear to merge inappropriately" domestic affairs with foreign operations.[7] The concern was that the Smith-Mundt Act of 1948 authorized the dissemination of propaganda abroad, but prohibited the military from using it to influence American public opinion except for recruitment and advertising purposes. To clarify any ambiguity, Congressman Paul Hodes (D-NH) sponsored a bill that would strengthen the federal ban on domestic propaganda. He stated, "It's not up to the Pentagon to sell policy to the American people."[8] The legislation never reached the congressional floor for a vote, however.

The Smith-Mundt Modernization Act of 2012 *repealed* the prohibition, and gave the government the legal authority to propagandize the American people. The bill was inserted into the 2013 National Defense Authorization Act (NDAA) by Congressmen Mac Thornberry (R-TX) and Adam Smith (D-WA), and was enacted with bi-partisan support. President Obama quietly signed it into law in December, 2013.

The nullification of the prohibition against the government's use of propaganda to influence American public opinion resulted in "unleash[ing] thousands of hours per week of government-funded radio and TV programs for domestic consumption," reported John Hudson of Foreign Policy.[9] Defense Department public affairs officers can now legally do what they have been covertly doing all along, that is, target the American public to "protect a key friendly center of gravity, to wit U.S. national will" with government-funded propaganda campaigns.[10]

Just as commercial advertisers' marketing strategies are based on the premise that the more times a consumer is exposed to a positive product advertisement, the more they are inclined to buy it, the Defense Department also adheres to the premise that failure to use repetition "to constantly drive home a constant message dilutes the impact on the target audiences."[11] Consequently, Americans are bombarded with relentless repetitions of military propaganda, causing them to support war from sources they have been conditioned to trust. The Government also uses the support-the-troops mantra as a mechanism to control, intimidate, and stifle dissent.

Aside from the spectacle generated by the alleged killing of Osama bin Laden, which conveniently gave President Obama the needed bump in public opinion to win reelection, the media frenzy surrounding the fake rescue of Private Jessica Lynch, heralded by the Pentagon as "G.I. Jane", from Iraqi forces in 2003 became one of the greatest Pentagon manufactured patriotic moments in modern military history. The 19 year old was injured in a truck crash and captured by hostile Iraqi forces without a single shot being fired. She was transported to a hospital where it is not disputed that she was given the best care available under the circumstances. She was never mistreated or abused by her captors.

William E. Cloud

When the Army learned where she was being held, it sent a Special Forces team to rescue her from the hospital. By the time they arrived, the Iraqi guards had fled. During the so-called "daring raid," according to the Pentagon, the rescue team came under fire and had to fight their way to where Lynch was held before whisking her away by helicopter.

The rescue was not nearly as heroic as the story the Pentagon supplied to the media. The truth is that the rescue team was not attacked. The only people it encountered were unarmed nurses and hospital staff. These facts didn't make a difference to the Pentagon/corporate media combine determined to make her an all-American heroine of the war. It's important to mention that this manufactured incident of valor occurred during a time when public support for the Iraq war waned. The sheeple had to be rallied.

"Her rescue will go down as one of the most stunning pieces of news management yet conceived. It provides a remarkable insight into the real influence of Hollywood producers on the Pentagon's media managers, and has produced a template from which America hopes to present its future wars."[12] The Pentagon, to this day, ignores Lynch's outspoken criticism of the exaggerated stories about her recuse. She rejects being deserving of heroine status, saying, "That wasn't me. I'm not about to take credit for something I didn't do...I'm just a survivor."[13]

The sad irony is our service men and women fighting abroad have little to do with keeping America safe. They are actuality expendable pawns used to advance the U.S. banking and corporate driven

William E. Cloud

agendas to consolidate the United States' hegemony over the world's natural resources and the international economic system; a system that has no allegiance to the United States or any other nation.

The Pentagon's propaganda campaigns successfully distort this sad reality. The nation's human condition, as a result, has been degraded instead of elevated by propaganda. Before any military intervention or invasion of an invariably militarily weak nation occurs, Americans are bombarded with misinformation and deception on television, radio, and in newspapers that demonize its leader. We are then told that removing him from power will keep America safe and bring democracy to the wretched land. Unfortunately, unconscious Americans fall for the hype that the lives of U.S. servicemen and thousands more foreign civilians are worth the price of ensuring their safety. Never mind the fact that the warmongers and their children never have to go to the front lines in the defense of their beloved country.

The U.S. Government and media operates as the Israeli Mossad foreign intelligence agency according to defector, Victor Ostrovsky. Its motto is "By way of deception, thou shalt do war." And, the public dearly pays for it while the corporations make a mint through government contracts and armaments sales. Despite the support the troops hype, American servicemen and women are the biggest losers because they are shipped off to fight and die in senseless wars. Soldiers who return home wounded receive substandard medical care in Veterans Administration hospitals before and after discharged and

William E. Cloud

then abandoned by the government because they are no longer of use to the war machine.

Postscript

The Discovery Communication's Military Channel found its viewership declining in an era when President Obama acknowledged the "tide of war is receding." In an attempt to maintain its relevance, the Discovery network made a meaningless modification to its Military Channel's mission by renaming it the American Heroes Channel because "heroism transcends the battlefield," according to the channel's general manager, Kevin Bennett. One new show, for example, *Against All Odds*, "tells the true stories of modern-day heroes whose courage and sacrifice made their deeds unforgettable."

The channel's superficial change from the military warfare paradigm to a hero worship format is intended to persuade the war weary American public to continue accepting and supporting U.S. military aggression by shifting its focus to individual gallantry. Actual changes in the channel's format, however, are imperceptible. It's still all things Hitler and Nazi. Americans are so brainwashed, however, they probably won't notice it's showing the same propaganda with a more palatable title.

William E. Cloud

CHAPTER 3

Defense Authorization Act is Authorization to Violate Due Process

No State shall...deprive any person of life, liberty, or property, without due process of law; nor deny to any person within its jurisdiction the equal protection of the laws.

~ Fourteenth Amendment to the United States Constitution

Writing this chapter could get me arrested and thrown in military prison indefinitely *"without trial, until the end of the hostilities"* ...which is anticipated to end the year after never.

President Barrack Obama quietly signed into law the National Defense Authorization Act of 2012 (NDAA) on New Year's Eve, 2011. Section 1021 of the act authorizes the military to arrest and detain American citizens in a military prison on the flimsiest suspicion or accusation that he or she supported a terrorist organization or "associated forces". A terrorist is whoever the government says is a terrorist. "This means that, in the near future, a controversial Twitter post, attending a peaceful protest, or publishing an anti-Congress critique or anti-TSA rant on Google could land you 'indefinite detention' for life, in the wording of the bill. No access to a lawyer, no access to trial."[1]

National Defense Authorizations, enacted annually, specify the budget and expenditures of the U.S. Department of Defense for the upcoming year. The provision causing angst states that any "person who was a part of or substantially supported al-Qaeda, the Taliban, or associated forces that are engaged in hostilities against the United States or its coalition partners, including any person who has committed a belligerent act or has directly supported such hostilities in aid of such enemy forces" can be detained by the military.[2] The catchall "associated forces" clause of the law is drawing the most fire. Senator Rand Paul (R-Ky.) argued in opposition to passage of the legislation, that a person could be suspected of terrorism if he was missing fingers, owns a gun, possesses waterproof ammunition or has stored enough food to last more than seven days.[3]

One of the pillars of this nation's legal system is that U.S. citizens on American soil cannot be taken into military custody. Section 1021 unconstitutionally strips away that basic freedom. High level law enforcement officials, including former Federal Bureau of Investigation (FBI) Director Robert Mueller, reportedly opposed the law because it confused the FBI and military's role in conducting investigations of terrorist activities in the U.S.

Leading civil liberty and human rights groups urged President Obama, a former constitution law professor, to veto the measure. That was an exercise in futility since it was he who pressured a reluctant Senate to include in the legislation the provision authorizing the detention of American citizens. It's not that he did not recognize the legislation was a serious assault on the First Amendment to the Constitution that guarantees the right to freedom of assembly, freedom of the press, freedom of religion, and freedom of speech, and the Fifth Amendment that entitles a person accused of a crime to presentment or indictment of a grand jury and a speedy trial. He intended to play fast and loose with our freedoms.

Instead of coming together to formulate a plan of action to fight for the repeal of the law, human and civil rights organizations merely lamented from the sidelines that it violated the Constitution. According to Human Rights Watch, had the Bush administration put forth the NDAA, it would have been deemed unreasonable to say the least. American Civil Liberties Union (ACLU) Executive Director Anthony Romero called the legislation "a stain on our democratic principles – one that will ultimately be viewed with embarrassment and shame."[4]

Obama attached a signing statement to the Act, which promised his "administration will not authorize the indefinite detention without trial of American citizens."[5] This was presidential window dressing. Signing statements are merely ceremonial exercises that praise or criticize the law or lawmakers. In this instance, it was "assert[ed] that the president will not enforce the law as written...[and] that he will interpret the law to avoid constitutional difficulties that he perceives."[6] There is no way this draconian law can be contorted to muster any degree of constitutionality. Besides, signing statements do not have the force or effect of law, and more importantly, are not binding on the president who signed it or future presidents.

It's difficult to give any credence to Obama's assurances that he would never use the law to detain U.S. citizens. He misled the public when he said that the government only spied on foreigners and that the NSA was only gathering meta-data when it turned out it was illegally intercepting and storing the content of every telephone call, text or tweet Americans made. According to documents leaked by whistleblower Edward Snowden, the NSA and its British minions even infiltrated video games and created characters to snoop on gamers. Let's not forget Obama's solemn assurance that subscribers the Affordable Care Act could keep their own doctor.

Another case to support the uselessness of signing statements is the Executive Order Obama signed on January 22, 2009, declaring, "The detention facilities at Guantanamo for individuals covered by this order shall be closed as soon as practicable, and no later than 1 year from the date of this order."[7] Mr. Obama obviously changed his mind about enforcing his own order to close the Guantanamo Bay prison since it is still open and running six years later. To be fair, "Congress inserted provisions in the 2012 NDAA, which makes it extremely difficult for the president, if he was so inclined, to release innocent detainees held in Guantanamo. The law prohibits the release of detainees unless the president certifies that he will not engage in terrorist activities in the future – a guarantee only God is capable of giving with any degree of certainty."[8]

Obama's poor track record for truthfulness inspires little confidence to journalists, bloggers, activists, and plain citizens that they will not be detained for simply being in the presence of someone the government regards as a terrorist. In other words, the military can arrest and detain anyone for interviewing a member of al Qaeda, Western-backed ISIS or anyone associated with any group opposed to U.S. domestic and foreign policy. If that doesn't put a damper on the right to express an opposing view on government policies, I can't imagine what does.

The controversial indefinite detention provision was challenged by a group of journalists, scholars, and political activists including Noam Chomsky, Daniel Ellsberg, Chris Hedges, Naomi Wolf, and Cornel West on the grounds that it provided no exemption for journalists and political activists who had direct contact with any organization on the State Department's terrorism list. They filed a lawsuit (*Hedges v. Obama*) on January 13, 2012 to strike down the law asserting, "The language is amorphous…anybody who 'substantially supports' – whatever that means – not only the Taliban or al-Qaeda, but what they term 'associated forces' is guilty." [9]

In May, 2012, U.S. District Judge Katherine Forrest of the Southern District of New York declared Section 1021 of the law was likely an unconstitutional violation of the First and Fifth Amendment rights of U.S. citizens. She rejected the Obama administration's argument that the NDAA merely reaffirmed existing law that recognized the military's right to perform certain routine duties. She granted the plaintiffs' request for a preliminary injunction that temporarily blocked the indefinite detention provision from taking effect. In August, 2012, the administration appealed the ruling and challenged the validity of permanent injunction. The Second Circuit Court of Appeals granted the administration's request for a stay on the ban, allowing the indefinite detention to remain in effect until it ruled on the appeal.

The appellate court overturned Judge Forrest's ruling in July, 2013, but sidestepped the question as to the constitutionality of the provision by ruling that the plaintiffs did not have standing to challenge the law because none of them had been imminently threatened or had a credible fear of arrest. The court's holding was not supported by the evidence introduced at trial which clearly proved that several plaintiffs had, in fact, been arrested and detained by the U.S. military, although not pursuant to Section 1021.

The plaintiffs filed a *writ of certiorari* to the U.S. Supreme Court requesting a review of the appellate court's decision. There is no guarantee the Court will grant plaintiffs' request. If it decided to hear the appeal, the court could squarely face the constitutional question or punt by affirming the Court of Appeal's ruling that the plaintiffs did not have standing to challenge it.

Many observers are skeptical that the conservative majority of the Supreme Court will be inclined to strike down the provision based on the perception that it will find it imperative the government has the ability to detain anyone it deems a threat to national security.

If the Court ducked the constitutional question by affirming the lower court's ruling that the plaintiffs lacked standing, it could be challenged again by anyone who was directly harmed by the law. With the detention provision in place, however, there is no guarantee that someone arrested pursuant to the law will get an opportunity to petition the court because the military could simply arrest them without warning and hold them in secrecy. Indeed, only the government knows whether it is already secretly holding someone in military detention. After all, this is the point of the law. This seemingly insurmountable hurdle for a detained person seeking relief from the court was described by one of the plaintiffs' attorneys, Bruce Afran:

"There's nothing that's built into this NDAA [the National Defense Authorization Act] that even gives a detained person the right to get to an attorney… In fact, the whole notion is that it's secret. It's outside of any judicial process. You're not even subject to a military trial. You can be moved to other jurisdictions under the law. It's the antithesis of due process."[10]

In the twelve years since the attack on the World Trade Center, those behind government and corporate media propaganda have ginned up an all-consuming fear in Americans that terrorists will strike the U.S. again. This dread is used to justify waging a permanent war against an undefined enemy. So far, U.S. taxpayers have been fleeced of $6.6 trillion to fight the un-winnable war on terrorism. Thus, only the *terrorists and war profiteers* are winning. By keeping the threat of terrorism at the forefront of the news, the power elite

William E. Cloud

have duped the nation to spend itself into bankruptcy to prevent future acts of terrorism. The military industrial complex is the main beneficiary of the taxpayer funded largess.

One thing certain is that al Qaeda has not attacked the United States, if it ever did, for nearly a decade and a half. The Obama Administration claimed Navy Seals killed Osama bin Laden, the alleged architect of 9-11, but the government continues to spend billions of dollars, not just to fight Muslim boogiemen abroad, but to also trample on our constitutional rights here at home. Both constitute a waste of already dwindling resources and a dangerous threat to world peace and individual freedoms. "The only way this changes is if citizens change the political incentives for politicians. Two-bit terrorists will always be around, sadly. This isn't a call to stop counterterrorism. Only when citizens make it acceptable for politicians to recognize that the threat of terrorism isn't so significant can the country finally get what it really needs, 10 years later: closure." [11]

Meanwhile, our constitutional rights hang in the balance while the case winds its way through the courts. If the Supreme Court lets this law stand – odds are it will – our civilian system of justice will be replaced with one run by the military. Journalists, activists, dissidents and ordinary citizens would be subject to being caught up in military dragnets, and secretly and indefinitely confined in military concentration camps.

Time is running out for Americans to protect their right to fight the tyranny that is threatening our liberties. If we don't start

William E. Cloud

aggressively challenging infringements on our rights "the president who claims the right to imprison or kill any person, of any nationality, any place on Earth, for reasons known only to him. The man who excelled George Bush by shepherding preventive detention through Congress – Barack Obama – is the More Effective Evil." [12]

Otherwise we're doomed.

Postscript

The Supreme Court predictably refused to review the case. "In declining to hear the case *Hedges v. Obama* and declining to review the NDAA," observed plaintiffs' attorney Carl Mayer, "the Supreme Court has turned its back on precedent dating back to the Civil War era that holds that the military cannot police the streets of America. This is a major blow to civil liberties. It gives the green light to the military to detain people without trial or counsel in military installations, including secret installations abroad. There is little left of judicial review of presidential action during wartime." The decision ushers in a post-constitutional era in which due process is rendered meaningless. The decision is definitive proof all three branches of government have been corrupted exclusively serve the corporate power elite.

This magnifies the urgency to assemble a militant mass movement to overthrow corporate tyranny. (Note: I am not advocating the violent overthrow of the U.S. government; I'm not trying to be charged with treason.)

William E. Cloud

CHAPTER 4

Bank of International Settlements is at the Apex of the International Banking Cartel

Allow me to issue and control a nation's currency,
and I care not who makes it laws.

~ Mayer Amschel Bauer Rothschild

Nearly every aspect of life on the planet, be it finance, government or culture, is either controlled or heavily influenced by immensely powerful international financial organizations. The elite class that controls these organizations has the world's economy in a death grip, and has contorted it at will to their benefit with detrimental consequences for the earth's population. The most powerful international banking institution in the world is the highly secretive and largely unknown Bank of International Settlements (BIS). As *guardian* of the world's monetary system it operates unimpeded because its activities are not regulated by any authority and rarely mentioned in the media. For example, the *Wall Street Journal*, America's premiere economic and international business news publication, lists only a handful of articles on the bank between 2010 and 2013. The *New York Times* and *Washington Post* mentioned the BIS during the same time period, but did not described its role, significance or impact on the world economy. The brief description of the BIS in the *Times* website in 2014 is so out of date, it erroneously stated that the United States is not a member of the BIS. In fact, it joined the board of directors in 1994.

The BIS is the apex predator in the international finance food chain. It owes its existence to the Rothschild family's banking and business dynasty that has dominated international banking since the early 1800's. It was established in 1930 by the Rothschilds to extract World War I reparations from Germany for payment to Britain and France. Their ownership interest in the BIS and central banks worldwide enabled it to "slither its way into each country on this planet, threaten every world leader and their governments and cabinets with physical and economic death and destruction, and then emplaced their own people in these central banks to control and manage each country's pocketbook. Worse still, the Rothschilds also control the machinations of each government at the macro level, not concerning themselves with the daily vicissitudes of our individual personal lives. Except when we get too far out of line."[1]

Despite being established by Jews, it was initially pro-Nazi at the same time Jews were being persecuted in Germany; a clear case of putting profit above the lives of their own people. Calls from the United States were made for its liquidation in 1944 based on accusations that it was laundering gold the Nazis stole during the occupation of Europe. The central bankers successfully made the

William E. Cloud

American resolution quietly go away. Its role and influence on the international monetary policy dramatically expanded afterwards.

The bank is a privately owned institution. Eight-six percent of its shares are owned by 60 privately owned central banks, including the Federal Reserve System, and 14 percent is owned by private individuals. Private BIS shareholders, whose identities are held in strict confidence, purportedly have no voting rights. Whether this is true or not, as the wealthiest, most powerful people on the globe, they most assuredly wield a great deal of influence in the decision-making process. Indeed, it would be well within the realm of possibility that a single utterance from their lips can profoundly affect the world's financial markets. Their power not only exceeds that of national political leaders, including the president of the United States, they control them.

The bank's net worth is a closely guarded secret. It is estimated to be $100 to $231 trillion...over half the wealth of the planet. The Rothschild BIS owns the London Gold Exchange that holds the world's largest stash of gold. In 2005, it was listed at 712 tons. It also sets the daily price of gold, giving it total leverage over the metal's price and the marketplace power it brings.

The BIS is described as the central banks' central bank. Its most important tool for achieving international monetary and financial stability is through control of currencies. As the coordinator of transactions between its member central banks, the BIS sets interest rates that determines the cost of borrowing, the speed of global currency transactions, and the level of reserves banks are required to hold. It also set the policies of the World Bank and the International Monetary Fund (IMF) which makes it the key cornerstone of the emerging one world economic system. It is believed to currently possess about 7% of the world's available exchange funds backed by the Swiss gold franc until it switched to artificial fiat money in 2003. It is important to understand that paper currency has no intrinsic value when not backed by physical reserves such as gold or silver; its value is based solely on peoples' faith. If this faith is lost, the money would become worthless in a flat downward hyperinflation spiral.

The BIS's control of foreign exchange currency and the price of gold gives it the power to determine the economic conditions of any country of its choosing or the world. Hence, it has unfettered power to trigger or remedy economic recessions; euphemistically called business cycles. The BIS and central banks thrive whether the world economy is in a boon or bust period. As mentioned, all decisions it clandestinely makes to intervene in the financial markets are final and unassailable because it is above the law. There is no oversight, its archives and documents are inviolable at all times and in all places, and its officers and employees have the advantage of complete immunity from criminal prosecution and civil liability without prior agreement of the bank.

Georgetown University professor Carroll Quigley wrote about the elites' ambitious plans for the bank.

"[T]he powers of financial capitalism has another far-reaching aim, nothing less than to create a world system of financial control in private hands able to dominate the political system of each country and the economy of the world as a whole. This system was to be controlled in a feudalist fashion by the central banks of the world acting in concert, by secret agreements arrived at in frequent private meetings and conferences. The apex of the system was to be the Bank for International Settlements in Basle, Switzerland; a private bank owned and controlled by the world's central banks which were themselves private corporations." [2]

Ellen Brown, an expert on the Federal Reserve System that is a BIS board member, explained how the bank has gained importance over the years.

"For many years the BIS kept a very low profile, operating behind the scenes in an abandoned hotel. It was here that decisions were reached to devalue or defend currencies, fix the price of gold, regulate offshore banking, and raise or lower short-term interest rates. In 1977, however, the BIS gave up its anonymity in exchange for more efficient headquarters. The new building has been described as 'an eighteen story-high circular skyscraper that rises above the medieval city like some misplaced nuclear reactor.' It quickly became known as the 'Tower of Basel.' Today the BIS has governmental immunity, pay no taxes, and has its own private police force. It is, as Mayer Rothschild envisioned, above the law." [3]

William E. Cloud

The world is in debt thanks to the owners of the BIS. Continents, countries, cities, towns, boroughs, individuals are all beholden to a small group of people who care not one whit about anyone but themselves. Our lives are not one of free will, as we must work hard to sustain ourselves with the basics of life while they unjustly prosper from our labor. The bible describes our condition in Proverbs 22:7 that, "The rich rule over the poor, and the borrower is slave to the lender." Our task is to rid the world of the international monetary system as it currently exists to level the economic playing field for all mankind. The opportunity to change this oppressive system may come with the impending worldwide economic collapse – a silver-lining in the disaster.

William E. Cloud

CHAPTER 5

Federal Reserve – Gonifs
(Yiddish for crooks or thieves) Extraordinaire

*The few who understand the system, will either be so interested from
its profits or so dependent on its favors, that there will be no
opposition from that class.*

~ Rothschild Brothers of London, 1863

The Federal Reserve System proves Mayer Rothschild's belief was correct that the elite few who understand and profit tremendously from the scheme will never be in favor of its abolishment. The Federal Reserve (Fed) is the U.S.'s central bank and controls its currency or monetary supply. By regulating the supply of money in circulation, it influences interest rates that have a direct bearing on the mortgage payments of millions of families. Interest rates theoretically cause the financial markets to boom or collapse, spurring the economy to expand or to contract into recession. Unfortunately, most Americans have only a vague understanding of its role in the regulation of the U.S. economy. "It is well that the people of the nation do not understand our banking and monetary system," warned Henry Ford, "for if it did, I believe there would be a revolution before tomorrow morning."[1] Former Congressman Ron Paul called them crooks, but they are far more evil. The bankers who control the Federal Reserve (Fed) are elite terrorists. The cozy symbiotic relationship between the politicians and bankers has enabled them to pull off the longest running financial hoax in history. They share a good deal of the blame for the imminent worldwide economic collapse. The only solution for putting an end to the fraud is to terminate the Fed and restore the government's control over U.S. currency.

There is truth in Thomas Jefferson's admonition that "banking institutions are more dangerous to our liberties than standing armies." He predicted in 1816 that, "If the American people allow private banks to control the issue of their currency, first by inflation and then by deflation, the banks and corporations that will grow up around them will deprive the people of all property until their children wake up homeless on the continent their fathers founded."[2] That chillingly describes the condition of today's U.S. economy.

The Federal Reserve System was surreptitiously created in 1913 and was given the official sounding title to mislead the public to believe it was a government agency. In fact, unless the percentage of shares have changed, since 1983 the majority eight owners of the New York Fed in order of the largest to smallest shareholders are Citibank, Chase Manhattan, Morgan Guaranty Trust, Chemical Bank, Manufacturers Hanover Trust, Bankers Trust Company, National Bank of North America, and the Bank of New York. Many of the shareholder banks are foreign owned by about a dozen European banking organizations, the Rothschild banking dynasty being the most notable.

The mainstream media perpetuates the public's misconception that it is a government agency working for the country's benefit. Actually, the U.S. government delegated issuing money directly and entrusted the Fed with the task. The Fed creates money out of thin air and then lends it to the government with interest. This arrangement should be too stupid to be true, but it is. It has contributed to the Fed becoming the most undemocratic and powerful institution in America. Indeed, it is now considered "the fourth branch of government" without the inconvenient constraints of checks and balances the other three branches operate under. Consequently, it has surreptitiously siphoned tens of trillions of American taxpayer dollars from the national treasury for more than a century.

Privately owned banks in control of the U.S.'s money supply is inherently suspicious. Banking, dating back to the Roman Empire, reveals that it has been historically evil and corrupt. Indeed, the biblical money changers, predecessors to bankers, demanded that the Messiah be crucified after he violently turned over their tables and chased them from the temple grounds. The history of central banks and the international banking system since then has been just as sordid.

Despite the sheer volume of available information on the Fed, the corporate media provides virtually no analysis of its impact on the national and world economies. The media also scrupulously avoids

William E. Cloud

reporting on the damage the Fed and the international banking cartel has inflicted on the American economy since the Great Recession.

"We are literally being robbed by illegal criminal banks as they laugh at the Greek riots, they are: the European Central Bank, IMF, Former Nazi bank – the Bank of International Settlements (BIS), Goldman Sachs, Wall Street, the corrupt financial system and the offshore Central Banks. They crashed the stock market, created the housing bubble (crashing it by design) then bailed us out with our own tax money, then robbed us all again. Our pension funds are now being plundered, all our money and rights stolen from us, they are trying to change all the laws (illegally) and as these central bankers try to get away with our trillions of hard earned money..."[3]

Having been designed to be independent from political influences, it shrouds its operations in secrecy with no oversight or accountability. Its virtually unlimited power to control the nation's money supply behind this veil of secrecy permits it to engage in all manner of theft on behalf of its shareholder banks. The nature and magnitude of the deceit rarely comes to the surface. Again, "[m]ost Americans have no real understanding of the operation of the international money lenders," said conservative Senator Barry Goldwater. "The accounts of the Federal Reserve System have never been audited. It operates outside the control of Congress and manipulates the credit of the United States."[4]

William E. Cloud

In 2007, the Fed launched a bond buying *con game* it called Quantitative Easing or QE, generously described as an "unconventional" monetary policy to stimulate the economy since everything has else failed. The program is actually a scheme to give free money to banks by buying their and other private financial institutions' assets. Financial assets are intangible assets, such as stocks and bonds, deriving their value from contractual claims traded on stock markets. Tangible assets, on the other hand, are land, buildings, machinery, inventory, etc. The value of intangible assets is completely dependent on the vagary of the financial markets; up one day, down the next. The gonifs purchased $85 billion dollars in assests a month for seven years until it ended the program in October, 2014. In three iterations, the Fed bought, strike that, gave banks $1.5 trillion during QE1, $600 billion during QE2, and $1.6 trillion during QE3; netting the banks $4 trillion of free money when the program ended.[5] The end result was the program artificially raised the assets' prices, making the banks even richer. The Fed's balance sheet essentially doubled to a record $4 trillion. Despite the ending of the unprecedented asset purchase program, "normality" has by no means returned. It did not stimulate the economy; it is still in the doldrums. Thus, there is no dispute that the Quantitative Easing scam was a roaring success for the crooked Fed and banks. American taxpayers, to put it indelicately, took it in the keister.

The QE program was chump-change when compared to the secret, colossal "loans" of $12.3 trillion of American taxpayer money the

Fed gave to international banks.[6] Put into context, this equals 75 percent of the $16.5 trillion U.S. national debt.

On top of that, in May, 2009 the Fed's Inspector General Elizabeth Coleman admitted that it could not account for $9 trillion in *off-balance sheet* transactions. An off-balance sheet transaction is bank parlance for *under-the-table* payment that's untraceable with an audit. In a hearing held by Rep. Alan Grayson to investigate the Fed, Coleman did not intelligently answer a series of questions put to her about the missing money. "Coleman could not tell Grayson what kind of losses the Fed has so far suffered on its $2 trillion portfolio, which has greatly expanded since September. She appeared unaware that the Fed engages in trillions of dollars in off-balance-sheet exchanges. She is not investigating the role of the Fed in allowing the collapse of Lehman Brothers. She did not know where the Fed has invested its $2 trillion on the liability side of the balance sheet. 'I do not know. We have not looked at that specific area at this particular point on,' she said."[7] Although the Inspector General's website definitively states that it "conducts independent and objective audits, inspections, evaluations, investigations, and other reviews related to programs and operations of the Board of Governors of the Federal Reserve System," Coleman testified her office did "not have jurisdiction to directly go out and audit reserve bank activities specifically."[8] She either did not understand her job or was simply playing the dumb card to avoid disclosing that the Fed robbed American taxpayers of trillions of dollars.

William E. Cloud

In an effort to tamp down congressional outrage stemming from its complete lack of transparency, the Fed "granted [the American people] the honor and privilege of finding out the specifics, a limited one-time Federal Reserve view, of a secret taxpayer funded 'backdoor bailout' by a small group of unelected bankers. This data release reveals 'emergency lending programs' that doled out $12.3 trillion in taxpayer money – $3.3 trillion in liquidity, $9 trillion in 'other financial arrangements'... and Congress didn't know any of the details...."[9] The Fed still refused, however, to disclose the terms and conditions of the so-called no interest loans.

No different than a pirate ship captain devoting up with the crew booty captured from an enemy ship, the Fed doled out the money plundered from the United States treasury to the usual suspects;

JP Morgan, Goldman Sachs, Bank of America, and Citigroup got the most generous shares of the financial bonanza, but central banks in Australia, Denmark, Japan, Mexico, Norway, South Korea, Sweden, Switzerland, and England also received substantial payments out of cuts the largesse, as did foreign primary dealers such as Credit Suisse (Switzerland), Deutsche Bank (Germany), Royal Bank of Scotland (U.K.), and Barclays (U.K). Many foreign banks that were in financial trouble received monies even though they had no dealings with the American banks.[10]

The *Financial Times*, a pro-business newspaper reported: "The initial reactions [of critics] were shocked at the breath of lending, particularly to foreign firms. But the details paint a bleaker and even more disturbing picture."[11] The loan was just a couple trillion shy of the $14 trillion total market value of products and services produced in the U.S. in 2009!

The Fed's shocking disclosure prompted Congress to pass the Dodd-Frank Act in July, 2010 which for the first time required the Fed to bi-annually disclose information about discount loans made to borrowers.[12] Prior to its passage, the identity of the borrower, the purpose of the loan, its amount and terms were kept secret, even from Congress. Some considered the legislation to be a step in the right direction, while its critics noted that the important restrictions on audits were unchanged since the Government Accounting Office (GAO) is still prohibited from evaluating the economic merits of its policy decisions, a critically important aspect of its operations. In other words, the law only required the Fed to tell the government what loans it made two years after the fact, but did not obligate it to disclose the basis for making the loans in the first place. Thus, the criticism some policy-makers and grass-root organizations like the Tea Party were well taken that the law did not go far enough to prevent another financial crisis or more bank bailouts.

The media marginalized 2012 presidential candidate, former Congressman Ron Paul, as a Tea Party-backed wacko who ran on reducing government spending, taxes, the national debt, and the federal budget deficit. He was also characterized by the media as fringe presidential candidate because he opposed the wars in Afghanistan and Iraq, and promised to bring the troops home if elected. The Jewish-controlled media was mum about the fact that Paul called for criminal prosecution of Wall Street bankers and the abolishment of the Fed because it diverged sharply from the interests of the business and banking elites. Thus, the media used negative propaganda to dismiss him as irrelevant.

Recognizing that legislation abolishing the Fed would go nowhere in a Congress owned by the banks, Paul introduced the Federal Reserve Transparency Act of 2012.[13] The act would have removed restrictions that prohibited the government from examining the Fed's deliberations and substantive details of lending transactions. Fed Chairman Ben Bernanke vehemently opposed the bill on the specious grounds that it would be "a mistake to eliminate the exemption for monetary policy and deliberations which would effectively, at least to some extent, create a political influence or a political dampening effect on the Federal Reserve's policy decisions."[14] This contention is absurd. The country's politicians should have controlling input on the formation of the nation's economic policy instead of leaving it to a self-serving third-party...the Fed. The Republican-controlled House passed the bill over Bernanke's objection in July, 2012, but the measure died before reaching the Senate floor due to Democrat and President Obama's opposition. They served their masters well.

President Obama's opposition to the bill is another example of his penchant to oppose anything that may negatively affect banks and Wall Street, as evidenced by his administration's failure to bring criminal charges against a single banker responsible for the banking crisis. With the defeat of this groundbreaking legislation, the Fed continues to perpetrate the most brazenly unimaginable crooked

William E. Cloud

schemes with no fear that the American people will find out what it was doing or that politicians will do anything about it.

It bears repeating that the Fed has complete control of the nation's money supply in large part because "there has been a virtual complete blackout of the facts and truths regarding money issuance and its vital importance to the nation...the coordinated control of the mass media in order to both suppress information and to indoctrinate the citizens of the nation as to how they will think, what they will believe, and how they will act. Due to [this], the information... regarding the truth of money issuance in our nation is not published in newspapers, discussed on television, spoken of on the radio, printed in magazines, or taught in college (or even any academic) courses. Even CPA's and many other professions with college degrees of advanced standing will not know of the simple and vital truths regarding the issuance of our nation's money..."[15]

A false flag is an operation designed to deceive the public into believing that something bad has been carried out by another entity. In 2012, the media went to extraordinary lengths to convince the nation that economy would go over the so-called "fiscal cliff" if a deficit reduction deal was not reached by January 1, 2013. Not coincidentally, Bernanke coined the term fiscal cliff to shift the blame for the bad economy away from the Fed where it belonged, to Congress and the Obama administration. The media pumped that farce like there was no tomorrow. January 1st passed with no deficit reduction deal or cataclysmic consequences...surprise, surprise! The

William E. Cloud

Fed-created fiscal cliff emergency, therefore, permitted it to avoid scrutiny of its substantial role in the deficit crisis.

The foreign-owned and controlled Fed wages financial terrorism against America. Economic stability would be restored to the U.S. if it was abolished. The nation would regain control over its money, the national debt could be markedly reduced, credit would be loosened, and recessions would be less frequent and milder. A revolution to change monetary policy is long overdue, but it's doubtful that a change will come anytime soon. The Fed is simply too powerful to bring under control because it owns the nation's politicians. That sounds defeatist, but it's the harsh reality.

U.S. presidents who dared to oppose central banking did so at their peril. President Andrew Johnson was shot in an attempted assassination two years after he stopped federal deposits into the Second Bank in 1832. Undeterred, he shut the bank down two years later. Many believe Abraham Lincoln was assassinated because of his opposition to the Rothschild's involvement in the financing of both sides of the Civil War. Lincoln stated,

"The money powers prey upon the nation in times of peace and conspire against it in times of adversity. The banking powers are more despotic than a monarchy, more insolent than autocracy, more selfish than bureaucracy. They denounce as public enemies all who question their methods or throw light upon their crimes. I have two great enemies, the Southern Army in front of me and the bankers in the rear. Of the two, the one at my rear is my greatest foe. Corporations have been enthroned, and an era of corruption in high places will follow. The money power of the country will endeavor to prolong its reign by working upon the prejudices of the people until the wealth is aggregated in the hands of a few, and the Republic is destroyed."[16]

President James Garfield, like Lincoln, also wanted to restore the government's right to control its money. "Whoever controls the volume of money in any country," he warned in 1881, "is absolute master of all industry and commerce." He was shot on July 2, 1881, and died that September. President John F. Kennedy signed Executive Order 11110 on June 4, 1963, which took away the Federal Reserve's power to loan money to the U.S. at interest.[17] The Treasury Department was given the authority to issue silver certificates backed by its silver reserves in place of the worthless Federal Reserve Notes. The order put the Fed out of business. On November 22, 1963, Kennedy was assassinated. Although the decree was never rescinded, the Fed immediately and illegally withdrew the Silver Certificate notes and resumed circulating its worthless Federal Reserve Notes. Critics dispute the connection between Kennedy's assassination and the abolishment of the Fed as baseless conspiracy theory. They point out that on the same time he signed an Executive Order delegating his authority to issue silver certificates under the AAA of 1933 to the Secretary of the Treasury, he also signed a law which repealed the Silver Purchase Act of 1934 (Public Law 88-36, 77 Stat 54) that "gave the Fed the authority to issue $1 and $2 notes (which it couldn't do before), and revoked the Silver Purchase Act. That's important because before PL 88-36 was signed, silver certificates could be issued either by the President (under the Agricultural Adjustment Act) or the Treasury Secretary (under the Silver Purchase Act)."[18]

In April, 2014, the Fed floated a trial balloon to gauge the public's reaction to a Fed research report that praised capital control systems operating in global markets. This may portend the end of the so-called free market economy and regulation of cash flows in and out of the U.S. Several countries experiencing a currency crisis have instituted capital controls that limit the amount of cash citizens can withdraw from their bank accounts and/or block foreign investors from selling their assets in the country.

The crisis in Ukraine caused dire financial consequences for its economy. While the corporate media's attention focused on Crimea, Russian President Vladimir Putin, and the economic sanctions imposed by the U.S. and Europe, it ignored that the Ukraine central bank pressured the country's domestic banks to give it complete control over their operations. Privatbank, Ukraine's largest bank with 45 million customers, was forced to limit over-the-counter teller and automated teller machine withdrawals to $103 per day. It ceased writing new loans, and all private and corporate credit lines, including credit cards, were suspended. It stopped accepting Crimean customers' debit cards to prevent a run on it.

Touting capital controls as an effective tool for managing financial stability, the Fed paper claimed that its implementation would guard the U.S. dollar against the effects of rapid cash movements. Johns Hopkins University professor of applied economics, Steve Hanke, believes that "[c]apital controls signal that a country is very worried about preserving its foreign exchange...That means bad things are in the wind."[19]

The U.S. dollar is the reserve currency of the global financial system. An international switch to another reserve currency – that China and Russia would welcome – and the imposition of capital controls would destroy the value of the dollar and accelerate the decline of the U.S. as an economic superpower. The trillions of dollars the Fed has printed and put into circulation with nothing to back it will cause inflation to rise exponentially. It would have to pay for imports in foreign currency like every other country in the world. Enormous debts could no longer be racked up and paid for by simply printing more money. Trouble is on America and the world's financial horizon. The Fed and its central bank cohorts are to blame.

In conclusion, since the political leaders are unable and unwilling to abolish the Fed, it's going to take a major revolution on the grassroots level to take back the nation's control of its money supply and economy. The urgency of the situation cannot be overstated because the country is on the brink of financial ruin.

It might take divine intervention to change the situation considering the Messiah was crucified for trying to control bankers.

William E. Cloud

CHAPTER 6

Ariel Sharon: A Western Revered War Criminal

It is not just Sabra and Chatilla. He committed so many crimes against Arabs everywhere. ... He is truly a butcher.

~ Adnan al-Mikdad,
a Lebanese man who lost both his parents in the massacre.

On January 11, 2014, former Israel Prime Minister Ariel Sharon, the "Beirut Butcher", died after being in a stroke induced vegetative state for eight years. Much of the Arab world celebrated his death. Reaction in the Western world was the opposite. President Obama released an obligatory statement about the death of the war criminal saying, "Michelle and I send our deepest condolences to the family of former Israeli Prime Minister Ariel Sharon and to the people of Israel on the loss of a leader who dedicated his life to the State of Israel."[1] He followed with the rote reaffirmation of America's unbending commitment to Israel's security. Vice President Joe Biden attended Sharon's funeral and said his passing felt "like a death of a friend," and praised his "courage".[2] In short, contrary to the worldwide consensus outside of the West that Sharon was a mass murderer, the Obama administration revered him as a respected leader and statesman.

In Obama's defense, as a Zionist sock puppet, he has no alternative but to publically honor one of the leading representatives of his overlords. United States' foreign policy is likewise dictated and unduly influenced by Israel, even when it is apparent that the Zionist agenda is not in America's best interest...and often detrimental. Indeed, Sharon once said, "Every time we do something you tell me Americans will do this and will do that. I want to tell you something very clear, don't worry about American pressure on Israel. We, the Jewish people, control America, and the Americans know it."

The corporate media conceded that Sharon was controversial, but predictably lionized him as a great warrior who also sought genuine peace with Israel's Arab neighbors. In a *Washington Post* article, it was written that he "epitomized the country's warrior past even as he sought to become the architect for a peaceful future."[3] Former U.S. Secretary of State Henry Kissinger, a war criminal in his own right, eulogized Sharon in his blog stating, "Arik Sharon started as a warrior. He ended his career on the way to being a peacemaker." He also wrote, "As prime minister, Sharon unexpectedly broadened his definition of security. He sought to bridge the gap between physical and political security with the same courage and decisiveness that had brought him victory in battle. He volunteered the largest withdrawal in Israel's history. He ended the Israeli occupation of Gaza and returned it to Arab self-rule as a unilateral act without reciprocity, abandoning even the Jewish settlements that had been established."[4]

William E. Cloud

This description of Sharon's personal transformation, if it were true, would make a very uplifting story. It could serve as the basis for a Hollywood movie in the spirit of the 1960 blockbuster hit *Exodus*, which provided a fanciful pro-Zionist account of the creation of the state of Israel absent the mass murder and expulsion of the Palestinians.

In reality, instead of Sharon's Israel making a sacrificial step toward peace, it's withdrawal from Gaza in the summer of 2005 simply reflected the abandonment of a costly and untenable position; the Israel Defense Forces (IDF) expending considerable resources to protect only 8,000 Jewish settlers living among 1.3 million Palestinians in a land area comprising just five percent of the overall Occupied Territories. As Middle East historian Juan Cole put it: "For Sharon, Gaza itself could be configured as an enormous slum. The withdrawal of the Israeli colonists from Gaza was simply a way of moving them into the gated community, so as to keep them safe more cheaply than military patrols and reprisals could hope to."[5]

Moreover, as has now become quite obvious, the Israeli withdrawal did not mean that Israel had given up effective control of Gaza. Rather, Israel still maintained full control of the water, communications, airspace, and all border entry and exit points. Israel also insists it has the right to intervene militarily inside Gaza at any time, with little or no provocation. Gaza has essentially become a jail for its inhabitants with Israel serving as its jailer.

Sharon was one of the leading proponents for physical security through the occupation Arab lands. Israel's occupation has completely isolated the Palestinians from the rest of the world. Yet, the mainstream media continues to portray him as someone seeking peace with the Palestinians. That portrayal is a revisionist lie that could not stray farther from the truth. The Zionist-owned media deliberately fails to mention Sharon's bloody war crime history. As the architect of the Israeli invasion of Lebanon in 1982 under false pretenses, a reported 20,000 Palestinians and Lebanese were killed. It was during that war that he committed his most infamous atrocity. He sent right-wing Christian paramilitary forces, known as the Phalangist militias, into Palestinian refugee camps in Sabra and Shatila, and stood by for three days while they massacred at least 3,500 Palestinian, mostly civilian men, women and children.

Despite international condemnation for his role in the massacre, he was elected president in March, 2001; three months after Bush started his presidency and six months before the events of 9-11. What does it say about a nation that elects a mass murderer as president? But then, again, the American people reelected George Bush to a second term.

No wonder much of the Arab world did not mourn Sharon's death. I say much because, incredibly, several Arab countries foolishly consider themselves Israel allies despite its plans to dominate them or even take their land. A Hamas spokeswoman in Gaza, on the other hand, predicted Palestinians will always revile him. "Sharon's death is a lesson for a bad end," she posted on social media.[6] Noam Chomsky could think of "nothing good to say [about Sharon],…He was a brutal killer. He had one fixed idea in mind, which drove him

William E. Cloud

all his life: a greater Israel, as powerful as possible, as few Palestinians as possible – they should somehow disappear – and an Israel that could be powerful enough to dominate the region."[7]

Israel President Shimon Peres eulogized Sharon as a "military legend" who in political life "turned his gaze to the day Israel would dwell in safety, when our children would return to our borders and peace would grace the Promised Land."[8] The borders Peres speaks of returning to encompasses much of the Middle East; a reaffirmation of Israel's founding fathers' vision to become a dominant regional powerhouse "Greater Israel" with borders encroaching into the territories of neighboring countries.

Sharon, just like the other Israeli leaders, have no intention of righting their wrongs or work with the Palestinians for a two-state solution. Their discussions are nothing but a ruse to placate the world and hide their true intentions. Their ultimate goal is for Eretz Israel, from the Nile to the Euphrates, killing every Arab in its path to take their land and resources. Israelis have a God-like complex…believing the lie that they are the chosen ones. They have used this to justify stealing the birthrights of another people.

Sharon is responsible for the continuation of Palestinian misery and will be remembered as such despite Western adoration.

William E. Cloud

CHAPTER 7

Susan Rice's Sordid Foreign Policy Record

I once naively criticized President Obama for passing over Susan Rice to replace Hillary Clinton as Secretary of State. I wrote,

"United Nations Ambassador Susan Rice's withdrawal from consideration for nomination to be the next secretary of state is actually an abandonment of a damsel in distress. In her letter of resignation to President Obama, Rice explained that she made the decision because she didn't want to subject the administration to a "lengthy, disruptive and costly" confirmation battle that archrival Republican Senator John McCain vowed to lead. Obama said he agreed with her decision and didn't try to convince her otherwise. From all indications, though, it was Obama who didn't want to wage the good fight to win her confirmation and nudged her to withdraw. Rice deserved to have been rescued from the dragon."[1]

How wrong could a Negro have been? Had I adequately researched Rice's background, I would have concluded that she would have been a terrible Secretary of State. This does not suggest that the president's selection of John Kerry was any better by any stretch of the imagination. The sad fact is that given past performance, chances are anyone Obama selects to be in his cabinet is next to worthless when it comes to serving the interests of *all* Americans.

My criticism of Obama is precisely what I accuse other Black folks of doing when they express extreme adoration and unflagging support for the president for no other reason than he is Black. In this instance, I too put the appearance of a Black face in high office over the substance of the person's character. I sincerely apologize.

In an article written by Glen Ford, executive editor of *Black Agenda Report*, entitled "The Shameless Vacuity of Susan Rice's Black Boosters," he said tragically, gullible Blacks "have rallied to the defense of a woman who has been mugging an entire continent since her appointment to Bill Clinton's national security staff in 1993...In their reflexive circling of the wagons around United Nations Ambassador Susan Rice, the U.S. Black Misleadership Class reveal a total absence of political or moral values beyond the narrow pursuit of group prestige through proximity to imperial power."[2] I, for one, was clearly among the overtrusting Blacks who were either clueless or didn't care about Rice's appalling political career that has left and continues to leave a wide swatch of death and destruction across Africa and the Middle East.

President Bill Clinton appointed Rice to his National Security Council staff before promoting her to be the Director of International Organizations and Peacekeeping at age 28. She eventually rose to become Senior Director for the Bureau of African Affairs in the U.S. State Department. Some wonder whether Rice's mercurial rise had anything to do with her father, Emmett J. Rice, being a former World Bank official and member of the Federal Reserve Board of Governors – chief gonifs.

As the director of African Affairs, in 1994 Rice stood by, almost as a casual observer, as the genocide in Rwanda took its horrible course. Indeed, she refused to describe the mass slaughter as *genocide*. Pursuant to the United Nation's convention on genocide, the U.S., and other signatory nations were obligated "to prevent and punish actions of genocide in war and in peacetime."[3] Rice played the word game, and was central in the decision-making process to avoid U.S. intervention in one of only three cases of genocide in the 20th century.

An estimated 800,000 to one million Tutsi men, women and children, as well as Hutu sympathizers, were massacred over 100 days of hell. [Note: See information in Prologue that questions the accuracy of the numbers killed in terms of ethnicity]. Bill Clinton didn't want to call it genocide and intervene because he wanted to avoid the possibility of a repeat of the embarrassment he experienced in Somalia where the awesome might of the U.S. armed forces was run out of the country by militants using artillery mounted on the beds of Toyota pickup trucks they called *technicals*. National politics also played into the decision to not interfere in the carnage because, according to Rice: "If we use the word 'genocide' and are seen as doing nothing, what will be the effect on the November congressional election?"[4]

In April, 1994, Hutu President Juvenal Habyarimana was killed when his plane was shot down. He was returning from peace negotiations with a Tutsi group in Tanzania. Although it was not clear at the time who was responsible, credible evidence has emerged that the order was given by Paul Kagame, head of the Rwandan Patriotic Front (RPF). Within hours of the president's death, enraged Hutus, who had already been primed by radio broadcasts and politicians to treat Tutsis as *cockroaches*, began a systematic campaign to totally annihilate the Tutsi population. To put the conflict into historical context, the catalyst for the violence was created by Belgian colonialists in the early 1900's. Employing divide and conquer techniques, preference was given to the Tutsi minority over the Hutu majority. The white Belgians considered the tall, thin, lighter-complexioned Tutsi similar to them and more intelligent. They were given better jobs and greater educational opportunities. The Belgians, and even the Tutsis, believed the darker-skin, short and stout Hutus were ethnically inferior. The distinctions between the two native groups were reinforced by government issued identity cards which classified them as Tutsi or Hutu. In an ironic twist, the coveted identity cards that bestowed a measure of privilege to Tutsis later marked them for death.

The resentment between the two festered and intensified over the decades, often leading to bloodshed and the forced exile of hundreds of thousands of Tutsis into neighboring countries. Barred from returning, Tutsi refugees in Uganda formed the Rwandan Patriotic Front (RPF), more commonly known as Inkotanyi, and invaded Rwanda when the government refused to enter into a power sharing agreement. French and Zairian forces helped the Rwandan military defeat the rebels. The Hutus blamed the Tutsis living in the country for the attack, and the Rwandan government retaliated by killing 2,000 Tutsi civilians.

Murdering one million people over a 100-day span took hard work and a maniacal sense of purpose. Six Rwandans died every minute; creating a death toll equaling the population of Dallas, Texas, the tenth largest city in America.

Because it is difficult to appreciate genocide in the abstract, it is essential to understand the horror of it through the words of the victims and the murderers. The following are a few of their graphic accounts selected from two books written by Jean Hatzfeld entitled, *Machete Season: The Killers in Rwanda Speak* and *Laid Bare: The Survivors in Rwanda Speak.*

The killers' prospective:

"The first day, a messenger from the municipal judge went house to house summoning us to a meeting right away. There the judge announced that the reason for the meeting was the killing of every Tutsi without exception. It was simply said, and it was simple to understand.

So the only questions were about the details of the operation. For example, how and when we had to begin, since

William E. Cloud

we were not used to this activity, and where to begin, too, since the Tutsis had run off in all directions. There were even some guys who asked if there were any priorities.

The judge answered sternly: 'There is no need to ask how to begin. The only worthwhile plan is to start straight ahead into the bush, and right now, without hanging back anymore behind questions.'

We would wake up at six o'clock. We ate brochettes of grilled meat and nourishing food because of all the running we had to do. We met up in town, near the shops, and chatted with pals along the way to the soccer field. There they would give us orders about the killings and our itineraries for the day, and off we went, beating the bush, working our way down to the marshes. We formed a line to wade into the mud and the papyrus. Then we broke up into small bands of friends or acquaintances."

~ Pio

"The club is more crushing, but the machete is more natural. The Rwandan is accustomed to the machete from childhood. Grab a machete – that is what we do every morning. We cut sorghum, we prune banana trees, we hack out vines, we kill chickens. The blade, when you use it to cut branch, animal, or man, it has nothing to say.

In the end, a man is like an animal: you give him a whack on the head or the neck and down he goes. Only young guys used clubs. The club has no use in agriculture, but it was better suited to their way of trying to stand out, of strutting in the crowd. Same thing for spear and bows: those who still had them could find it entertaining to lend them or show them off."

~ Elie

"Killing could certainly be thirsty work, draining and often disgusting. Still it was more productive than raising crops, especially for someone with a meager plot of land or barren soil."

~Ignace

"The Thursday when we went to the church in Ntarama, the people just lay there in the dim light, the wounded visible between the pews, the unhurt hiding beneath the pews, and the dead in the aisles all the way to the foot of the altar. We were the only ones making a commotion.

Them, they were waiting for death in the calm of the church. For us, it was no longer important that we found ourselves in a house of God. We yelled, we gave orders, we insulted, we sneered. We verified person by person, inspecting the faces, so as to finish off everyone conscientiously. If we had any doubt about a death agony, we dragged the body outside to examine it in the light of heaven,"

~ Alphonse

William E. Cloud

"When we spotted a small group of runaways trying to escape by creeping through the mud, we called them snakes. Before the killings, we usually called them cockroaches. But during, it was more suitable to call them snakes, because of their attitude, or zeros, or dogs, because in our country we don't like dogs; in any case, they were less-than-nothings.

For some of us, those taunts were just minor diversions. The important thing was not to let them get away. For others, the insults were invigorating, made the job easier. The perpetrators felt more comfortable insulting and hitting crawlers in rags rather than properly upright people. Because they seemed less like us in that position."

~ Adalbert

Resigned that no one would be coming to their rescue, Tutsis did their best to hide from gangs of killers. Those that were young and fit enough tried to outrun their Hutu pursuers while the elderly, sick, and parents with young children hid for days among the tall papyrus in the mud of the marshes waiting for death.

The survivors' perspective:

"In the morning, we could not even give ourselves a little moment to dry out in the rising sun. We went off again, soaked through, to deposit the children in little groups under the cover of the papyrus. We told them to stay as nice as fish in the ponds – meaning not to put more than a head out of the water and not to cry. We gave them muddy water to drink, even if it were sometimes tinged with blood.

Then, in our turn we covered ourselves in mud. Sometimes, we would glimpse one another through the surrounding foliage. We asked ourselves why God had forsaken us here, in the midst of snakes, which fortunately did not bite anyone.

We went down very early. The little ones hid first, the grown-ups acted as look-outs and talked about the disaster that had befallen us...they were the last to hide. Then there was killing all day long. In the beginning, the Hutus played tricks in the papyrus, for example they said, 'I've recognized you, you can come out' and the most innocent got up and were massacred standing. Or else Hutus were guided by the cries of little children, who could not stand the mud anymore.

The killers worked in the swamps from nine to four, half past four, as the sun would have it. Sometimes, if it rained too much, they came later in the morning. They came in columns, announcing their arrival with songs and whistles. They beat drums, they sounded very cheerful to be going killing for an entire day.

One morning, they would take one path, the next day another path. When we heard the first whistles, we disappeared in the opposite direction. One morning, they cheated, they came from all sides springing traps and ambushes; and that day was a very dispiriting one because we knew that that evening there would be more than the usual number of dead.

William E. Cloud

In the afternoon they (the killers) would not sing anymore because they were tired, but chatting away, they returned to their homes. They fortified themselves with drink and by eating the cows that they had slaughtered at the same time as the Tutsis. These were truly very calm and accomplished killings. If the RPF liberators had delayed one week more on the road, there would not be a single Bugesera Tutsi left living to deny the lies, such as the criminals' so-called drunkenness."

~ Angélique Mukamanzi"

In the evening, after the killings, we scattered out into the night to dig in fields, collect manioc and beans. It was also the banana season. We ate raw for a month, hands filthy with mud, like louts. It was the same fate for adults as for little children, who no longer had the opportunity to drink maternal milk or other nutritious substances. So, many people, even though not struck by machetes, were sprung by a deadly weakness. In the morning, we woke and we found them, lying beside us, stiffened in their sleep. And we, without a word of farewell for them, without a last gift from time, were unable to cover them decently. We made the most of rainy nights by rubbing ourselves down with palm leaves, cleaning away the thickest coatings of refuse and the mud filth. Then we lay down on the ground. We talked of the day, wondered who had died that day, asked ourselves who was to die the next. We discussed the evil

William E. Cloud

fate that had fallen on our heads. We did not exchange many words of joy, but many despondent ones."

~ Angélique Mukamanzi

"During the evening assemblies, we could catch hold of no news from anywhere because radio sets no longer blared out, except in the killers' homes. Still, we understood by word of mouth that the genocide has spread over the country, that all Tutsis were suffering the same fate, that no one would come to save us anymore. We thought that we would all have to die. As for me, I no longer concerned myself with thinking about when I would die, since we were going to die anyway, only with how the cuts would hack at me; only about how long it would take, because I was very frightened of the suffering machetes bestow."

~ Francine Niyitegeka

"On certain evenings, when the evil-doers had not killed too much that day, we gathered around glowing embers to eat something cooked; on other evenings, we were too dispirited. In the marsh, at dawn the next day, we found the same blood in the mud...corpses going off in the same places.

These corpses offended our spirits to such an extent that, even amongst ourselves, we did not dare speak of them. They all too bluntly showed us how our own life would end. Which is the reason why our utmost wish in the morning was simply to make it through to the end of the afternoon one more time."[4]

Révérien Rurangwa raptly watched a French news clip, taken three weeks after the genocide began, of a child sitting among bodies laid out in a Kabgayi hospital. Seated in front of a dead woman, "he is shockingly injured, even under his bandages. He is missing an arm and his forehead is badly disfigured by swelling. His mouth is an agonized O. A dressing covers the place where his left eye should be, but what fixates Révérien when he watches the footage is the other eye, a large, black marble petrified by disbelief."[5] He's the child in the footage, and 15 years later still cannot believe what happened to him and his family. A Hutu neighbor, who his family knew and sometimes went to the local bar he owned, one day calmly hacked to death 43 members of his extended family. The U.N. rescued 30 nuns and two priests the day before, but left the Tutsis to their doom. Sure enough, his neighbor showed up with a group of men and they slaughtered his family "one by one inside the goat shed they had hidden in for a fortnight, but Révérien survived despite horrific wounds. 'I just couldn't seem to die,' he says. 'And when I asked them to kill me, they laughed and taunted me. They said, 'Look at the cockroach crawling.' They said, 'Hey, dead-on-legs, can't you go any faster?' They took bets on how long I would live.' The killers then set fire to everything and burned the bodies of his parents, sisters and other relatives. 'So, I sat among their teeth, the only thing that was left of my family.'"[6]

William E. Cloud

Some Tutsis *luckily* met their fate with a bullet instead of machete. One gentleman was spared the agony because he was a good man, according to his daughter who described what happened when the order came to kill her elderly father:

"[A]ll the killers refused. They said we cannot kill such a holy man. And they told those responsible for the killings, 'you go and kill him yourself, we cannot go an attack this man because he is like our father.' They said 'this man is a good man, he did good to all of us. How can we go and kill him?' He said, 'go and kill him.' They refused. They went to find a policeman; people who didn't know him. They went and they bought them and they came. Before killing him they said, 'Moses we are coming to kill you, but we ask you to forgive us. We don't know you, we haven't seen you, but we have heard you are a good person. You have so much respect in this community, but it is an order. We have been given an order. We have been given an order to come and kill you and go. But please forgive us. But because you are a good man, we will not kill you with a machete. We will not kill you with a spear. We will shoot you.' And he said, 'before you kill me can I ask a favor?' They said 'yes.' 'Can I call my wife and talk to her for the last time?' They said, 'yes.' He said, 'give us some minutes.' They apologized to one another. They told each other what they needed to tell each other. He said after that, 'now we are ready, you can kill us now.' And they shot him.

William E. Cloud

And he was lucky to not have been hacked to death. Others were killed by nail hammers. He was killed by [unintelligible]. They shot him and they left him and the rest were killed; really, it was very bad. Cutting to pieces and torturing. So, this way you understand how he was. Yeah." [ld]

Rape was the rule, not the exception in the genocide. An estimated 250,000 to 500,000 women and girls were raped. "Sexual violence occurred everywhere, and no one was spared," according to a United Nations report.[8] "Grandmothers were raped in front of their grandchildren; girls witnessed their families being massacred before being taken as sex slaves; fathers were forced to have sex with their daughters. Many women were murdered following rape. Almost all of the women who did survive the genocide were victims of sexual violence or were profoundly affected by it."[8]

Genocide is the gravest crime that can be committed against humanity. Article Two of the U.N. Convention on Genocide defines it as "any of the following acts committed with the intent to destroy, in whole or in part, a national, ethnic, racial or religious group, as such: Killing members of a group; Causing serious bodily or mental harm to members of the group; Deliberately inflicting on the group conditions of life calculated to bring about its physical destruction in whole or in part. The convention imposes a general duty on signatory states to 'prevent and to punish' genocide."[9]

Although there has been some debate as to how the convention should be interpreted, there is no real dispute that it occurred in

Rwanda. As previously mentioned, in total disregard of international law, Susan Rice refused to describe the mass murder of a million Tutsis and Hutu sympathizers as genocide because to do so might have had adverse ramifications for upcoming congressional elections. For Rice, the risk of losing some Democrat congressional seats trumped stopping the killing of hundreds of thousands of innocent civilians. Let the Rwandans "deal with that...The only thing we have to do is look the other way," Rice is quoted as saying.[10] If looking the other way wasn't enough, the Clinton administration agreed with the U.N. Security Council to refuse a request by a Canadian U.N. commander to deploy 5,000 troops to quell the violence. Instead, it endorsed putting only a skeleton force of 270 soldiers on the ground; who were powerless to stop the bloodbath.

The Clinton administration's refusal to take action to quell the genocide shirked the U.S.'s responsibilities to the international community. More than that, if the prosecution at Nuremberg of Nazis responsible for failing to prevent the killing of Jews during the holocaust set any precedent, Clinton and Rice's failure to protect Rwandans constituted war crimes.

Is there any doubt that Clinton or Rice would not hesitate a nanosecond to scream genocide to the rafters if a miniscule fraction of Israelis were being killed by Palestinians or Iranians? Surely, they would not have opted to do nothing if something far less horrific was happening to the residents of London? They would have brought to bear the full force of the U.S.'s military might on the perpetrators.

William E. Cloud

Rice later admitted that it was a mistake to not intervene in Rwanda to stop the killings. "I swore to myself that if I ever faced such a crisis again, I would come down on the side of dramatic action, going down in flames if that was required," she said.[11] Before becoming Obama's U.N. ambassador, Rice backtracked in an effort to absolve herself from direct culpability. She shifted the blame to U.S. policy and directives. "No policymakers in Washington or on Capitol Hill or any editorial boards, for that matter, were advocating U.S. military intervention in Rwanda," explained Rice. "It wasn't an option that was ever credibly contemplated, whether or not that would have been the right option."[12] Rice was duty bound to refuse to carry out illegal directives of the president. Instead, as point person, she should have exerted more pressure on Clinton to use U.S. power to stop the violence as well as attract international attention to the unfolding tragedy – or quit. "In other words, she could have done more to minimize the scope, duration and magnitude of the genocide but failed miserably and allowed genocide of a biblical proportion to take place on her watch with indifference. That is undeniable historical fact!"[13]

"[T]o this day she espouses polices in the eastern Congo that obscures US support for those that endorse, supply, and encourage the M23 genocidal actions there—the same forces that promoted the Rwandan genocide."[14] While not a power unto herself, Rice has slavishly and unabashedly pursued the warlike policy objectives of American globalization of Africa.

William E. Cloud

Clinton appointed Rice as Assistant Secretary of State for African Affairs in 1997 where her views toward using military intervention for humanitarianism morphed into a hawkish agenda for American empire building.

After leaving the government in 2001, Rice became managing director and principal at Intellibridge, a strategic analysis firm in Washington, D.C. Her partners in the firm were well connected in the highest echelons of the intelligence and business communities, including Anthony Lake, Clinton's national security advisor; David J. Rothkopf, an acting under secretary in the Commerce Department; and John M. Deutch, who was director of the Central Intelligence Agency.[15] The Rwandan government was one of Rice's major clients, and she befriended its strongman, President Paul Kagame.

Moving through the revolving door back into the government, Rice signed onto the Obama campaign, and was rewarded with the appointment as U.N. ambassador after he was elected in 2008. It was apparent from jump that she favored dictators over multi-party governments. Indeed, Rice never met a despot she didn't like, provided, of course, he was willing to give the U.S. total access to his country's raw materials and allow a military presence in its territory.

Rice denies her work with Rwanda at Intellibridge, and close relationship with Kagame compromised her objectivity according to her spokesman. "Ambassador Rice's brief consultancy at Intellibridge has had no impact on her work at the United Nations. She implements the agreed policy of the United States at the U.N."[16]

William E. Cloud

This is not borne out by her indefensible protection of Kagame. When the U.N. moved to publically censure him, Rice came to his defense like a junkyard dog. In a meeting with the French envoy Gerard Araud in October, 2012 Rice took him to task for "explicitly 'naming and shaming' Mr. Kagame and the Rwandan government for its support of M23, and to his proposal to consider sanctions to pressure Rwanda to abandon the rebel group."[17] "Listen Gerard," she reportedly said, "This is the D.R.C. [Democratic Republic of the Congo]. If it weren't the M23 doing this, it would be some other group."[18] This demonstrates why some in the diplomatic community call Rice's negotiating style rude and abrasive and callous.

For weeks, she blocked the U.N. report that denounced Kagame's support for the M23 rebel army, and opposed any direct reference to Rwanda in its statements and resolutions on the grave humanitarian crisis. Rice lobbied the Security Council to tone down the resolution language that "strongly condemned the M23 for widespread rape, summary executions and recruitment of child soldiers."[19] The resolution expressed *deep concern* about external actors supporting the M23, but Ms. Rice prevented the resolution from explicitly naming Rwanda when it was passed."[20] When it comes to dictators in league with the U.S., Rice is a staunch believer in constructive engagement instead of public censure. As one observer noted this was a "case of condemning the rape but not the rapist."[21]

As Obama's ambassador to the United Nations, Rice was at the vanguard of the call for U.S. military intervention in the 2011 Libyan civil war, which the U.S. instigated, unless Muammar Gaddafi and his aides stepped down. Rice falsely accused Gaddafi of committing atrocities against his own citizens. Her accusation was intended to cover-up the real motivations for removing him from power. Gaddafi was planning to introduce a single African currency, the gold-backed Dinar, and demanded that it be used to purchase oil instead of the worthless Federal Reserve note. That posed a grave threat to the international monetary system and Western economies, especially the United States' financial stability. He refused to create a Rothschild controlled Federal Reserve type central bank and encouraged African nations to establish their own central bank. The West also disliked him because wanted to create an African development bank which would have seriously diminished the World Bank and the International Monetary Fund's ability to dictate onerous terms for African development assistance. Of course, the U.S. wanted Libya's vast oil reserves, but it also coveted its 144 tons of gold bullion. Indeed, "the U.S., France, the U.K., Canada and other NATO war criminals [were] pouring into Libya to steal the Libyan people's gold. U.S. and British troops [were] already on the ground (in violation of the UN Resolution 1973) to extract the gold bullion. It is the stolen gold that Barack Obama is offering to bail out the bankrupt European Union with stolen Libyan gold."[22]

Without any evidence, Rice sought to persuade the UN Security Council to approve a resolution to intervene in the Libyan conflict on the grounds that Gaddafi was "doing reprehensible things" such as the absurd claim that he was giving Viagra to his loyalists so that they could use rape as a terror weapon. Her rape allegations were directly contradicted by U.S. military and intelligence officials who told MSNBC that there was no basis to support her claim.[23] "While rape has been reported as a 'weapon' in many conflicts," according to *Antiwar blog*, "US officials say they've seen no such reports out of Libya."[24] Rice lied.

Rice and Secretary of State Hillary Clinton overcame internal opposition by top administration officials, including Defense Secretary Robert Gates, counterterrorism advisor John Brennan and security adviser Thomas Donilon, to push a UN proposal to impose a no-fly zone over Libya and authorize other military actions as necessary. Prior to the Security Council's approval of the resolution, Rice took an even more aggressive posture saying, "We need to be prepared to contemplate steps that include, but perhaps go beyond, a no-fly zone at this point, as the situation on the ground has evolved, and as a no-fly zone has inherent limitations in terms of protection of civilians at immediate risk."[25] Rice won out.

The intent of a no-fly zone is to protect civilians, however, the so-called no-fly zone imposed on Libya was an iniquitous ruse to launch a massive aerial bombardment by NATO of "some 26,000 sorties including some 9,600 strike missions and destroyed about 5,900 targets before operations ended."[26] To hide the magnitude of the atrocities, Western media reported that the U.S. and NATO took great precautions to avoid civilian casualties. Depending upon the source, the number of civilian deaths widely varied. "In the end, according to the numbers presented, a total of 14,572 to 18,873 deaths have been reported, of which some have not been independently confirmed."[27]

William E. Cloud

The opposition initially stated in 2011, that 25,000 people had been killed, but revised down the number in 2013 to 4,700 rebel supporters dead and 2,100 missing.[28] The number of Libyan casualties caused by NATO bombing will never be known because it failed to properly investigate the civilian deaths it caused. How convenient! "NATO officials repeatedly stressed their commitment to protecting civilians," Donatella Rovera, Senior Crisis Adviser at Amnesty, said in a statement. "But they are trying to brush aside the deaths of scores of civilians with some vague statement of regret without properly investigating these deadly incidents."[29]

NATO's claim to have taken great steps to avoid civilian casualties was a lie. Libya is a small, militarily third-rate country. Commonsense dictates that NATO's massive aerial bombardment was in and of itself overkill. Libya could not possibly have had that many military targets. This was a repeat of President George Bush's *shock and awe* attack on Iraq to instill fear into the populous by killing tens of thousands of civilians and destroying the infrastructure short of complete destruction. NATO has yet to respond to Amnesty's demand to "determine whether any civilian casualties resulted from a breach of international law, and if so, those responsible should be brought to justice."[30] Whatever the death toll is, Susan Rice bears a share of responsibility for Libyan civilian and military deaths.

The annihilation of Libya let other resource-rich countries know the consequences for challenging the Western powers and their almighty dollar. But, the greater purpose rarely spoken about is that it's all a part of Eretz; Israel's plan to break up neighboring countries so they are easier to control and to gain more territory.

Despite a Pew Research Center poll that indicated a surge in the American public's opposition to striking Syria, the Obama administration made Rice the point person for going to war with Syria anyway. Rice delivered a speech to the New America Foundation, a Washington think tank and proponent of foreign wars, that was riddled with myths.[31] She used inflated casualty numbers, and claimed that there was no doubt President Bashar Assad's government was responsible for chemical attacks on rebel held territory. According to an *Associated Press* report, the American public has "yet to see a single piece of concrete evidence – no satellite imagery, no transcripts of Syrian military communications – connecting the government of President Bashar Assad to the alleged chemical weapons attack last month that killed hundreds of people."[32] Rice's assertions that military intervention would "not be the United States launching another 'war'" were ludicrous. What would bombing a country be if not starting another war? Her claim that "there will be no American boots on the ground – period," is probably not true because intelligence operatives and Special Forces units would surely have to locate and take control of weapons in a combat environment. Rice was also misleading when she said, "The Arab League foreign ministers have called for 'deterrent and necessary measures.'"[33] Aside from Saudi Arabia, not one Arab country publically called for U.S. military action.

William E. Cloud

Rice strongly condemned Russia and China for vetoing a Security Council resolution calling for Bashar to step down. "They put a stake in the heart of efforts to resolve this conflict peacefully, she said. "We the United States are standing with the people of Syria. Russia and China are obviously with Assad," adding "the United States is disgusted that a couple of members of this Council continue to prevent us from fulfilling our sole purpose."[34] Rice's performance in the Rwandan genocide matter, her "intimate involvement in the murder of six million Congolese, her frenzied campaign to bomb and block Sudan, her successful instigation of regime change in Libya, and her bloody-handed role in the ongoing torture of Somalia," wrote *Black Agenda Report's* Glen Ford, made for an astoundingly destructive career.[35] This constitutes overwhelming evidence that she is unsuited to be secretary of state, unless the position's function is to create wars. Rice was not a damsel in distress who needed to be rescued from a dragon. She is the dragon.

Postscript

New intelligence discredit the accepted U.S. version of the events surrounding the Rwanda genocide in 1994. For twenty years the Western media has reported the history of the Rwanda genocide largely from the perspective of the "RPF victors." It has hid U.S. foreign policy that made it complicit in the slaughters in Rwanda and the Congo. Unfortunately, the real truth was not revealed until after

William E. Cloud

this chapter was written. The following corrects the disinformation campaign.

A plane carrying Hutu Rwandan President Juvénal Habyarimana was shot down as it approached Kigali, the capital of the central African nation on April 6, 1994. Everyone aboard the jet perished. His assassination was the catalyst that ignited long simmering tensions between the Hutu majority and the Tutsi minority. *Official* reports variously cast suspicion for the attack on Hutu extremists, Habyarimana's elite presidential guard and the Rwandan Patriotic Front (RPF), a Tutsi rebel group that was fighting a civil war to restore the Tutsi minority to power. Many speculated the plane was shot down on orders of RPF leader Paul Kagame, who later became president of Rwanda. Until now, no definitive finding as to the identity of the perpetrators was ever reached; prompting a British journalist to conclude the identities of the assassins "could turn out to be one of the great mysteries of the late 20th Century."[36]

The Western media reported Hutus killed an estimated 800,000 to one million Tutsi civilians and some Hutu *sympathizers* – the implication being the Hutus killed many more Tutsis than fellow Hutus. The Clinton administration, in which Susan Rice was the Director of the Bureau of African Affairs in the U.S. State Department, was blamed for negligently failing to stop the genocide which ranks among the most horrifying events in the 20th century. Kagame has been portrayed as the savior who intervened to stop the genocide, rescued the country from disintegration, and restored peace and stability. The media justified the subsequent attacks he launched

William E. Cloud

against refugee camps in neighboring Democratic Republic of Congo that were occupied by Hutu civilians who fled there to escape the violence on the grounds that Hutu rebels were operating from the camps. Finally, the media minimized Kagame's role and U.S. complicity in what is known as the Great War of Africa that began in 1996 and still continues; killing six million people.

An October, 2014 documentary entitled *Rwanda's Untold Story* broadcast on BBC casts serious doubt on the long accepted propaganda.[37] Interviews with former members of Kagame's inner-circle confirmed he ordered Habyarimana's plane shot down to spark ethnic violence between the Hutu and Tutsi which would give him an excuse to invade Rwanda. Instead of peace with the Hutu government, he wanted to overthrow it.

The corporate media lied and kept secret that the Hutus were not responsible for the majority of the 800,000 to one million Tutsis and Hutu sympathizers killed during the genocide. Not to minimize the senseless loss of life, the Hutus could only have killed 100,000 to 200,000 Tutsis. This is based on pre-1994 Rwandan government data that just 500,000 Tutsis were in the country before the conflict of which 300,000 survived. "If a million people died in Rwanda in 1994 – and that's certainly possible – there is no way that the majority of them could be Tutsi. Because there weren't enough Tutsi in the country," concluded Allen Stam, a well-respected professor and researcher at the University of Michigan who was interviewed in the documentary.[38] "[T]hat means 800,000 of them were Hutu" killed by Kagame's invading RPF forces.[39] Furthermore, the killings had stopped long before RPF forces invaded Rwanda. Thus, the U.S. government and corporate media have deliberately misled the world with the false scenario that the Hutu were the sole perpetrators of the genocide against the Tutsis when, actually, the overwhelming number of victims were Hutus killed by RPF forces. This is 180 degrees opposite to Western media's propaganda that blamed the Hutus while concealing the real truth.

It is illegal in Rwandan to tell this truth. In fact, denying genocide is a serious crime in Rwanda. Victoire Ingabire, a leading Hutu opposition leader who intended to run for president against Paul Kagame was convicted in a politically motivated treason trial for *denying* and *belittling* the genocide. Her crime was to question why memorials to the victims of the genocide failed to include Hutu who were the vast majority of genocide victims. She was sentenced to eight years in prison. "[T]o claim that a genocide occurred is closer to the politics of surrealism than to the truth," declared: Antoine Nyetera, a high-ranking Tutsi and U.N. official who doubts genocide of the Tutsi took place.[40]

The Western press has falsely portrayed Kagame as hero, humanitarian and respected African leader. Nothing could be further from the truth. He sacrificed the lives of several hundred thousand of his Tutsi brethren to create a justification to invade Rwanda. According to the documentary, his forces' incursion into Rwanda was launched long after the killing of the Tutsis had stopped, and that the indiscriminate slaughter of Hutus that followed may have quadrupled the number of Tutsis killed. The media not only suppressed the war crimes Kagame committed in Rwanda, but also in the Congo during the deadliest conflict worldwide since World War II, that killed six million quintupled the deaths in Rwanda.

All the while, Kagame has enjoyed the U.S.'s military support and economic aid as a member of its new generation of African puppet regimes that got his start with Bill Clinton, with flunky Susan Rice at his side. President Obama, the first president of African descent, continues to support this monster.

William E. Cloud

CHAPTER 8

War Criminal Bush's Illegal Iraq War

No matter how many policies you put on paper, in reality, there are no rights and wrongs in war. War itself is a crime. War cannot be justified.

~ Thisuri Wanniarachchi

L ife is wonderful for former President George W. Bush. In April, 2013, his daughter, Jennah, an NBC *Today Show* news personality, gave birth to his first grandchild, Mila. Photos of the proud grandfather snuggling and intently gazing into his granddaughter's eyes during a Halloween gathering of the Bush clan was uploaded to his Facebook page to share with the world. In April, 2014, he hosted the opening of an exhibit of his paintings of world leaders, including a self-portrait, in his presidential library and museum in Dallas. He told his daughter during a *Today Show* interview that he said to himself, "There is a Rembrandt trapped in this body, and it's your job to unleash it." [1] He turned his man cave into a studio where he spent much of the last few years painting portraits. Yes, Bush is enjoying the good life.

Since leaving office as one of the most unpopular presidents in history, Bush took a low profile, but recently signaled his desire to come out the political wilderness. The media is working full-tilt to persuade the public to forget he's a war criminal and was a terrible president. If recent polls are accurate, it seems to be working. Bush's approval rating among Americans is steadily improving. His surge back into the spotlight is also calculated to create a political atmosphere more conducive for his brother Jeb's run for the presidency in 2016; the continuation of the Bush family dynasty of thieves and butchers seeking to control the nation's fate once again.

Life for Iraqis, especially children, has not been good since the Bush Administration illegally invaded their country in 2003, virtually destroying it over the course of nine years. The destructive impact of his war on the Iraqi society is staggering, and its ravages are predicted to plague the country for decades. There are no definitive statistics on the number of children killed in military action, but the general consensus is that it is several hundred thousand. Tens of thousands more were wounded or maimed. Millions lost one or both parents and grandparents. Untold numbers of children live on the streets, are internally displaced or stranded in neighboring countries as refugees, often victims of crime, violence, exploitation, and abduction. Between one and three million children live in single parent households headed by widows who struggle for the survival of their families. They lack fundamental necessities such as food, clean water, shelter, health, and education. More children between the ages of five to 14 work instead of attending school. Unlike the great future promised adorable granddaughter, Mila, Bush, along with his

William E. Cloud

handlers, murdered or irreparably destroyed the lives millions of Iraqi children.

The Iraqi invasion was predicated on the lies that Iraq possessed weapons of mass destruction (WMD) and was six months away from developing a nuclear weapon. "I don't know what more evidence we need," he concluded in September, 2002 speech.[2] However, his assertion was at odds with a report from the International Atomic Energy Agency (IAEA) that Iraq's nuclear weapons program had been "efficiently and effectively" eliminated. Bush and his British flunky, Tony Blair, demanded IAEA inspectors to reconfirm their earlier findings. A team of inspectors reported back that Iraq was still in full compliance. Determined to not let the truth undermined his nuclear threat claims, Bush demanded the weapons inspectors be allowed back. Neither Bush nor the media fully disclosed "that the UN inspectors were never expelled by the Iraqis, but withdrawn only after it was revealed they had been infiltrated by US intelligence."[3] There's now no doubt that the corporate media knew he was lying, and parroted the administration's propaganda that Saddam posed an imminent threat to his people and world peace.

The profound words of war journalist and author Chris Hedges in an article in The Nation magazine deserves to be replicated at length here:

"The reasons for war are hidden from public view. We do not speak about the extension of American empire but democracy and ridding the world of terrorists — read "evil" —

William E. Cloud

along with weapons of mass destruction. We do not speak of the huge corporate interests that stand to gain even as poor young boys from Alabama, who joined the Army because this was the only way to get health insurance and a steady job, bleed to death along the Euphrates. We do not speak of the lies that have been told to us in the past by this Administration — for example, the lie that Iraq was on the way to building a nuclear bomb. We have been rendered deaf and dumb. And when we awake, it will be too late, certainly too late to save the dead, theirs and ours.

The embedding of several hundred journalists in military units does not diminish the lie. These journalists do not have access to their own transportation. They depend on the military for everything, from food to a place to sleep. They look to the soldiers around them for protection. When they feel the fear of hostile fire, they identify and seek to protect those who protect them. They become part of the team. It is a natural reaction. I have felt it.

But in that experience, these journalists become participants in the war effort. They want to do their bit. And their bit is the dissemination of myth, the myth used to justify war and boost the morale of the soldiers and civilians. The lie in wartime is almost always the lie of omission. The blunders by our generals — whom the mythmakers always portray as heroes — along with the rank corruption and perversion, are masked from public view. The intoxication of killing, the

William E. Cloud

mutilation of enemy dead, the murder of civilians and the fact that war is not about what they claim is ignored. But in wartime don't look to the press, or most of it, for truth. The press has another purpose.

Perhaps this is not conscious. I doubt the journalists filing the hollow reports from Iraq, in which there are images but rarely any content, are aware of how they are being manipulated. They, like everyone else, believe. But when they look back they will find that war is always about betrayal. It is about betrayal of the young by the old, of soldiers by politicians and of idealists by the cynical men who wield power, the ones who rarely pay the cost of war. We pay that cost. And we will pay it again."[4]

When no WMD or evidence that Saddam was working on a nuclear bomb were found after the invasion, the media doubled-down harder to push the party-line that Bush should not be held responsible for going to war because he relied on faulty intelligence while ignoring highly persuasive evidence to the contrary. According to Paul R. Pillar, a former CIA official who coordinated U.S. intelligence on the Middle East from 2000 to 2005, the Bush administration "was 'cherry-picking' intelligence on Iraq to justify a decision it had already reached to go to war, and ignor[ed] warnings that the country could easily fall into violence and chaos after an invasion to overthrow Saddam Hussein.[5] Pillar claimed that any mistakes made by the U.S. intelligence agencies' conclusion that

Hussein's government possessed WMD was not the driving motivation behind the administration's decision to invade. "It has become clear that official intelligence was not relied on in making even the most significant national security decisions, that intelligence was misused publicly to justify decisions already made, that damaging ill will developed between [Bush] policymakers and intelligence officers, and that the intelligence community's own work was politicized,"[6] Pillar wrote. Richard C. Clarke, former member of National Security Council also confirmed that the Bush administration made a decision to invade Iraq before the 9-11 incidents.

It would be futile to list the enormous amount of intentional disinformation put out by the media in the lead up to and throughout the Iraq war, but suffice to say that those who knew the truth failed to inform the country and the international community that Bush's case for going to war was weak. The media suppressed the fact that the United Nations did not authorize automatic war without further consultation with the Security Council or that the U.S. and Britain were determined to go to war with or without U.N. backing or international support. Despite overwhelming international opposition to the U.S. going to war with Iraq, the mainstream media minimized the divide and split in opinion. Any questionable claims made by Bush administration officials and Blair were unchallenged by the media, not the least of which the legality of the decision to go to war without the approval of the Security Council.

William E. Cloud

The Bush administration did a thoroughly effective job in controlling media reports on the war. It learned from the Viet Nam war that it was dangerous to permit war journalists to roam freely around combat zones because they could not be controlled. To counter dealing with reporting from independent journalists, the administration came up with a brilliant strategy borrowed from the public relations industry. As Katie Delahaye Paine explained, "The better the relationship any of us have with a journalist, the better the chance of that journalist picking up and reporting our messages."[7] Embedding journalists enabled the Pentagon to portray the U.S. military as an overwhelming force of good against an outmatched evil foe.

Broadcasts of grainy television footage of reporters hunkered down with troops in the belly of a tank or through a Humvee roof opening as it dodged bombs known as improvised explosive devices or IED's planted on roadways was good entertainment for the voyeuristic American public which has been methodically primed to expect action, as opposed to factual information about the death and destruction being meted out to the civilian population. Reports of the resulting civilian casualties were either understated or not addressed. A National Security Council memorandum in support of allowing journalists to report live from the front lines argued,

"Our people in the field need to tell our story. Only commanders can ensure the media get to the story alongside the troops. We must organize for and facilitate access of

William E. Cloud

national and international media to our forces, including those forces engaged in ground operations. To accomplish this, we will embed media with our units. These embedded media will live, work and travel as part of the units...to facilitate maximum, in-depth coverage."[8]

The military expelled American and foreign journalists who strayed from the approved propaganda. At the end of the day, this worked out well for the Pentagon.

The compliant media made minimal effort to investigate the number of Iraqi military or civilian casualties. In their defense, this would have been difficult to measure due in part to the destructive power of the weaponry used. One thing was certain, the so-called Coalition forces made keeping the civilian death count hidden an utmost priority so as to not lose public support. That attitude was no different from the position taken by former Secretary of State Colin Powell when he was Chairman of the Joint Chiefs of Staff, the highest ranking general during the Gulf War in 1991. He quipped in response to a New York Times reporter's question about civilian casualties that, "It's really not a number I'm terribly interested in."[9] That same attitude carried over to the Bush administration. General Tommy Franks, of the U.S. Central Command, stated, "We don't do body counts."[10] Thus, as did his father during the first Gulf War, Bush cared little about how many people he was responsible for killing. The corporate media, for propaganda reasons, not only ignored the issue, but criticized the methodology of the most prestigious

William E. Cloud

independent research estimates. Because of media's lies and omissions in its reports to the public, the world may never fully grasp the enormity of civilian deaths or understand the sheer barbarism caused by corporate-led governments.

John Hopkins University researchers estimate that as of 2006, 655,000 civilian Iraqis were killed. Other studies put the death toll upwards to one million souls. There are no reliable statistics on the number of civilians wounded. An estimated 870,000 Iraqi children were orphaned, and millions more displaced.

The needless loss of life, human suffering and the devastation of Iraq's infrastructure caused by the U.S. that will take generations to rebuild should and never will be forgotten by the Iraqi people.

It's critically important to understand that the media willfully failed to report the real threats Bush perceived Saddam posed. Hussein previously announced that Iraq would no longer accept dollars for oil because he didn't want to exchange it for the enemy's currency; which would have shaken the petrodollar system that enriched America to the detriment of other nations. If implemented, the U.S. dollar would no longer be the world's benchmark currency which would ultimately lead to the collapse of the American economy. Also, his refusal to allow the establishment of a Jewish-controlled central bank to take control of the Iraqi economy spelled his doom. Finally, he was an impediment to Israel's plans for territorial expansion and regional hegemony.

Bush came into office with a preconceived plan for regime change in Iraq. The media could have exposed that fact, but didn't. Key

William E. Cloud

members of his foreign policy team were ultraconservative, staunch supporters of Israel, and dedicated to the annexation of Iraq. They were responsible for making Saddam Hussein's nonexistent WMD the administration's justification for his immediate removal from power. Regime change in Iraq would advance Israel's expansionist plans, guaranteed continued access to Iraq's vast oil reserves, and give the international banking cartel power over its economy. The Israel and the American Jewish lobby privately urged Bush to topple Saddam. They were able to take a low profile in the debate leading up to the war because Bush's foreign policy wonks gave it significant informal influence in the shaping of American Middle East policy. Thus, Israel was confident that U.S. foreign policy would be favorable to its interests. Indeed, Bush's Iraq policy followed to the letter his warmonger advisors' advice to go to war with Iraq based on the WMD lies and the invented connection between Saddam and al Qaeda.

Richard Perle, chairman of the administration's Defense Policy Board Advisory Committee from 2001-2003, led the pro-Zionist Middle East foreign policy troika. A self-described neoconservative, Perle believed that Israel's key objectives were the removal of Saddam, expanded conduction of armed incursions into Lebanon, and label Arab states as undemocratic. David Wurmser, a Swiss-born American Jew, served as Vice President Dick Cheney's Middle East advisor. Seven years before pushing for war on Iraq, he co-authored with Perle and Douglas Feith a 1996 report for incoming Israel Prime Minister Benjamin Netanyahu entitled, *A Clean Break: A New*

Strategy for Securing the Realm, which called for Saddam's removal, pre-emptive strikes against Syria and Iran, and the abandonment of traditional "land for peace" negotiations with the Palestinians. In 1999, he wrote *Tyranny's Ally: America's Failure to Defeat Saddam Hussein*, and contributed to the drafting of *Ending Syria's Occupation of Lebanon: the US Role?* in 2000, which falsely claimed that Syria, not Iraq, was developing WMD. That propaganda was conveniently flipped to justify attacking Iraq.

In 2004, he, Feith, and Paul Wolfowitz, Deputy Secretary of Defense, were targets of FBI counterintelligence investigators on suspicion that they illegally passed classified information to (AIPAC), the most powerful Jewish lobbying/unlicensed foreign agent. Wurmser's Israeli-born wife, Meyrav, also an ultraconservative neocolonialist, wrote her Ph.D. thesis on revisionist Zionism. In 1998, she and Yigal Carmon, a former colonel in the Israeli Defense Force (IDF) Intelligence and advisor to three Israeli prime ministers, including Netanyahu, started the nonprofit Middle East Media Research Institute (MEMRI). Carmon once said that negotiations with the Palestine Liberation Organization mark (PLO) "the most revolutionary change in the history of the State of Israel" and that Netanyahu's actions "teach the PLO that pressure pays, that violence works."[11] MEMRI's website describes itself as an organization that provides translations which "bridges the language gap between the West and the Middle East and South Asia, providing timely translations of Arabic, Farsi, Urdu-Pashtu and Dari media, as well as original analysis of political, ideological, intellectual, social, cultural, and religious trends."[12]

Several people voiced their skepticism about MEMRI. Brian Whitaker of *The Guardian* newspaper stated, "it is not quite what it seems."[13] He sensed that there is a recurring construct, the translated articles either vilifies Arabs or advocates for Israel. Ibrahim Hooper of the Council on American-Islamic Relations said, "Memri's intent is to find the worst possible quotes from the Muslim world and disseminate them as widely as possible."[14] MEMRI's only concern is Israel.

Under Secretary for Defense Policy David Feith, the third member of the pro-Israel trio, was born to Dalck Feith, a member of the Betar, a revisionist Zionist youth organization. Dalck migrated to the United States during the Second World War, where he made a fortune. He became a philanthropist, and made major donations to Jewish and Israeli organizations and the Republican Party. Feith co-founded the Washington, D.C. lobbying law firm of Feith & Zell which represented the Israeli government. He urged Bush to make the destruction of Saddam's nonexistent WMD the administration's public justification for the immediate invasion of Iraq. He was also behind the decision to commit lower troop levels than the generals requested, which he candidly admitted made the military function at a limited capacity. He concealed that the real reason for deploying fewer troops was to prolong the war so as to increase the devastation to Iraq's infrastructure and economy; creating political instability that would ripen it for Israeli domination. The Bush administration's Iraq policy did not deviate from the recommendations of its pro-Israel advisers. Because American media is virtually controlled by Jews, it would not benefit them to tell the truth that Americans were being used by the Illuminati to benefit Israel and the corporate-run military industrial complex.

As noted, Saddam came within the U.S's crosshairs because he challenged the supremacy of the dollar and the international banking cartel. In 2003, Iraq was one of only seven countries that was not a member of the BIS, along with Libya, Syria, Iran, Sudan, and Somalia; countries the U.S. is currently involved militarily. The Rothschild's BIS, the central bankers' bank in Switzerland, is nothing to trifle with.

Bush repeatedly and with hubris lied to the world that Iraq possessed WMD and sponsored terrorism through its links with al Qaeda, posing a sufficient threat to international security to warrant an invasion. Vice President Dick Cheney, National Security Advisor Condoleezza Rice, and Secretary of State Colin Powell concurred with their boss. Powell has since expressed remorse, but stopped short of apologizing, and still maintains that he did not intentionally mislead the world. Instead, he contends that the administration relied on faulty intelligence reports. The truth just isn't in him!

"The immortality of the United States and Great Britain's decision to invade Iraq in 2003, premised on the lie that Iraq possessed weapons of mass destruction has destabilized and polarized the world to a greater extent than any other conflict in history," concluded

William E. Cloud

Desmond Tutu, the retired Anglican bishop, outspoken opponent of apartheid in South Africa, and Nobel Laureate.[15]

My grandson is named after his uncle who died in combat in Iraq as a way of keeping his memory alive. He was one of 4,500 American soldiers killed in the act of aggression against Iraq by the Western governments. More than 32,000 of our military men were wounded. While they deserve our deepest gratitude for answering the call to duty, and in too many cases for making the ultimate sacrifice, it is morally indefensible that they were ordered to go to war based on lies and deceit. Powell's belated regret does not bring back my grandson's uncle and the thousands of others who were killed or wounded. Our servicemen were duped into making tremendous sacrifices of life and limb for no good reason. Bush put them in harm's way and sacrificed my grandson's uncle and thousands more for no other reason than to further U.S. and Israel hegemony and the power elite's world domination agenda. They, along with their families, are victims of Bush's war-making folly. The western media downplayed and ignored the criminality of Bush and his advisors.

In September, 2012, Tutu called for Bush and Blair to face war crime charges in the International Criminal Court (ICC) for their roles in the illegal invasion of Iraq. He explained in a letter that he could not appear on the same stage with Mr. Blair at a leadership summit in Johannesburg. He wrote, "On what grounds do we decide that Robert Mugabe should go [to] the International Criminal Court, Tony Blair should join the international speakers' circuit, bin Laden should be assassinated, and Iraq should be invaded, not because it possesses weapons of mass destruction, as Mr. Bush's chief supporter, Mr. Blair, confessed last week, but in order to get rid of Saddam Hussein?"[16]

The Bishop's reason for criticizing the West's call for Zimbabwe President Robert Mugabe to be tried by the ICC is because he refuses to be their patsy. Furthermore, so far, only African leaders have been brought to its docks for war crimes prosecution. He and other African leaders are demanding Western heads of state and officials also be held accountable for their commission of war crimes. Indeed, the international community as well must demand Western leaders be held to the same standard. However, given its record, the ICC is but another organization that singles out for criminal prosecution African leaders who do not bow down to the West. Powerful, moneyed, and weapon stocked Anglo nations always escape justice. Protecting the people of the world from criminality, they set it up for their benefit, that is, to maintain control over the darker and resource loaded nations. It would be naïve to think that the U.S. or European country would voluntarily turn over Bush or Blair for prosecution. The issuance of international warrants for their arrests which could be executed should either be found elsewhere, however, would subject them to detention and extradition to the ICC to face charges, trial, and punishment if convicted. That would give the Court credibility.

This almost happened to former Chilean dictator General Augusto Pinochet when he was arrested on an Interpol warrant in a London hospital in 1998, six days after he was indicted by a Spanish magistrate on charges of killing, torturing, abduction, and war crimes

William E. Cloud

he committed in the early 1970's. Pinochet was put in place by the West after an illegal coup. As a right-wing puppet, he masterfully followed the orders of his controllers. The Spanish judge indicted him for human rights violations. He detained for a year and a half before he was ordered released in early 2000 by the British government on questionable *humanitarian* grounds of ill health.

In 2002, a Chilean judge ordered former secretary of state Henry Kissinger to answer questions about his involvement in the atrocities. This sent a chilling message to all government officials who hide behind sovereign immunity that they should be very selective in making travel plans. Indeed, Kissinger has left the safety of the U.S. only once when President Bush took him along to the Chinese Olympics. To remedy this, the ICC's jurisdiction should be expanded to provide for prosecution in absentia. If found guilty, criminal penalties could be imposed, including fines, restitution and prison sentences that can be effectuated when the court gets personal jurisdiction of the convicted fugitive from justice.

Bush, in particular, is just as culpable for his crimes against humanity as the Nazi officials convicted in the Nuremberg trials. Not a single Bush administration official has been charged, much less convicted. Bush and many other war criminals are living wonderful, prosperous lives.

That travesty begs to be corrected.

William E. Cloud

CHAPTER 9

Israel: Palestinians are Never Going to Get a State

We Jews, we are the destroyers and will remain the destroyers. Nothing you can do will meet our demands and needs. We will forever destroy because we want a world of our own.

~ Jewish Author Maurice Samuels

Israeli Prime Minister Benjamin Netanyahu recently demanded the Palestinian leadership recognize Israel as a Jewish state. This ultimatum was said to be a non-negotiable prerequisite to reaching a *framework* agreement to guide peace negotiations, as oppose to authentic, fair, and rational negotiations that could lead to a two-state solution. In a March, 2014 speech before AIPAC, Netanyahu stated directly to the Palestinians, "In recognizing the Jewish state you would finally make clear that you are truly prepared to end the conflict…So recognize the Jewish state, no excuses, no delays. It is time."[1] Ceding upfront the right to their ancestral land is but another condition Israel insists the Palestinians must accept as a precondition to actual negotiations. Netanyahu, the embodiment of Israel's permanent right-wing majority and future, is the first Israeli leader to make nation state recognition, among other demands, a litmus test for agreeing to enter negotiations is the latest iteration of the peace process charade the Zionists have used for sixty years to avoid relinquishing any territory to the Palestinians. This is an irrational mandate demanded by a rational man who does not want a peace agreement.

Joe Lockhart, a Clinton White House spokesperson called in Netanyahu "one of the most obnoxious individuals you're going to come into - just a liar and a cheat. He could open his mouth and you could have no confidence that anything that came out of it was the truth."[2] Even an exasperated Clinton once asked, "Who the fuck does he think he is? Who's the fucking superpower here?"[3] In October, 2014, an Obama administration official called Netanyahoo a "chicken shit" prime minister.

Palestinian Authority (PA) President Mahmoud Abbas rejected Netanyahu's ultimatum, "We won't recognize and accept the Jewishness of Israel. We have many excuses and reasons that prevent us from doing so."[4] This was an apparent reference to the Palestinian Authority's belief that recognition of "Israel as a '*Jewish state*' would de jure declare the Palestinians living in Palestine as illegitimate, possibly exposing them to discrimination. It would also effectively eliminate any 'right of return' for the millions of Palestinians who were forced from their homes after Israel was granted state status by the United Nations in 1948."[5] Besides, "Since 1988, we [Palestinian Authority] have recognized international legitimacy resolutions" [on

Israel]...And in 1993, we recognized the State of Israel," Abbas explained to Obama in the Oval Office in March, 2014.

Although the PA refused to recognize Israel as a state in advance of negotiations, it reiterated its willingness to accept a resolution to the conflict with the establishment of a Palestinian state based on 1967 borders, with the proviso that East Jerusalem be its capital. In addition the Authority required the right of return authorized by U.N. Resolution 194 of 1948; the right given to 711,000 of the 900,000 Palestine Arab residents who fled or were forced from the territories during the 1948 Palestinian War. As of today only about 30-50,000 original refugees are alive, but by definition of the mandate, their patrilineal descendants, estimated to number 4,950,000, also have the right of return.

Successive Israeli governments have consistently rejected the right of return as a condition for resolving the impasse. As late as December, 2013 Netanyahu told his cabinet that unity of Jerusalem verses a Palestinian right of return are incompatible and cannot be a part of any final agreement for a two-state solution. "We ascribe importance to the unity of Jerusalem and, of course, to the cancellation of the right of return," declared Netanyahu.[6] Despite Netanyahu's unequivocal rejection of any right of return, in January, 2014 Secretary of State John Kerry proposed a compromise to Abbas, encouraging him to accept a limit the right of return to 80,000 refugees. This was the same warmed-over proposal President Clinton made during the Camp David peace talks in 2000 that Israel rejected outright. Abbas is said to be holding out for the return of 200,000

William E. Cloud

refugees, ill-advisedly forever depriving 4.7 million Palestinians from returning to their ancestral land. Even in the unlikely event Israel capitulated and agreed to the weak compromise Abbas proposed, Hamas would presumably never accept the disenfranchisement of millions of Palestinians. In any event, what kind of autonomy would any independent state have if 4.5 million of its people are permanently dispossessed of their land, thus, denying it of the power to determine who could or could not live within its borders?

The parties' deadlock on the question of whether East Jerusalem would be the capital of Israel or a future Palestinian state is still and always will be a major impediment to reaching any agreement. As one Israeli official put it, "gaps are still wide concerning the permanent status of Jerusalem, borders, settlements, refugees and the Jewish state."[7]

The Israeli proceedings throughout its short history plainly reveal in no uncertain terms that it will *never* agree to a Palestinian state. Pretending to want peace is the historical hallmark of Israel's chicanery. The short and long of it is that Israel is using the so-called peace process as a delaying tactic to give it time to expand its borders well beyond the Palestinian enclaves. Its endgame is nothing short of the expropriation of the territories of neighboring countries and Middle East hegemony.

The Obama administration's July, 2013 initiative to restart Israeli-Palestinian settlement negotiations, if sincerely desired, is delusional, but more likely shows that it is in cahoots with Israel. Obama set a

William E. Cloud

low bar for any expectation that a breakthrough was possible by conceding before the negotiations started that reaching an agreement on Palestinian statehood is an *elusive goal*. Secretary of State John Kerry was slightly more optimistic that the stalemate could be broken. "This is not mission impossible. This can be happen."[8] Considering Israel's intransigence and U.S. complicity, it may not be impossible, but it is highly improbable.

Looming in the background is the absence of Hamas, which controls the Gaza Strip. It has been left out of peace negotiations. Israel and the U.S. consider Hamas a terrorist organization that supports the eradication of Israel and its Jewish population from Palestine; but without Hamas every accord is doomed to failure. In 2011, at a ceremony commemorating the 24th anniversary of Hamas, its leader, Ismail Haniyeh, asserted that they will work for, "interim objective of liberation of Gaza, the West Bank, or Jerusalem."[9] The considered goal is to eliminate Israel. "The armed resistance and the armed struggle are the path and the strategic choice for liberating the Palestinian land, from the [Mediterranean] sea to the [Jordan] river, and for the expulsion of the invaders and usurpers [Israel]...We won't relinquish one inch of the land of Palestine."[10] Accordingly, Hamas almost certainly will never recognize a State of Israel; the position Netanyahu is banking on because without the incorporation of the Gaza territory the creation of a unified Palestinian state is impossible.

Israel's latest obstacle to negotiating in good faith brings into sharp focus the insincerity of its claim to seek peaceful co-existence with the Palestinians and the regional Arab countries. Israel's master plan, since conception, has been to make it an exclusively Jewish state with territorial borders well beyond the frontiers approved by the 1947 U.N. General Assembly resolution. In the words of David Ben Gurion, the father of Israel, only the Jewish "right to the whole of this country is valid, in force and endures forever. And until the Final Redemption has come, we will not budge from this historic right."[11] In Judaism, the final redemption means the end of days when God redeems the Israelites from their various exiles, signaling the coming of the Jewish Messiah and the afterlife. In other words, Jews believe they have the sole right to Israel until the end of the world.[12]

Israel is an ethnocratic state, according to Max Blumenthal author of *Goliath* and critic of Israel. He believes the Zionists are working on the premise that Israel "belongs to the white man." He continued, "The rhetoric of mainstream Israeli politicians, which is bellicose, paranoid and racist, is so rarely conveyed to the American public."[13] To ensure a Jewish majority, Israel established a 70 percent Jewish demographic threshold maintained by perpetual ethnic cleansing and deportation of non-Jews. This also applies to Israel's relationship to Gaza "because 80 percent of its population [are Palestinian] refugees who have legitimate claims to the land and property inside what is now the state of Israel," noted Blumenthal.[14]

Prawer Plan legislation was introduced in 2013 to cleanse the land of tens of thousands of the Bedouin nomadic peoples of the Middle East deserts who reside in *illegal communities* and hypocritically not acknowledged by Israel as citizens. Had mass protests not forced the Israeli government to withdraw the legislation in December, 2013,

Bedouin land would have been expropriated and they would have been forcibly transferred to reservation-styled villages in the Naqab desert, south of present-day Israel. This does not mean that "the bill has been shelved or just temporarily postponed," reported the *Haaretz* newspaper.[15] But, if top Israeli officials like Foreign Minister Avigdor Lieberman's opinion that the plan is too generous to Bedouins, the matter is sure to be revisited.

Under the terms of the 1948 Balfour Agreement, Britain gave European Jews the right to establish a state in Palestine, completely disregarding the rights of the Arab people who occupied the territory for centuries. As already mentioned, Ben Gurion was determined that Jews would forever maintain exclusive and absolute sovereignty over the entire land. "What we want is that the whole and unified land be *Jewish*," [his emphasis] declared Ben Gurion, adding "a Jewish state on only part of the land is not the end but the beginning."[16] He was instrumental in devising an incremental, slow but deliberate approach to Jewish settlement of the entire country "through agreement and understanding with our Arab neighbors, or through other means."[17] Given Israel's penchant for resorting to force at the slightest provocation or no provocation at all, a reasonable interpretation of what he meant by *other means* would be with an advanced defense force...a superior army which no doubt will be one of the best armies in the world.

Just prior to Israel's establishment, a small group of Jewish leaders drew up detailed preparations for the mass expulsion of Palestinians to make it easier to steal their land. Elaborate maps and intelligence were compiled about each village to enable systematic ethnic cleansing of vast areas of the country through "large-scale intimidation; laying siege to and bombarding villages and population centers; setting fire to homes, properties, and goods; expelling residents; demolishing homes; and, finally, planting mines in the rubble to prevent the expelled inhabitants from returning," according to an intelligence document.[18] They created a power vacuum by rounding up and often summarily executing Palestinian village leaders. In a handful of months, Jewish terrorists emptied and destroyed 531 villages and 11 urban towns. Over 750,000 Palestinians, half the native population, were expelled and made refugees. It's clear that Israeli leaders had no intention to ever brook a Palestinian presence, much less national sovereignty, authority or power. Israeli post-independence claims that the territory would be a bi-national state proved false.

Six months after Palestine was partitioned, the Jewish National Council composed of the major Jewish factions met in Tel Aviv to ratify a proclamation declaring the establishment of the State of Israel and the formation of a provisional government. The Palestinians were denied statehood when they refused to accept the compromise two-state solution proposed by the U.N. that was favorable to Israel. They went to war against Israel and lost.

Ben-Gurion anticipated an international outcry if Israel annexed the whole of Palestinian land. To keep condemnation tamped down, Israeli leaders have historically professed a commitment to partitioning off a Palestinian state, provided its security was guaranteed. This is a ruse intended to delay the division of any of its land for a Palestinian state while it used military and diplomatic means to implement its ultimate goal to reunify all parts of "Greater Israel" under Jewish sovereignty; encompassing Syria, half of Iraq, Jordan, a large part of Saudi Arabia, and a portion of Egypt. This is further proof that Israel's assurances regarding a two-state solution is a disingenuous ploy Obama, as did the presidents before him, has been forced by Zionist to foist on the world…lest their transgressions be exposed or be assassinated. As my mother might have said, "Obama got the can't help its!"

Since partition 60 years ago, Israel has opposed recognition of a Palestinian state on the pretext that its leadership refuses to acknowledge its right to exist, reject terrorism, and negotiate a settlement. These objections are contrived to indefinitely postpone reaching a partition accord. The condition that the parties must negotiate a two-state solution, for example, is a *catch 22* because Israel can endlessly prevent Palestinian statehood by merely refusing to negotiate in good faith, as it has done for six decades and counting. "If I were an Arab leader, I would never sign an agreement with Israel," said Ben Gurion. "It is normal; we have taken their country…we have come and we have stolen their country. Why would they accept that?"[19] Netanyahu, more so than every Israeli leader preceding him is of the same ilk as Ben Gurion, and would never consider, let alone accept the establishment of an independent Palestinian state. The strategy always has been to indefinitely prolong the peace process while consolidating and implementing their plan to dominate the region.

In a dramatic ceremony in 1993, President Clinton beamed as Israeli Prime Minister Yitzhak Rabin and Palestinian Liberation Organization leader Yasser Arafat historically shook hands following the signing of the Oslo Accords. The problem with the spectacle was that Arafat lacked the consensus of the Palestinian people to enter the agreement. Hamas immediately denounced Arafat as an Israeli lackey and declared annulled the accords and any other agreement he signed. Arafat subsequently caved to U.S. pressure to amend the Palestine Liberation Organization (PLO) Charter to accept that the Jewish state would comprise 80% of historical Palestine, leaving the Palestinians the rest. He sold out his people, and by design, the interminable peace talks between Israel and the newly created PA have not progressed one iota toward establishing a Palestinian state in the 21 years since. The so-called peace negotiations, therefore, have been a total sham from the very beginning.

Israel denies Palestine the means to create a productive economy. To survive, the PA is dependent on billions of dollars in budgetary support and humanitarian aid from the U.S. and the European Union. Therefore, out of need and greed, Abbas continues to traitorously collaborate with the Israeli oppressor. A report issued by the United Nations Conference on Trade and Development found that Israel was depriving the Occupied Palestinian Authority (OPT) of approximately $300 million annually which is "buttressing Palestinian dependence on Israel, and gravely undermining its

William E. Cloud

competitiveness by refusing to transfer to the Palestinian treasury revenues from taxes on direct and indirect imports and on smuggled goods into the OPT from or via Israel."[20] If Israel transferred to the Palestinian treasury the revenue it was entitled, it could expand its growth by four percent and create over 10,000 jobs per year. Otherwise, it will always owe its existence to financial aid donors, making it highly vulnerable and susceptible to outside detrimental influences.

On the other side of the equation, the Palestinian elite also heavily rely on external support to maintain their lavish lifestyles while the rest of society suffers. So, to ensure no disruption in financial support, the Palestinian Authority has willingly participated in the deliberately unproductive U.S.-sponsored peace process, which is contrary to the Palestinian Authority's Negotiations Affairs Department's (PANAD) assessment of the situation that the peace negotiations brought nothing but disappointment. "This year marks 20 years of shattered hopes and unfulfilled obligations; of promises betrayed and of illegal colonization that not only continues to intensify but has inched us ever closer towards permanently ending any hope for a peacefully negotiated two-state solution."[21]

Israel's continued access to Palestinian water is apparently another insurmountable obstacle to a viable two-state solution. Israel's main source of groundwater comes from the Mountain Aquifer that lies almost entirely beneath the Palestinian territories. As part of the Oslo II Accord, Arafat treasonously agreed to give Israel full control of its water. Since then, Israel has monopolized access to

William E. Cloud

water within the territories, routinely denying Palestinians the right to drill wells or repair existing ones. Israel is highly dependent upon this water which today constitutes about 80% of Israel's total supply. Some water officials estimate that Jewish use of water is up to 69 gallons per day whereas Palestinians in Gaza and the West Bank use an average 18 gallons of water a day. The difference mainly attributable to large-scale Israeli industrial and agriculture use, which barely exists on the Palestinian side. The Coastal Aquifer is the only source of natural fresh water for Gaza, but has been over-exploited, and its salination has been compromised as a result of seawater intrusion. Israel has intentionally hampered the development of seawater desalination, some critics say it is its desire to limit Arab population growth in the area.

Israel's has taken an uncompromising position on its control of the water resources in the occupied territories is to ostensively maintain its security. In an article entitled "The Politics of Water in the Middle East: An Israeli Perspective on the Hydro-Political Aspects of the Conflict", Martin Sherman cited a 1989 study published by the Israeli Ministry of Agriculture that concluded, "It is difficult to conceive of any political solution consistent with Israel's survival that does not involve complete, continued Israeli control of the water and sewerage systems, and of the associated infrastructure, including the power supply and road network, essential to their operation, maintenance and accessibility."[22] Water is the lifeblood of a nation. A fully autonomous Palestinian state Israel fears would

William E. Cloud

markedly increase its vulnerability and could even jeopardize its very survival. Israel would never subject itself to these perceived risks.

Palestinian threats to take Israel to the ICC on charges that its military committed war crimes in Gaza and the West Bank if peace talks fail concerns Israel. Considering the Palestinian's financial dependence on the West, such a move would be tantamount to dropping an "atomic bomb," according to senior PLO executive committee leader, Hanan Ashrawi. Alan Baker, former Israeli ambassador to Canada, dismissed the threat as a huge bluff because it was unlikely the Palestinians could persuade the Court to hear the case. His assumption is correct. Notwithstanding its mandate to be "an independent, permanent court that tries persons accused of the most serious crimes of international concern, namely genocide, crimes against humanity and war crimes," it has unfairly targeted only Africans for prosecution.[23] More than that, since the U.S. and Israel are not state parties to the Criminal Court convention neither has legal obligations to the Court. Likewise, it is unlikely either would submit to the Court's jurisdiction and would block a U.N. Security Council resolution to refer a matter to the ICC.

Under pressure from the *United States of Israel*, the PA agreed, as a condition to entering the latest rounds of negotiations, to not join the more than 60 United Nations and other agencies, including the ICC. This was to forestall any further international embarrassment they already experienced when the U.N. General Assembly, over the objections of the United States and Israel, overwhelmingly voted to grant Palestine non-member observer state status following a failed bid for full statehood recognition in September, 2011. The grant of observer status had symbolic importance in that it came on the 65th anniversary of the General Assembly's vote to partition Palestine into a Jewish and Arab state.

Netanyahu declared after the vote, "The decision at the U.N. today will change nothing on the ground."[24] Only direct talks will result in Palestinian statehood, he insisted, and any other tactic "will not advance the establishment of a Palestinian state...it will push it off." Then U.S. Secretary of State Hillary Clinton seconded the prime minister, saying, "We [U.S.] have been clear that only through direct negotiations between the parties can the Palestinians and Israelis achieve the peace they both deserve: two states for two people, with a sovereign, viable and independent Palestine living side by side in peace and security with a Jewish and democratic Israel."[25]

During the two-decades since the Oslo Accords, Israel has consistently stalled negotiations while it confiscated large tracts of Palestinian territory, leaving little land for a viable Palestinian state, even if against all odds an agreement is ultimately reached. Palestinian commentator Edward Said wrote in an article published in the *London Book Review* that:

"[T]he Oslo Agreements granted Israeli control over the territories it has been expanding towards up to the eve of the 1967 war, and further allowed Israel the right to negotiate on the remainder of the territories that it annexed by power during the Six Day War. Israel did not really give anything in return, and it established its security demands over those of the Palestinians in a way that allowed for aggressive settlement activities and the elimination of reparations for Palestinians."[26]

Since the 1967 war, Israel has built housing on occupied land for more than 700,000 settlers. Construction was up 70 percent in the first six months of 2013. Its future building plans further undermine the possibility of a viable Palestinian state, much less a contiguous one. U.N. Secretary General Ban Ki-moon expressed unease and dissatisfaction that Israeli building in this sensitive area "would represent an almost fatal blow to the remaining chances of securing a two-state solution."[27] Netanyahu flatly rejected the criticism and stated that Israel would continue to build as long as there is a tactical benefit to do so. Out of arrogance, he disregards the devastating outcome for the Palestinians. What places are of strategic interest to Israel?

Since the start of the 2013 so-called framework negotiations, Israel magnanimously agreed to "show restraint" in building in its West Bank settlements, which most of the world views as illegal. "The partial freeze would apply to the issuing of government tenders for housing; projects underway would be allowed to continue, and institutional projects like schools could still move forward. East Jerusalem, which Palestinians consider the capital of their future state, would not be included in the freeze."[28] If Israel was sincere, it would halt the confiscation of all Palestinian land while negotiations continued. It's refusal to stop building in Jerusalem has to be particularly galling to Palestinians who believe it is the holiest place for Muslims and cannot change ownership. Jerusalem is just as important to the European Jews who consider it a Holy City that God chose for the building of His temple. It is also the where the Jewish faith started and is the center of their national life for about 3,000 years. According to Vladimir Lenin, "A lie told often enough becomes the truth."

The 2013-14 negotiations were doomed to be a spectacular failure. Israel's treatment of Palestinians, which considers them sub-human, violates the legal, moral, and ethical principles, standards and norms of civilized society. The grandfatherly looking late Israeli Prime Minister Golda Meir hatefully said the Palestinians "never existed."[29] The irony is that the descendants of the exaggerated Jewish Holocaust are dedicated to committing steady and comprehensive genocide against Palestinians.

Israel's deplorable treatment of the 1.7 million souls in the Gaza Strip is intended to generate Palestinian loathing and an incentive for them to give up. In 2007, Hamas defeated the U.S./Israel-backed PA to govern the Gaza Strip. Hamas handily defeated the PA, but despite being democratically elected, Israel and the U.S. refused to recognize the Hamas government, and designated it as a terrorist organization that advocated the destruction of Israel. Although Hamas softened its position after taking control over Gaza, Israel and the U.S. have not. As collective punishment, Israel pulled out its settlers, and troops in 2005 and imposed a military economic blockade around Gaza that trapped the entire Palestinian population, including children who make up half the inhabitants. The nearly two million people are in

William E. Cloud

limbo and crowded together under inhuman conditions on a strip of land just 25 miles long and 6 miles wide. According to Article 33 of the Fourth Geneva Convention adopted in 1949, "No persons may be punished for an offense he or she has not personally committed. Collective penalties and likewise all measures of intimidation or of terrorism are prohibited."[30] But since Israel has never abided by any U.N. mandate or international law in the past there is no expectation it will comply in the future.

Israeli treatment of the Palestinians clearly violates international law. The Geneva Convention (IV) relative to the Protection of Civilians in Time of War in cases of partial or total occupation of the territory obliges an occupying power to meet the basic needs of a people under occupation, even if the state of war is not recognized by one of them, and the occupation meets with no armed resistance. The blockade tripled the number of Gazan refugees living in abject poverty. Because Israel strictly limits the importation of food, eighty percent of the residents are practically dependent on international humanitarian aid for survival. Indeed, the U.N. estimates that more than 60 percent of households are food insecure. More than 10 percent of the children suffer from chronic malnutrition, and most families don't have adequate access to clean drinking water. It is also the Jewish state's policy to severely restrict the type and amount of humanitarian supplies international aid organizations are permitted to donate. A recurrent shortage of cooking gas required the implementation of a rationing scheme, exempting hospitals and bakeries. Medical supplies and equipment headed for hospitals, however, are often denied entry without explanation by Israeli border officials. People with medical conditions who cannot be treated in Gazan hospitals due to the shortage of medical supplies and equipment are forced to go through a torturous application process for a permit to seek treatment outside the territory. Israeli authorities frequently delay or deny issuance of permits, again, with no explanation. There are no available detailed statistics documenting the number of people who died as a result of not being able to be treated in a Gaza hospital or denied an exit permit to be treated elsewhere. Still, many believe the death toll is in the tens of thousands.

The Census Department of the Palestinian Ministry of Detainees reported in December, 2013, that 3,874 Palestinians, including 930 children, were kidnapped by Israeli authorities in that year alone. Thousands of Palestinian political prisoners held in Israeli prisons are tortured, abused, and their rights are systematically denied. Four detainees died in custody in 2013, under suspicious circumstances; strongly suggesting they were tortured and murdered.

Fearing widespread and growing resentment of its persecution of the Palestinians, especially Gazans, the Israeli government attempts to avoid the charges that it is committing genocide. But many are in agreement with Jeff Halper, an author and activist that, "Palestinians [are] a centimeter above starvation…a controlled experiment in how to keep people hungry, to punish them, to keep them just a centimeter above the line of starvation." He added, "The thing behind it – and it's true of the West Bank as well – is that Israel is trying to impose a permanent occupation. Everything that Israel is doing is an attempt to break the resistance and the will of Palestinian people, so in the end they give up and accept whatever Israel wants. But that is not succeeding."[31] This was confirmed when an Israeli court granted Gisha, a human rights organization's "request for the government's planning document 'for putting the Palestinians on a diet' without risking the bad press of mass starvation," according to Juan Cole.[32]

"The document, produced by the Israeli army, appears to be a calculation of how to make sure, despite the Israeli blockade, that Palestinians got an average of 2,279 calories a day, the basic need. But by planning on limiting the calories in that way, the Israeli military was actually plotting to keep Palestinians in Gaza (half of them children) permanently on the brink of malnutrition, what health professionals call 'food insecurity'. And, it was foreseeable that sometimes they would slip into malnutrition, since not as many trucks are permitted to enter the territory daily then that recommended by the Israeli army (106 were recommended, but it was often less in the period 2007-2010)."[34] Israel's policy of keeping Gazans near starvation constitutes a crime against humanity because it woefully falls short of supplying their critical nutritional needs.

As late as July, 2014, high Israeli government officials and leaders came out of the closet and openly called for genocide. Ayelet Shaked, a senior lawmaker in the Habeyit Hayehudi (Jewish Home) party that is a faction of Israel's ruling coalition published a call for genocide of the Palestinians on social media after the killing of three Israeli teenagers allegedly by Palestinians. Shaked declared that "the entire

Palestinian people is the enemy," which justifies the destruction of "its elderly and its women, its cities and its villages, its property and its infrastructure."[34]

Palestinian woman should be particularly singled for murder, in her opinion, because they give birth to "little snakes." Her post meets the legal definition of genocide, but received little local or international condemnation. To the contrary, more than a thousand people shared her post, and at the time of this writing it received more than 5,000 "likes." Shaked apparently got her inspiration from Uri Elitzur, a now deceased leader of the settler movement, speechwriter, and close advisor to Netanyahoo who she referred to in the post.

Elitzur was a rabid hater of Palestinians who he viewed as mortal enemies that warranted their complete annihilation and destruction. There was no such thing as an innocent Palestinian in his mind. "[T]he enemy soldiers hide out among the population, and it is only through its support that they can fight. Behind every terrorist stand dozens of men and women, without whom he could not engage in terrorism. Actors in the war are those who incite in mosques, who write the murderous curricula for schools, who give shelter, who provide vehicles, and all those who honor and give them their moral support. They are all enemy combatants, and their blood shall be on all their heads. Now this also includes the mothers of the martyrs, who send them to hell with flowers and kisses. They should follow their sons, nothing would be more just. They should go, as should the physical homes in which they raised the snakes. Otherwise, more little snakes will be raised there."[34]

William E. Cloud

Despite these shocking words, and their reiteration by a high government official, the message to the Israeli public is that Palestinian genocide is not only a moral duty, but an imperative obligation to ensure the survival of Israel. The lessons of the so-called Holocaust have been lost on the Israeli government. Killing all the Palestinians and be done with the problem forever is gaining traction with a majority the Israeli populous, as evidenced by its overwhelming support for the government's murderous assault on Gaza during the summer of 2014.

It's noteworthy that the EU relieves Israel of its legal responsibilities to the Palestinians by footing a significant part of bill for its occupation of the territory. In early 2014, the EU threatened to cut the $622 million a year in assistance to the Palestinians if the latest peace negotiations failed; something they have no control over short of agreeing to a one-sided deal. It can be inferred from Lars Faaborg-Anderson, the EU ambassador to Israel, that the payment to the Authority provided stability in the occupied territories. "I think it is realized in Israel that this money is key to the stability of the West Bank and in Gaza," he said. "If we don't provide the money, I think there is a great likelihood that Israel would have to provide far more."[35] Why is the EU helping Israel oppress the Palestinians?

The Libyan envoy to the U.N. accurately described the situation in Gaza to be as bad as Nazi Germany's punishment concentration camps. "It's worse," Ibrahim Dabbashi said in statement urging the Security Council to take action on the humanitarian crisis in Gaza. "It is more than what happened in concentration camps because...there are the bombing, daily bombs, military bombs on Gaza. It was not in the concentration camps."[36] Unable to refute the facts, Israeli officials, as always, lamely condemned his opinion as "an outrage" and "a disgrace." In tandem with Israel, the U.S. ambassador called the statement "morally insensitive, historically inaccurate and fundamentally at odds with efforts to try to make peace in the Middle East."[37] Truth be damned.

Vatican officials and many American politicians agreed with the Libyan ambassador, however. The Vatican's justice and peace minister, Cardinal Renato Martino, speaking for Pope Benedict XVI, told an Italian newspaper that conditions in Gaza "increasingly resemble a big concentration camp."[38] Conservative Republican Patrick Buchanan, a most unusual suspect, described Gaza as an "Israeli concentration camp...When you cut off 1.5 million people's food, energy, and contact with the outside world and you have human waste pilling in the streets and half of children with dysentery that does indeed resemble a concentration camp." [39] Congressman Ron Paul in an interview on Iranian state television likened Gaza to a "concentration camp" and denied the Hamas government was the aggressor.[40]

Helen Thomas, 89, the former granddame of the White House press corps urged the Israelis to "get the hell out of Palestine."[41] The Obama White House immediately denounced her remark as anti-Semitic and questioned whether her White House credentials should be revoked. During her 57-year career, she covered the administrations of eleven U.S. presidents from Eisenhower to

Obama, earning her a reserved seat in the White House briefing room. Within a week after her remarks, she was forced to resign her position as columnist for Hearst newspaper and threatened with the revocation of White House credentials. A Jewish lobbyist acknowledged Thomas had "the right as a private citizen under the First Amendment to speak her mind, even as an anti-Jewish bigot, but not as a member, much less privileged member with a reserved seat, in the WH press corps."[42] Ms. Thomas commented afterward that, "You cannot criticize Israel in this country (USA) and survive."

In retaliation for Israeli transgressions and self-defense, Hamas resorted to rocket attacks on areas just inside Israeli territory. It's difficult to condemn the Palestinians because "a wounded animal yet bears teeth." And it's an undisputable fact that Israel literally and figuratively has had them hemmed-in for years with few choices other than to hit back or surrender...the latter never being an option for them.

In 2008, the media began reporting that without provocation, Hamas was firing rockets into uninhabited areas in Israel just over the Gaza border. The firing of rockets was portrayed as an extremely serious threat to Israel's security even though they are rudimentary, short-ranged and unguided with far less destructive capability than Israeli sophisticated munitions. Months of rocket fire caused one death of an unidentified, probably non-existent, Israeli.

In response, Israel resorted to its Dahiya doctrine, a government sanctioned plan to target civilians to pressure political leaders, Hamas, and retaliated with a disproportionate ferocious assault on

Gaza code-named Operation Cast Lead. It deployed fighter jets to make round-the-clock bombing and missile attacks, as well as drone missile attacks and artillery bombardments on alleged military targets such as weapons caches and suspected rocket firing teams. Israel also attacked places that had, at best, marginal military value, including 24 police stations, government buildings and political headquarters.

Israel's fierce onslaught on defenseless Palestinian civilians was the most appalling aspect of that war which unfortunately set a pattern for conflicts that followed. It rained down air-bursts of artillery-fired white phosphorous shells over Gaza City in flagrant violation of the Fourth Geneva Convention, which outlaws their use against civilian populations. More destructive than napalm, phosphorous artillery shells are incendiary weapons of mass destruction. They indiscriminately kill on a larger, more devastating scale than ordinary bombs. To maximize kill count, the shells detonate high above the target and shower contrails of phosphorous over the area the size of several football fields. The most horrific aspect of phosphorous is that it continues to burn and smolder after making contact with human flesh. If victims survive the strike, they are left horrifically maimed. Inhalation of the chemical literally sets the digestive system afire, resulting in the passage of phosphorus-laden stool; the *smoking stool syndrome.* Despite the fact that Israel committed war crimes by illegally bombing civilians with phosphorus bombs, the U.S. pressured the U.N. Security Council to not condemn Israel's white phosphorus attack on Gaza.

William E. Cloud

Israeli ground forces also fired hundreds of cluster bombs into open areas occupied by civilians. "The use of cluster bombs – which have a large footprint when initially dropped and then remain a threat for decades – in a location like the Gaza Strip which is so packed with people is horrifying,"[43] wrote Siun in the *FireDogLake* blog. The UN decried the use of the indiscriminate anti-personnel munition as *completely immoral*, but like the phosphorus atrocities, at the U.S.'s insistence, the Security Council failed to denounce Israel's barbarism.

The Israeli assault killed 1,477 civilians, including at least 308 children, during what the Palestinians refer to as the January Massacre or Black Saturday. Palestinian deaths were grossly disproportionate to just 13 Israelis casualties, four were from friendly fire and only three were civilians.

Then Secretary of State Condoleezza Rice cynically attempted to lay the blame for civilian deaths on Hamas, falsely alleging it fought from populated structures using civilians as human shields. Hamas sought to stop hostilities, but Rice voted to block the approval of a U.N. Security Counsel statement calling for an immediate halt to Israel's ground operations and a cease fire. In defiance to mounting world outrage, the U.S. leadership stuck to its position that no ceasefire should take effect until Hamas' ability to defend Gaza, no matter how anemic, was destroyed.

It's worth mentioning that Operation Cast Lead took place as the U.S. was in the midst of an administration change over. The neo-con Bush administration supported Israel with no conditions attached;

however, the Israelis were not as certain that the Obama Administration would do the same. The attack ended just days before Obama took office. As it turned out, Israel's concern that Obama might not be as supportive of Israel's barbarism toward the Palestinian people was unfounded because he is willing to kiss more Israeli butt than any president before him.

Israel withdrew its troops out of Gaza in 2009, but remained a de facto occupier by imposing a blockade and erecting a barrier, further isolating Gazans from contact with the outside world. It maintained control of Gaza's airspace and water, denied fishing rights, limited trade, and prevented or severely restricted the importation of essential and none essential goods ranging from food and medical supplies to basic building materials. Gaza was rendered even more destitute when international aid dried up after the attack as a result of Israeli pressure on donors. Palestinians continued to be terrorized after the operation. Raids, air attacks, murders, vandalism, robberies, home destruction, olive grove damage or uprooted altogether, land theft, illegitimate detentions, kidnapping, persecution, and limited travel was intensified; an escalation of misery even the Palestinians were not accustomed to.

Then Senator Obama expressed sympathy for the Palestinians, but switched sides after he won the Democratic nomination. President-Elect Obama refused to weigh-in on the atrocities being committed on the Palestinian people on the grounds that there could only be one president at a time, and it would have been inappropriate to second guess War-Criminal-in-Chief Bush. This copout conflicted with his

William E. Cloud

numerous comments, often negative, on Bush's handling of the economic crisis. As president, Obama continued the Bush policy of giving Israel free reign and military support to oppress the Palestinians, no matter how brutal. Not to give Obama a free pass, but it is well documented that U.S. Presidents have no power. For his life's sake, he had to go along to get along, or be removed. He had no choice but to bow down to the shadow government controlled by money masters of this world that put him in power.

In November, 2012, a long-term ceasefire agreement was near completion when Israel *deliberately* derailed it by assassinating Hamas military commander Ahmed al-Jabari just hours after he reviewed the draft proposal. Israel also wanted to test the performance of its new American-funded Iron Dome missile defense shield to remind the Gazans and other potential foes of their vulnerability to its military might. In other words, Netanyahoo nixed the ceasefire agreement to provoke a war. The provocation worked. Hamas resumed firing rockets into Israel, which gave Netanyahoo manufactured justification to launch Operation Pillar of Defense. The destruction in the 2012 bombardment was not as extensive as the one in 2008, but 160 Palestinians and six Israelis were still killed in violation of any sense of morality and international law.

At the conclusion of Israel's assault on Gaza, it was reported in the *Jerusalem Post* that the Beirut Butchers' son, Gilad Sharon, boasted that the purpose of the war was to send "a Tarzan-like cry that lets the entire jungle know in no uncertain terms just who won, and just who was defeated."[44]

William E. Cloud

In the aftermath of Israel's murderous assault on Gaza, Obama reaffirmed for the umpteenth time that the U.S. is "fully supportive of Israel's right to defend itself" and that peace in the region must begin with "no missiles being fired into Israel's territory."[45] He predictably ignored the fact that Israel provoked the war when it assassinated the Hamas leader who, incidentally, was in favor of finalizing a ceasefire agreement with Israel.

Israel, formerly known as Palestine, is only about the size of New Jersey, about 290 miles long, 85 miles wide at its widest point and 35 miles wide at its narrowest point, but is considered the Middle East mini-superpower...economically and militarily. It possesses the state of the art arsenal, including a formidable cache of nuclear weapons supplied by the United States. Acquiring weaponry was the only way that Israel could expand its territorial footprint...as most Europeans have done throughout history. The one with the most guns wins every time. Fair trade or buying at face value is not in their genetics. As always, land was stolen.

The creation of a Greater Israel requiring the occupation or control the territories extending from the Nile Valley to the Euphrates was rarely discussed in public until quite recently. Eretz Yisrael Ha-Shlema, literally "the whole land of Israel" is the expansionist doctrine calling for the seizure of all the oil-rich lands from the shores of the Euphrates to the banks of the Nile, including the annexation of virtually all of Syria, half of Iraq, Jordan, a large part of Saudi Arabia, and a portion of Egypt. Hebrew scholar Levnoch Osman believed the Torah described Israel, "not as a long, narrow strip of land with wavy,

William E. Cloud

crooked borders, but as a state with broad natural borders."[46] In 1952, Israeli terrorist and former defense minister Moshe Dayan said, "Our task consists of preparing the Israeli army for the war approaching in order to achieve our ultimate goal, the creation of an Israeli empire."[47] Rabbi Avrom Shmuleviv, on behalf of For the Homeland Movement, said in 2009, "The process of national revival of the Jewish people is irreversible and has internal logic. We shall have no peace as long as the whole territory of the country of Israel will not return under Jewish control...A stable peace will not come then, when Israel will return itself all its historic lands, and will thus control both the Suez and the Ormudz Channel...We must remember that Iraq oilfields too are located on the Jewish land."[48] The outright lies these people tell are absolutely astounding. European Jews did not exist in the Middle East during biblical times. Israel is part of Africa, and so its original inhabitants were African. Never forget this fact, and always forget their fiction.

The so-called peace process collapsed in April, 2014, and cannot be resuscitated because Israel never has been serious about reaching any sort of agreement to create an independent Palestinian state. To the contrary, the absorption of Palestinian land is just a stepping stone toward fulfilling what used to be a closely held plan to extend Israel's boundaries well beyond the Palestinian territories. The two decade peace negotiations have been a grand charade to buy time for Israel to achieve its ultimate objective to incorporate a large swatch of the Middle East for the creation of *Greater Israel.*

William E. Cloud

Tragically, the Palestinians have only one option available to them as a Palestinian diplomat involved in the talks lamented, "We know there is no Palestinian state coming our way; we know it but we have to do something at least to improve the quality of the lives of our people under occupation."[49] Unfortunately, that's a realistic appraisal of the situation barring the unlikely event something extraordinary is brought into the equation. Otherwise, the prospect of statehood is bleak for the Palestinians.

In conclusion, the latest peace process was an abject failure because it was never meant to succeed. The two parties are negotiating from two vastly different positions with no balance of power. One entity, namely Israel, has backing of the U.S. and the West, military weapons of mass destruction, and financial resources. The Palestinians have none of this. Israel is in complete control, and when the Palestinians ask for anything or go outside of Israel for help, they face further restrictions or are attacked. Yet, the Palestinians activists and freedom fighters are labelled as terrorist for wanting their land back and to live in peace.

William E. Cloud

CHAPTER 10

The United States of Israel's Constructive Chaos in the Middle East

It lies upon the people's shoulders to prepare for the war, but it lies upon the Israeli army to carry out the fight with the ultimate object of erecting the Israeli Empire.

~ Moshe Dayan, Israel Defense and Foreign Minister

The British Yinon Plan was designed, according to Mahdi Darius Nazemroaya in a 2011 *Global Research* article, to ensure the continuation of the United States of Israel's domination of the Middle East. Regional superiority would be accomplished through the balkanization of the surrounding Arab states into smaller and weaker states. A policy of *constructive chaos* was devised to meet the challenge by fermenting internal political divisions, stirring up sectarian and ethnic strife, arming militias, creating refugees through social dislocation, sabotage, and direct military intervention. The sheer breath of it and the West's plans for the Middle East and Northern Africa can be found in maps published in the U.S. military's *Armed Forces Journal* in 2006 and the 2008 issue of the *Atlantic* magazine which closely resembles the Yinon Plan, except it expands the territorial boundaries to Iran, Turkey, Somalia, and Pakistan. The Plan also called for dissolution in North Africa from Iraq, spilling over into Egypt, Libya, Sudan, and the rest of the region.

Israeli leaders' calls over the last 65 years for expansion beyond the original territorial boundaries is difficult to dismiss or ignore when put in the context of its unwillingness to tolerate a Palestinian state within its boundaries. Israel and the U.S.'s enlargement strategy is quite simple, i.e., instigate, agitate, and perpetuate political turmoil in the countries they have their sights on so that it's easier to maneuver their way in or manipulate to bring the region within their sphere of influence. Their mutual cooperation almost assures successful hegemony of the region.

It is not a coincidence that there is turmoil and instability in all the countries comprising the planned Greater Israel – Iraq, Syria, Egypt, Lebanon and Jordan. This also explains Israel's gung-ho madness to neutralize Iran's nuclear capability, even though there is no definitive proof that it intends to build atomic bombs.

Iraq was number one on the list of countries to be conquered. Its vast oil reserves and territory made it the biggest prize, but also posed the greatest strategic challenge, not just to the United States of Israel's geopolitical goals, but its financial interests as well. Saddam Hussein's plan to price Iraqi oil for Euro currency of the EU seriously threatened the U.S. dollar. His refusal to create a central bank in defiance to the international banking mafia sealed Iraq's fate as the initial takeover target. The plan entailed deposing Saddam, destroying much of the country's infrastructure, and splintering the

William E. Cloud

country into weak Kurdish, Arab Shiite, and Sunni Muslim states before moving onto the rest of the Middle East and the Arab World. The U.S. invasion of Iraq, therefore, had nothing to do with the 911 attack or nonexistent weapons of mass destruction.

The tragedy of the calamitous sectarian turmoil and violence that led to the destabilization of Iraq, Syria, Libya, Sudan, and elsewhere is the product of Israel's Oden Yinon plan to balkanize the Middle East. For example, Netanyahoo openly supports the "Kurdish aspiration for independence" in hopes of successfully achieving Israel's plan to fan sectarian strife to set the stage for the fragmentation of Middle Eastern countries. The destruction of Iraq would give Israel the two-fold bonanza of eliminating the geo-strategic threat posed by a united Iraq and control over the lion's share of oil an independent Kurdistan would facilitate. Indeed, Israel has been establishing alliances in Kurdistan for years in anticipation of dominating its oil and marketing it via a pipeline to Israel. Israel's plan is to dismember Middle East nations that would lead to an explosion of the regional through a series of interlinked civil wars. The U.S. officially opposes the Oden Yinon plan, but behind the scenes is working hand-in-hand with Israel to fragment the Middle East because its foreign policy is dictated by Zionists, regardless whether it is in the best national interests of America. The sad reality is that even if the U.S. wanted to promote peace and stability in the Middle East, which it does not, the world's sole superpower is destined to remain forever an abject slave of Israel unless it decides

William E. Cloud

to assert its own interest instead of allowing Israel to pursue the Oden Yinon plan to its detriment.

In January, 2011, the Egyptian Arab Spring revolution started, and within days, President Hosni Mubarak was forced out of office by the military. His loyalty as a stooge for the West did not prevent Israel from coveting the land or the U.S.'s desire to open up its economy for investment and exploitation by multi-national corporations. The Arab Spring turmoil was a win for both countries. The political situation in Egypt was fluid and uncertain after Mubarak was deposed until the Muslim Brotherhood's Mohammad Morsi was elected president in 2012. It seemed that he was not going to be a lackey like Mubarak and he supported the Palestinian struggle. This was not good for his longevity as Egypt's leader. He was overthrown in a military coup d'etat led by Army General Adbel Sisi in 2013.

Egypt was receiving $2 billion in military aid annually from the United States. Under U.S. law, no U.S. foreign aid may flow to "any country whose duly elected head of government is deposed by military coup d'etat or decree." [1] There are limited exceptions, but compliance cannot be waived without Congressional approval. The Obama administration and Israel refused to describe the coup as a coup so that it wouldn't have to cut off Egypt's military aid and jeopardize losing its influence because they believed Sisi would reinstate Mubarak's draconian policies, especially with regard to continuing the isolation of the Palestinians in the Gaza Strip. Sisi did not disappoint his masters. Curiously, the May, 2014 military coup in Thailand drew swift condemnation from the administration.

William E. Cloud

Secretary of State John Kerry said in a blunt statement that, "[t]here is no justification for this military coup," and that the U.S. was reviewing its military aid and other dealings with its closest ally in Southeast Asia.[2] Some coups are coups; some others are not.

Mouammar Gaddafi's Libya posed no military threat to Israel or the U.S., but the Zionists believe Israel has a God-given claim to the country, especially its vast oil reserves and maybe equally important, its enormous geological store of water found below it, Egypt, Chad, and Sudan; holding about 500 years of the Nile's flow. On top of that, his proposed oil and banking policies threatened the Western economies and the international banking cartel. Soon after the U.S.-NATO attack, at the behest of Israel, the oil companies, and the international banking mafia, the race to control the oil fields began, the national bank was transformed into the Central Bank of Libya and Gaddafi's murder recorded on cellphones went viral.

In May, 2013 Israel struck Syria three times, purportedly to prevent it from delivering weapons to Hezbollah, its arch enemy dedicated to its destruction. Israel has avoided direct involvement in the civil war, but it and the U.S. have undoubtedly provided militarily support to the *rebel* forces fighting Hezbollah, which is allied with the Syrian government. Obama threatened to attack Syria to prevent the Bashar Assad regime from deploying or using chemical or biological weapons against rebels, despite persuasive evidence that the rebels were the culprits.

Syria's civil war is one of the worst humanitarian disasters in recent history. Four years after the start of the Syrian civil war, fierce fighting on both sides has raged. The estimated death toll varies between 150,000 and 220,000, including thousands of children. More than nine million innocent people fled their homes, including a million refugees living in severely stressed neighboring countries. An untold number of families have been torn apart, communities razed, schools and hospitals wrecked and power, sewage, and water systems destroyed. Syria's military capacity has been seriously put to the test, but was winning the Western-instigated civil war.

Yet, there seemed to be a lack of urgency by the U.S. and Israel to directly intervene to stop the cruelty and carnage in Syria if President Assad was allowed to remain in power. Israel certainly has no incentive to intervene in the chaos it created and is benefitting from. Instead, it's in a defensive castle mode as the maelstrom of destruction swirls around it. Its strategy was described by Yaakov Amidror, who recently stepped down as Israel's national security adviser. He said, "What we have to understand is everything is going to be changed...What we see now is a collapsing of a historical system, the idea of the national Arabic state. It means that we will be encircled by an area which will be no man's land at the end of the day...Wait, and keep the castle safe."[3] Israeli spymaster Efraim Halevy, saw it the same way, "If you look all around, compared to what it was like six months ago, Israel can take a deep breath...The way things are at the moment, if you want to photograph it, it looks as if some of the potential is there for an improvement in Israel's strategic position and interests. It's more than ever a see and wait, and be on your guard, and protect yourself if necessary."[4]

William E. Cloud

Meanwhile, Israel celebrates its self-proclaimed status as the "'Villa in the Jungle' while the wild beasts out there tear each other to shreds," observed Noam Chomsky. "And, of course, Israel under this picture is doing nothing except defending itself. They like that picture and the US doesn't seem too dissatisfied with it either. The rest is shadowboxing." [5]

The United States of Israel is executing with satanic aplomb its hegemony game plan for sewing chaos throughout the Middle East.

Post Script

The chaos in the Middle East exponentially intensified in July, 2014 with the emergence of the Islamic State of Iraq and the Levant, sometimes referred to as ISIS or ISIL. In July 2014, ISIS controlled a third of Syria's territory and most of its oil and gas production, thus establishing itself as the major opposition force. The U.S. will certainly use ISIS to intervene militarily in Syria to oust Assad.

William E. Cloud

CHAPTER 11

Gadaffi's Sin: African Economic Independence

This chaos in Libya was deliberate because Libya was a stable African society in North Africa, where the leader of Libya wanted to use the resources of Libya for the reconstruction of Africa—the water resources, the oil resources, the financial resources, and the intelligence of the Libyan people.

~ Paul Jay, Real News Network

"We came, we saw, he died," then Secretary of State Hillary Clinton arrogantly commented about the overthrow and murder of Libya's Muammar Gadaffi in October 2011. This was a tacit admission that regime change was the United States' main objective in going to war against Libya, which contradicted her boss, Barack Obama's, big lie that he had to go because he was a crazy, brutal dictator who robbed and killed his own people. The U.S. and its European allies terminated Gadaffi primarily because he threatened the Zionist-controlled international financial system. The aftermath is that Libya is in complete turmoil.

Years after Gaddafi's removal, the Republicans continue to express fake outrage, anger, and frustration that the Obama administration did not properly respond to the September, 2012 *terrorist* attack on the U.S. embassy, operating as a CIA hub, in Benghazi that resulted in the deaths of four American diplomats, including the U.S. ambassador. Critics claimed that the administration perpetrated a massive cover-up of the events related to the Benghazi affair. Master warmonger, serial complainer, and dunce, John McCain, the Republican senator and Zionist shill stated, "There are so many answers we don't know." The Benghazi brouhaha is nothing more than a Republican effort to create a scandal for the Obama administration that does not exist, at least not with respect to the deaths of the U.S. diplomats.

The real scandal is that an estimated 30,000 Libyan civilians were killed and 100,000 injured in another war instigated by the West. [1] American officials and the corporate media kept under wraps that before the attack on the embassy in Benghazi, the Rothschild banking mafia had already taken control of the country's gold and wealth, and established a central bank.

The brutal assassination of Gaddafi by a rebel mob on October 10, 2011, was graphically memorialized through the lens of a cellphone that went viral on the internet. That afternoon from the White House Rose Garden, President Obama told the world that Gaddafi's death was "a momentous day in the history of Libya...[that] marks the end of long and painful chapter for the people of Libya, who now have the opportunity to determine their own destiny in a new and democratic Libya...For four decades, the Qaddafi regime ruled the Libyan people with an iron fist. Basic human rights were denied.

Innocent civilians were detained, beaten and killed. And Libya's wealth was squandered. The enormous potential of the Libyan people was held back, and terror was used as a political weapon. Today, we can definitively say that the Qaddafi regime has come to an end. The last major regime strongholds have fallen. The new government is consolidating the control over the country."[2]

During the news conference, Obama reiterated the lie that the United States only got involved in the Libyan conflict to prevent Gaddafi from committing mass atrocities against his own people. His statements could not have been farther from the truth. Obama's speech was a repetition of the false propaganda that the corporate media bombarded the American public with to gin up support for the continuation of U.S. imperialism, despite the total lack of credible evidence to substantiate the claim that Gaddafi was a threat to his own people. The Bush administration trotted out the same lie against Saddam to justify attacking Iraq.

Gaddafi was overthrown by Western recruited bands of ragtag fighters to fight alongside mercenaries hired by the CIA. The fact that the United States' primary mission in Libya was regime change was conclusively proven in emails leaked by WikiLeaks. The government contracted with the Blackwater security provider to send mercenaries "to fight alongside rebels in Libya, and was even involved in the killing of Muammar Gaddafi."[3] Heavily armed and equipped rebel ground forces combined with an intense seven month U.S. bombing campaign, cinched Gaddafi's demise. While the administration falsely claimed that no American troops' boots were on the ground, it also falsely maintained it did not muster the rebels. American troops and CIA-hired mercenaries clearly were involved in the proxy war in Libya. Given the Obama administration's aversion to transparency, the public may never know about its true involvement in the hostilities because the information would be classified top secret. WikiLeaks snatched off the veil of secrecy and exposed the lies.

The only truth in President Obama's speech was that the new government was consolidating control over the country. Indeed, the *rebels* were accomplishing the international banking mafia's objective to consolidate control over the country's banking system, gold reserves, oil fields, and water resources before the war ended. Gaddafi's overthrow was a great moment for the international bankers, not the Libyan people.

Gaddafi refused to sell out his country to the international banking families and the U.S. corporatocracy, a coalition of banks, corporations, and government officials that control the planet's national economies and natural resources. Not only could he not be paid off or extorted, he defiantly rebuffed their efforts with proposals that could have turned the world of international finance upside down. In order to maintain their diminishing hold on world economic domination, the Western powers at the behest of the international banking mafia decided Gaddafi's termination with extreme prejudice was absolutely necessary. If his plans were successful they would have at a minimum propelled Africa toward economic self-determination to the detriment of the world's financial system and

Western economies. They were not willing to permit that to happen under any circumstances.

Obama lied to the war-weary American public to garner its support for the intervention efforts to *save* the Libyan people, arguing the U.S. was morally obligated to rescue the Libyans from a brutal, tyrannical dictator bent on massacring his own people. The truth is that America only feels *morally* obligated to rescue someone if it has something to gain by doing so.

Gaddafi was certainly not the most benevolent leader and made his share of serious mistakes, but even his harshest critics concede that he inherited the poorest country in the world and transformed it into Africa's richest. Libyans enjoyed the highest standard of living in Africa as noted by *Fleet Street* journalists, David Blundy and Andrew Lycett, who observed,

"The young people are well dressed, well fed and well educated. Libyans now earn more per capita than the British. The disparity in annual incomes...is smaller than in most countries. Libya's wealth has been fairly spread throughout society. Every Libyan has a job and a decent salary. He gets free, and often excellent, education, medical and health services. New colleges and hospitals are impressive by any international standard. All Libyans have a [rent free] house or a flat, a car and most have televisions, video recorders and telephones. Compared with most citizens of the Third World countries, and with many in the First World, Libyans have it very good indeed."[4]

Libya's high standard of living was achieved through Gaddafi's economic policy that mandated oil profits seep down to benefit the Libyan people, as opposed to other oil producing countries that hoarded oil profits for the few. Libya's Great Man-Made River project, which Gaddafi called "the eighth wonder of the world," was the premier centerpiece of the country's agricultural revolution. The 248 mile pipeline brought drinking and agricultural water to 70 percent of the people. Huge underground pipes from aquifers beneath the Sahara, enabled Libya to develop large scale agricultural projects designed to achieve self-sufficiency in food production, thereby reducing dependence on imported foodstuffs from overseas. Although far from being a utopia, contrary to western propaganda, Libyan society benefitted from the country's oil wealth, and through direct participation in the decision-making process they enjoyed a freedom that citizens are denied in many other nations.

With the launch of a telecommunications satellite in 2006, Gaddafi showed his commitment to African economic development. Prior to that, the entire African continent was dependent on European companies for access to satellite communications at a cost of $500 billion annually; making Africa the most expensive place in the world to make a telephone call. For years, African governments pleaded with banks and the IMF to fund a communications project. It was widely believed that their requests were rejected because the lenders wanted to protect the profits of European satellite providers. Even if the international banks financed the project, they would have demanded unfair terms and conditions at usurious interest rates which would have saddled the Continent with more debt than it could ever repay.

The project languished until Gaddafi stepped up with $300 million of the $400 million needed to finance a Russian and Chinese built communications satellite. The successful launch of Africa's first satellite provided all of Africa with access to reasonably priced telephone, broadcasting, and internet service. It's safe to say that the loss of $500 billion in annual revenue did not endear Gaddafi to European telecommunications companies and international banks. This extraordinary accomplishment was also troubling to the West because it demonstrated that a unified Africa was capable of getting out from under the boot of European economic colonialism.

His proposal of four initiatives posed greater danger to the international economic system, however. He sought to introduce the gold dinar, in Gaddafi's words, "a single African currency made from gold, a true sharing of wealth."[5] Under the plan, Libyan oil could only be purchased with dinars instead of dollars. Indeed, he urged African and other developing nations around the world to likewise demand all purchases of their resources be made in gold dinars. Thus, a country's wealth would be measured by how much gold it had to trade, as opposed to how many dollars it had. "Analysts say introducing the gold dinar as the new medium of exchange would destroy dependence on the U.S. dollar, the French franc and the

British pound and threaten the Western world," reported Brian E. Muhammad of the *Final Call*. "It would finally swing the global economic pendulum that would break Western domination over Africa and other developing economies." [6]

In May 2011, Anthony Wile, founder and Chief Editor of the *Daily Bell* stated in an interview with *Russia Today* that,

> "If Gaddafi had an intent to try to re-price his oil or whatever else the country was selling on the global market and accept something else as a currency or maybe launch a gold dinar currency, any move such as that would certainly not be welcomed by the power elite today, who are responsible for controlling the world's central banks. So yes, that would certainly be something that would cause his immediate dismissal and the need for other reasons to be brought forward from moving him from power." [7]

Gaddafi also proposed creating two major banks financed by Libyan investments in the United States. The African Monetary Fund (AMF) would have eliminated the need for the IMF and the World Bank, depriving them of the power to coerce African governments to accept unrealistic and unpopular measures to qualify for loans such as the privatization of natural resources that guaranteed neocolonialists the ability to keep Africa eternally poor and dependent on the West.

William E. Cloud

Gaddafi's vision of an African Central Bank (CAB) constituted the most serious and unacceptable challenge to the international banking system. Headquartered in Nigeria, the bank would have gone into operation in 2011 had Gaddafi not been murdered. The gold dinars it intended to print and circulate would be backed by 144 tons of gold held in Libyan vaults. The bank's creation would free the Continent from the clutches of international bankers. The banksters feared, and rightfully so, that this would start a bad precedent.

Lastly, Gaddafi envisioned the formation of the United States of Africa, spanning from Cape Town to Cairo. This would diminish the negative impact of the national borders arbitrarily drawn up by European imperialists that still inhibited travel, trade, and is a source of conflict between nations. Like Gaddafi's other proposals, an African commonwealth provided a path toward self-determination. "The US, the other G-8 countries, the World Bank, IMF, BIS (Bank for International Settlements), and multinational corporations do not look kindly on leaders who threaten their dominance over world currency markets," notes John Perkins, author of "Confessions of an Economic Hit Man".[8] So, Gaddafi was playing with dynamite when he threatened the very existence of the western banking, energy, and weapons lobbies. The West had to eliminate him...to protect their inhuman hegemony and to show others not to challenge or attempt to thwart their supremacy. Secretary of State Hillary Clinton put the U.S's intentions succinctly with her snide quip about the brutal execution of Col. Gaddafi.[9] Her inadvertent gaffe, of course, was not challenged by the media.

William E. Cloud

The uprisings in the border countries of Tunisia and Egypt gave the West a convenient opportunity to overthrow Gaddafi while making it appear to be a continuation of the Arab Spring. "The CIA's early involvement with Libyan rebels, along with early support for the rebels by French and British intelligence, indicates that the Libyan rebellion was not based on events of neighboring Tunisia and Egypt, but was designed to authorize the rebels to militarily strike at Gaddafi when a favorable situation presented itself," wrote Wayne Madsen in an article entitled "The Illegal War on Libya".[10] Western intelligence agencies, especially the CIA, worked on the ground to manipulate Libyans, orchestrate protests, and assemble a collection of renegades, traitors, and western collaborators, who could be counted on to form a friendly, subservient government after Gaddafi was ousted. Former Italian Prime Minister Silvio Berlusconi accurately called the conflict in Libya a fake revolution. There was no dispute that the western countries completely orchestrated the revolt from the beginning to the end for the sole purposes of removing the troublesome Gaddafi and gaining control of Libya.

Although the West claims al Qaeda is the preeminent terrorist organization, many anti-Gaddafi rebels were affiliated with the group. Indeed, al Qaeda fighters were easily recruited to do the West's dirty work in Libya because Gaddafi always considered it an enemy of Libya. Before and after the September, 11, 2001 incident, Gaddafi provided the West with intelligence about its activities. Notwithstanding this, the Obama administration supplied thousands of al-Qaeda irregulars with weapons and other support in rebel-controlled eastern Libya. Thus, when it came to destabilizing Libya and removing Gaddafi, the U.S., and European interests had no compunction about arming and using terrorist forces to do the deed.

With few exceptions, the corporate media reports on the war were pro-rebel. The sentiments and opinions of the vast majority of Libyans who supported Gaddafi were ignored. The media concealed the high standard of living most Libyans enjoyed, the country's phenomenal economic development and the progressive visions Gaddafi had for the creation of an economic self-sustaining Africa. Instead, it fanned racial hatred with despicable lies that Gaddafi was using African mercenaries against his people. The Africans referred to were actually men who had come to the country seeking construction jobs who took no part in the fighting.

"Yusuf Suleiman Hassan, a 25-year-old native of Chad, says he came to Benghazi, in eastern Libya, six months ago to find work. He eventually joined dozens of his countrymen in grueling construction work," reported Babak Dehghanpisheh of the *Daily Beast*. "When the violent uprisings broke out in Libya last month, he knew it was time to go. 'There was a lot of fighting,' says Hassan, who's wearing a muddy light blue jacket and brown sandals. 'I'm a poor man and I just want to go home.'"[11] The media's fabrication that Gaddafi was using African mercenaries was to further legitimize intervention in Libya. Sadly, this false rumor was responsible for the massacre of hundreds, maybe thousands of innocent Africans civilians.

When the *rebels* took time out of their pitched battle against Gaddafi to establish a central bank headquartered in Benghazi to replace Libya's state-owned authority, the Obama administration's deceitful humanitarian cover story for intervention was revealed. They also created a new state oil company. Many banking experts believe that was the first time in history a revolutionary group created such institutions before the end of hostilities. "This suggests we have a bit more than a ragtag bunch of rebels running around and that there are some pretty sophisticated influences," noted Robert Wenzel, an analysis for the *Economic Policy Journal*.[12] They, meaning the globalist, private international financiers of Europe, American and Britain, are the actual agitators. To date, the ownership of the newly-created Central Bank of Libya bank has not been revealed, according to its website, with the exception of a stake held by the Arab Banking Corporation, a universal bank headquartered in Bahrain.

In any event, more than two years after Libya's Interim Transnational National Council established the bank, no chairman or officers had been installed on the board, and rules as to how it would be governed were not formulated due to government infighting.

That is all academic, however, since then, 144 tons of gold bullion securely locked up in Libyan vaults disappeared without a trace. To avoid the risk of confiscation, Gaddafi refused to store it in the BIS, New York, or London central banks. He also refused to exchange it for paper currency. So, the banking cartel resorted to the old fashioned way of stealing it by military conquest. Considering one of the banking cartel's objectives of the war of aggression was to take Libya's gold it so coveted, it would be ludicrous to believe that it would permit a motley crew of pretend freedom fighters to take custody of billions of dollars in gold bullion. It would be infinitely more likely that the gold was taken to the Fed or U.K. for safe keeping, euphemistically speaking. Despite the new Libyan central bank's halting start, when it becomes operational, the banking vultures will swoop in to take over and *reform* the country's monetary system with huge injections of worthless dollars. Chaotic inflationary cycles inflationary cycles are sure to follow. The high standard of living that Libyans were accustomed to will be more. Gaddafi's vision for an economic independent Africa is likewise gone for the foreseeable future, and it will remain hopelessly dependent on its cruel neocolonial masters.

The rebel's new Libyan Oil Company, also based in Benghazi, was given permission from the Obama administration to sell oil in its control, provided it was transacted through the new oil corporation. This strongly suggests the rebellion was most likely a major play for oil and gold, with the true disaffected rebels being used as puppets and cover while international bankers and the West solidified control over the country's natural resources and finances. One writer sarcastically wrote about the rebels' ability to multi-task.

"What a skilled bunch of rebels — they can fight a war during the day and draw up a new central bank and a new national oil company at night without any outside help whatsoever. If only the rest of us were so versatile!...Apparently someone felt that it was very important to get pesky matters such as control of the banks and control

William E. Cloud

of the money supply out of the way even before a new government is formed."[13]

CNBC senior editor John Carney marveled "how extraordinarily powerful central bankers have become in our era."[14]

There is no genuine dispute that Gaddafi's ambitious plans for an economically independent and self-sustaining Africa posed a clear and present danger to the world's monetary system. Global financiers and market manipulators don't tolerate any type of independence. The Libyan government's ability to create its own money and control it through its own central bank, therefore, was problematic for the globalist banking cartel. It put them in a position they were not accustom to being in, that is, having no domination or power-broking ability over Libyan and African affairs. The downfall of the Gaddafi regime was not the momentous day for the Libyan people as President Obama triumphantly proclaimed, but will go down as a monstrous day for the vultures.

Three years after the U.S. orchestrated the termination of Gaddafi's rule, the rebels it used to remove him have proved difficult to control. The country spiraled into lawlessness and chaos. The human rights situation deteriorated, extremists groups fought each other, and the threat of civil war loomed, jeopardizing neighboring countries. The weak, and largely dysfunctional transitional government, comprised of Western puppets, has been incapable of maintaining law and order, which was the intended purpose to enable the Western nations to take over and carve it up.

William E. Cloud

In October, 2013, Prime Minister Ali Zeidan was kidnapped from his hotel in Tripoli by a group of former rebels amid anger that the government had some involvement in a U.S. Special Forces raid that seized a Libyan al Qaida suspect. Thousands were driven out of towns the rebels considered pro-Gaddafi and resettled in squalid refugee camps. Thousands more were indefinitely detained because the criminal justice system shut down due to the attacks and murder of judges, prosecutors, lawyers, and witnesses.

A police force is nonexistent, and an every-man-for-himself atmosphere prevailed. The weak government tried to maintain the peace by appeasing 160,000 militiamen, often members of violent gangs, to act as an informal police force with payments of $1,000 a month. They turned out to be undisciplined thugs who terrorized instead of protecting Libya's citizenry.

Militia rule emboldened the warlords. One "took control of eastern oil terminals, demanding autonomy and more resources for Cyrenaica, the long-neglected oil-rich east of the country. Oil exports collapsed from about 1.5m barrels a day to fewer than 500,000, costing the country billions of dollars."[15]

In March, 2014, former rebels and militias hijacked the oil tanker Morning Glory, full with crude oil, in defiance of the government. That was the last straw for the Obama administration. Under no circumstances would the tolerate anyone to cease and control the oil it went to great lengths to steal. U.S. Special Forces were ordered to board and seize the tanker as it sailed off the coast of Cyprus. "The dispute over the ship underscored the weakness of the Libyan government and the extent to which the Obama administration is willing to use military force to support an oil-rich nation still reeling from the aftermath of its civil war."[16]

Obama was prepared to go even further in protecting American interests in Libya. The transitional government installed by the U.S had not brought the stability and peace needed to accomplish its ends. Aside from its oil reserves, Libya has enormous strategic value to the U.S., as it is essentially in the center of the Middle East and borders on many countries it has an interest in, allies and foe, notably Iran. Regime change was in order. The CIA called up its backup dictator in waiting, Khalifa Hifter, who was involved in the coup that brought Gaddafi to power in 1969. Hifter changed sides and became leader of the Libyan National Army, an anti-Gaddafi rebel group financed by the U.S. He subsequently sought refuge in the U.S., became an American citizen, and voted regularly in Virginia elections. Hifter and his family lived a comfortable life in a pricey five-bedroom home in Vienna, Virginia, a short distance from CIA headquarters. An acquaintance said, "Nobody knows what his source for compensation was…Hifter's family was not originally wealthy."[17] He bided his time until the start of Libyan war in 2011, and was presented with an opportunity to return at the behest of the CIA. He kept in the shadows until his handlers tapped him to take over the government. Calling himself the "Commander of the New Libyan Army," Hifter began roaming around Libya with a band of supporters, "probably hired mercenaries funded by the U.S., and he was viewed as a foreign stooge by the Islamist militias."[18] From all indications, Hifter will be

William E. Cloud

Libya's next strongman. Deplorably, there is always someone ready and willing to take money and accept a position of illusionary power, to the detriment of his own people. Also, the West created a favorable environment to take over the Libyan government through the use of *militants*, and the bewildered and bamboozled *rebel* fighters fall for the same false promises every time.

In August, 2014, Libya's ambassador to the United Nations warned that the low-level civil war was on the verge of becoming full-blown if an immediate cease-fire was not reached. Rooted in rivalries between Islamists and non-Islamists, and powerful tribal and regional allegiances, the country currently has two governments with competing parliaments. The situation was further complicated when the United Arab Emirates and Egypt secretly executed airstrikes against Islamist militias inside Libya. This came a month after violent clashes between militias forced the U.S. and Canada to evacuate their diplomats from the Libyan capital Tripoli. "[D]ue to the ongoing violence resulting from clashes between Libyan militias," a U.S. State Department spokesman explained, embassy personnel were evacuated because "the location of our embassy is in very close proximity to intense fighting…between armed Libyan factions."[19]

Human Rights Watch warns that, "Libya has been sitting on the international community's back burner as the country has slipped into near chaos."[20] A divided Libya is a weak Libya, susceptible to easy exploitation. Thus, religious, ethnic, tribal, and political turmoil in Libya is *mission accomplished* for U.S. hegemony there.

William E. Cloud

Muammar Gaddafi was a man who defied the West. He was a true solider for the good of all Africans. His goal was a united Africa, one without European influence. He used the oil wealth of the country to benefit Libya's people, nothing that any European controlled country has ever done. Predator nations, America, Europe, Israel, and France, bombed the hell out of Libya to thwart his plans for a financially self-sustaining Africa, steal its vast wealth, protect the petro-dollar, and install a Rothschild's central bank. What a wicked world we live in when entire countries of color are destroyed to the benefit of the American and European power elite.

William E. Cloud

CHAPTER 12

The Never Ending Rape of Haiti

The international community is so screwed up
they're letting Haitians run Haiti.

~ Luigi R. Einaudi (US career diplomat)

In low-key ceremonies around Haiti, survivors of the cataclysmic 7.0 magnitude earthquake that devastated the country on January 12, 2010 commemorated the deaths of more than 300,000, an equal number injured and the over one million left homeless. The fourth anniversary of the worst natural disaster in recorded history was ignored by the Western media, and vaguely remembered by most Americans. Already the poorest, least developed country in the Western Hemisphere, the pre-earthquake-suffering of the Haitian people can be directly traced to centuries of U.S., French, and British white racist policies forced on the nation that were calculated to fail. The earthquake magnified Haitian misery. True to form, the U.S. and the international community did not fulfill or reneged entirely on their promises to donate humanitarian and reconstruction aid. Non-governmental organizations (NGOs), Americans, and the elite Haitian carpetbaggers exploited the tragedy by stealing or

William E. Cloud

misspending the aid that was received with confidence that the Haitian people were powerless to do anything about it. Meanwhile, multinational corporations descended on the country like vultures to pursue business interests including, garment manufacturing sweatshops, tourism, gold mining, and production of the country's sizable reserves of natural gas.

The rebuilding of Haiti's housing and the infrastructure has progressed at a snail's pace. Consequently, the country remains in ruins, and hundreds of thousands continue to live a subsistence existence in tent encampments and earthquake damaged buildings. Eighty percent of Haiti's population live below the poverty line, 54% live in abject poverty, and unemployment tops 70%. Crippling poverty, high unemployment, corruption, low levels of education, and the ever present vulnerability to natural disasters are serious impediments to its recovery.

Four years after the earthquake, there is scant evidence that the U.S. stepped up to help the beleaguered nation. The combined pledges of long-term assistance totaled nearly $10 billion. Shamefully, most of the international donors barely fulfilled or welshed entirely on their pledges of financial assistance. There are no accurate figures on the amount of aid Haiti received, but whatever expenditures international donors made only marginally benefited the Haitian people, if at all. The United States and the international community should be condemned for failing to adequately address this continuing humanitarian crisis.

William E. Cloud

In the aftermath of the disaster, President Barack Obama told *Newsweek,* "In the last week, we have been deeply moved by the heartbreaking images of the devastation in Haiti; parents searching through rubble for sons and daughters; children, frightened and alone, looking for their mothers and fathers. At this moment, entire parts of Port-au-Prince are in ruins, as families seek shelter in makeshift camps. It is a horrific scene of shattered lives in a poor nation that has already suffered so much." [1] He promised a massive relief effort, saying "We act for the sake of the thousands of American citizens who are in Haiti, and for their families back home; for the sake of the Haitian people who have been stricken with a tragic history, even as they have shown great resilience; and we act because of the close ties that we have with a neighbor that is only a few hundred miles to the south. But above all, we act for a very simple reason: in times of tragedy, the United States of America steps forward and helps. That is who we are. That is what we do."[2] The Haitians' trust that Obama would keep his word was for naught.

Although there was no threat to the peace and stability on the devastated island, Obama's first order of business was to militarily invade Haiti. Within two hours after the quake, and before the after-shocks stopped, an armada of U.S. warships, including the biggest aircraft carrier, the Carl Vinson, steamed toward Haiti to join the contingency of United Nations' Minuatah force of 9,000 *peacekeepers* that occupied the country since 2004. The UN forces were initially deployed to control the populous after the U.S, France and Canada kidnapped Jean-Bertrand Aristide, Haiti's democratically

William E. Cloud

elected president. Their real purpose was to keep Haiti under the boot of imperialism. The U.S. military commandeered the main airport in Port of Prince and the seaports to facilitate the invasion. Days later, 10,000 U.S. soldiers had either landed on Haitian soil or were stationed offshore on warships. Meanwhile, no relief supplies were allowed to be delivered to the desperate people.

Haiti, known in the 18th century as Saint Dominque, was France's most prosperous overseas colony due to slave labor. It was the leading producer of cotton, sugar, coffee, indigo, and tobacco; accounting for 20% of France's revenue. In fact, France couldn't then economically survive without brutally exploiting the colony's slave labor, nor is it doing well without pilfering from African peoples of the world, as evidenced by its flat growth and the financial crisis it was experiencing in 2014. The slaves revolted in 1791. Described as the most successful rebellion in the Western Hemisphere, they soundly defeated the white slave-owners and declared Haitian independence in 1803, becoming the second independent nation in the Americas after the United States. France retaliated by refusing to recognize it politically and economically unless it agreed to an extortion demand of 150 million francs as reparations to the ousted white slaveholders in compensation for their loss of slaves and property as a result of the revolution. No other victorious party in a revolution to secure liberty has been coerced to pay the vanquished.

Fearing international isolation, in 1820 the fledgling republic agreed under duress to France's extortion demand. Although the payment was reduced to 60 million francs, it still exceeded the economically destitute, war-torn nation's ability to pay without causing severe damage to its economy and its peoples' welfare. Indeed, by 1900, eighty percent of its national budget was spent on repayments, forcing it to borrow money from American and other foreign banks on onerous terms and usurious interest rates. "For Haiti, this debt did not signify the beginning of freedom, but the end of hope...[and] [t]hese payments may have permanently affected Haiti's economy and wealth."[3]

Haiti's relationship with the United States isn't much better. The U.S. bears a large measure of responsibility for the impoverished condition of its Caribbean neighbor. Its poor response to the humanitarian crisis was, therefore, predictable. To understand this, it's important to put in perspective the historical relationship between the two countries. American foreign policy towards Haiti was extremely hostile after it defeated the French and declared its independence. The successful slave rebellion sent shock waves throughout the American South. Plantation owners feared it might inspire their slaves to revolt. The U.S. refused to recognize Haiti for almost fifty years after its founding, and the vestiges of this resentment forms the insular political culture that continues to plague its relationship with Haiti.

American animus toward Haiti was recently confirmed by a former United Nations special envoy to Haiti, Paul Farmer, who acknowledged that the United States and the island nation have "been very uneasy neighbors for the past 200 years...The thing that's striking to me is that any historical view of the problems we're seeing in Haiti shows that we don't have a long and distinguished history of good-neighbor policy towards Haiti."[4] Considering America's historical cruelty and mistreatment of the defenseless island nation, that's an understatement. For example, using the pretext of bringing stability to the Haitian government, arch-racist President Woodrow Wilson ordered a Marine invasion of the country in 1915. Many American officials believed that the occupation was necessary to peaceful governance of the country because Haitians were incapable of governing themselves. White racism was actually the key factor. Explaining the paternalistic attitude toward Haiti, one official said "these people had never heard of democracy and couldn't have comprehended it had they heard." [4] Militant peasant leaders, like Charlemagne Peralte who resisted occupation, were murdered, and their mutilated corpses were publically displayed for days as a reminder of American military might. U.S. armed forces killed more than 15,000 civilian Haitians before troops withdrew in 1934, after two decades of occupation. The U.S. maintained economic control of the nation until 1947. That was not the last time the U.S. interfered in Haitian affairs or tried to impose democracy by undemocratic means.

For decades after the withdrawal of U.S. forces, a succession of juntas, coups, and puppet mulatto and black dictators terrorized Haitians. The most notorious dictators were Francois "Papa Doc" Duvalier, who was president from 1947 to his death in 1971, and his son, Jean-Claude "Baby Doc" Duvalier. With the support and backing of the U.S., both dictators brutally ruled Haiti with iron fists while poverty on the island remained the most widespread of any country in the Western Hemisphere. Relations between Baby Doc's regime and the U.S. deteriorated during the Carter Administration, but his anti-communist stance brought him back in U.S. favor during the Reagan Administration. In 1986, he was overthrown and went into exile in Paris.

In 1990, Jean Bertrand Aristide, a populous ex-priest, was elected president. During three terms in office, he worked to bring democracy to the country through proposals for fundamental populist changes that gave more voice to the poor, raised the minimum wage, and forced businesses to pay taxes, among other things. He was also a frequent and vocal critic of America as being a major negative influence on Haitian affairs. That was perceived as a serious threat by powerful forces in the U.S. "He wasn't going to be beholden to the United States, and so he was going to be trouble," warned Senator Christopher J. Dodd, "[w]e had interests and ties with some of the very strong financial interests in the country, and Aristide was threatening them."[5] In 2004, President George Bush ordered American troops to abduct Aristide. Randall Robinson described in his book *An Unbroken Agony: Haiti, from Revolution to the Kidnapping of a President*, how Aristide was forced aboard an airplane that flew him to the Central African Republic.[6] He resettled in South Africa where he remained in exile for six years.

On the eve of the 2010 Haitian presidential elections, Aristide came out of exile and returned to Haiti over the objection of President Obama, who personally urged South African President Jacob Zumba to delay his departure. Obama was concerned that Aristide's presence in Haiti could upset the presidential election the U.S. was covertly rigging in favor of its hand-picked mulatto stooge, Michael "Sweet Mickey" Martelly. Just before the election, Baby Doc also returned to Haiti and brazenly acted as though he and his father had not "waged war on Haiti's poor, ruled brutally with dictatorial harshness, and amassed wealth the old-fashioned way like his father – he stole and extorted it, including massive amounts of US and international aid, notably from the World Bank, IMF, International Development Bank (IDB), and USAID."[7] Baby Doc's horrid human rights record was irrelevant to Obama. In contrast to his objection to Aristide's return, he was silent about Duvalier coming back to the country he ravaged.

In February, 2014, the Haitian Court of Appeals reinstated charges against Duvalier on the grounds that his commission of crimes against humanity was governed by international law, which has no statute of limitations, thereby reversing a lower court decision that the charges were barred by Haiti's statute of limitations. The court ordered further investigation into the extensively documented abuses he committed during his 15-year reign.[8]

Sweet Mickey Martelly, a singer with rightwing leanings, mostly lived in Florida before running for president. Despite having no political experience and a close supporter of Baby Doc, he was elected president in May, 2011. The *Black Agenda Report* noted that he won "in a forced election marred by irregularities and low voter turnout. More importantly, he is the face – and backbone – of a resurgent Duvalierism."[9] This explains why parliamentary and local elections have not been held or a voting date announced since

Martelly took office three years ago. The Haitian government is dysfunctional mess.

Curiously, former President Bill Clinton who did nothing meaningful for the Haitian people during his terms in office finagled an appointment as special envoy to Haiti in 2009 from his friend United Nations Secretary General Ban Ki-moon. Since his appointment came prior to the earthquake, it's clear he was motivated by something other than humanitarianism. Clinton saw underdeveloped Haiti as a promising business investment opportunity. The earthquake was a literal blessing in disguise for him to open Haiti for economic exploitation.

Clinton wasted no time taking advantage of the tragedy. Before the dust settled, he began pursuing economic development projects and liberalization of trade restrictions. For example, even though rice is the country's main crop and staple of the Haitian diet, he forced the Haitian government to drop tariffs on imported U.S. subsidized rice imports. The elimination of the tariff put Haitian rice farmers out of business because they could not compete with the cheaper, subsidized American imports. Consequently, Haiti lost its ability to maintain self-sufficiency in rice production, and is now totally dependent on imports. In 2010, Mr. Clinton acknowledged during a hearing held by the Senate Foreign Relations Committee that, "'It [tariff cuts on imported U.S. rice] may have been good for some of my farmers in Arkansas, but it has not worked. It was a mistake…I had to live every day with the consequences of the loss of capacity to produce a rice crop in Haiti to feed those people because of what I did; nobody else.'

William E. Cloud

Although a generous mea culpa, at the end of the day Clinton went on with his life while Haiti had to pay the price of Clinton's benighted policy towards President Aristide as well as the economic prejudice he fostered on the island."[10]

Obama inexplicably, or maybe not, appointed former President George Bush to coordinate with Clinton on humanitarian relief efforts and fund-raising for Haiti. Appointing Mr. Clinton is arguably logical considering he did have a limited familiarity with Haiti, even though as noted by Randall Robinson, he supported economic policies that created sweatshops instead of uplifting the human condition of the Haitian people. But Bush's appointment as co-chair of U.S. relief efforts was baffling given the fact the he forced the country's democratically elected president into exile. Moreover, his infamous mishandling of the New Orleans relief effort in the aftermath of hurricane Katrina in 2005 should permanently disqualified him from involvement in any other disaster relief program.

Rebuilding Haiti would have conservatively cost $14 billion. So, from the start, donor pledges of $10 billion were $4 billion short even if all the money pledged materialized. As of December, 2012, only $7.5 billion in donations is said to have been received; half of which was spent on relief aid.

The most pressing problem created by the earthquake continues to be safe, stable housing for the displaced people. One hundred and five thousand houses were destroyed and 208,164 homes were badly damaged, rendering 2.3 million homeless. One and a half million people internally displaced, gathered in 1,555 makeshift camps, and another 600,000 were forced to move to areas unaffected by the earthquake.[11] As of 2014, more than 400,000 people were still trapped in wretched tent camps or buildings that are dangerously unfit for habitation, while thousands more have moved into the hills where they live under tarps and in rusty corrugated metal huts. The U.S. completed building only 2,649 permanent homes, far short of the 15,000 homes promised, before it terminated the construction program in December, 2013. In its place, USAID said it would begin extending Haitians direct financing to build their own homes. "There was definitely a shift, because USAID began to realize that building houses here is very complicated," said mission director John Groarke in an interview with *The Associated Press*. "We feel that we can reach and help more people through creative financing."[12] That's asinine. In view of the fact that the country's unemployment rate still hovers in the high fifty to seventy percent range, there is no amount of creative financing the Haitians can afford. How will they pay the mortgages? They can't. The USAID's plan to offer creative financing, therefore, is doublespeak to say the U.S. is out of the house building business in Haiti.

Of the roughly $3.6 billion the U.S. allocated for relief, only $1.3 billion was earmarked for reconstruction. To put this into perspective, America's contribution to rebuilding Haiti is less than half the cost of a $3 billion stealth bomber.[13] This raises serious questions about America's priorities when the cost of a single platform of death and destruction is more than its contribution to help the victims of an epic natural disaster in a neighboring nation that's less than 500 miles

William E. Cloud

from Florida. Further contrast this with the government's response to super storm Sandy that struck the East coast in October, 2012 which killed 125, destroyed 72,000 homes and businesses, and left 3,500 families displaced in New Jersey alone. Obama immediately declared the area a disaster, and the federal government promptly provided storm victims with temporary housing. In recognition that the expeditious provision of relief aid to storm victims was paramount, within three months Congress authorized $50 billion in relief aid with a promise of an additional $10 billion. Haiti needed just $14 billion to rebuild the *entire* country. The U.S. did not display the same compassion in its response to the death and destruction in Haiti that dwarfed the damaged caused by Sandy.

The Haitian government got less than 1% of the money. Likewise, extremely little went to Haitian companies or Haitian NGOs. Haitians, by and large, were not even consulted about the relief efforts. Most of the money spent went to outside governments, international aid agencies, big well-connected NGOs, and for-profit companies that specialized in disasters. "A lot of the pledged money has never been actually put up. And a lot of the money that was put up has not yet been spent."[14] The reality is that disaster aid rarely benefits the devastated country. The Western *saviors* take the whole pie, and what crumbs that fall off their bloated bellies goes to those who need the most funding.

Richard Morse, Martelly's cousin and spokesperson, resigned in December, 2012 "because of corruption in the palace, and infrastructure sabotage," he said.[15] He witnessed fake checks being

William E. Cloud

given to people who no longer worked for the government. Nothing was done when he brought this corruption in the palace to the attention of administration officials. "Rather than fight the corruption, I feel like they have embraced it," he added.[16]

The perception of pervasive corruption is a reason most donors used to circumvent sending money directly to the Haitian government. Indeed, Baby Doc Duvalier took millions in loans, saddling Haiti with appallingly odious debt before he was overthrown. World lenders were in the process of forgiving the debt before the earthquake hit. In fact, $1.2 billion in debt was written off a few months before the earthquake. Cancelling the debt, according to Congresswoman Maxine Waters, was "one of the simplest but most important things we can do to help Haiti." Instead of rebuilding the country, the largest part of the U.S.'s relief expenditure of $245 million was used to reduce the debt. The multilateral institutions made out like bandits. Haiti still owed lenders $828 million when the earthquake struck. Since Martelly took office, his administration has put the country back in debt with an additional $657 million in loans…with little to show for it.

Unfortunately, there is an issue of transparency with the way the Martelly administration is spending Haiti's $1 billion in annual foreign aid and loans. It has resisted, and sometimes flatly refused, to disclose the information even to members of Congress. "The lack of specific details in where the money has gone facilitates corruption and waste," complained New York Congresswoman Yvette Clark, adding, it "creates a closed process that reduces competition and

William E. Cloud

prevents us from assessing the efficacy of certain taxpayer-funded projects." Some of the secrecy, though, is attributable to USAID's instructions to the Martelly government to "wait for formal clearance...before releasing any information" on projects.[17]

Most of the money immediately allocated following the earthquake did not reached Haiti. Right off the bat, the U.S. kept 33% of the money to reimburse itself for the 22,000 troops it sent to Haiti for the unnecessary invasion. As for the total relief aid following the first allocation, the Department of Defense got $655 million; the Department of Health and Human Services paid individual States $220 million to cover the cost of services provided to Haitian evacuees; USAID reimbursed $350.7 million to International Disaster Assistance (IDA); the US Department of Agriculture received $150 million for emergency food assistance; the State Department Contributions to International Peacekeeping Activities expenditure of $96.5 million was paid back; the U.S. Coast Guard got a $45 million cut; and the Department of Homeland Security charged back $15 million for immigration fees. The majority of relief aid, therefore, was actually kicked back to U.S. coffers.

Forty-two percent of the money was paid to well-connected private and public NGOs such as the American Red Cross, the U.N. Food Program, and Save the Children, to name a few. The American Red Cross, for example, notorious for playing games with donations, claimed that as of January, 2012, it spent or contractually obligated $330 million of the $486 million it received in donations for Haiti. Although the specifics as to how it spent the money are sketchy, much of it was used to purchase food exclusively from U.S. companies, including highly subsidized rice.

The American business community also lost no time in capitalizing on the disaster. Within a month after the quake, U.S. Ambassador Kenneth Merten heralded in a cable that: "THE GOLD RUSH IS ON." [19] Two weeks after the quake, retired General Wesley Clark met with the former president of Haiti to hawk foam core houses built by a Miami-based company. A high ranking USAID relief coordinator, Louis Lucke, quit his job and joined a Florida corporation at a salary of $30,000 per month. He said at the time that "it became clear to us that if it was handled correctly the earthquake represented as much an opportunity as it did a calamity." [20] He was ultimately instrumental in securing more than $20 million in contracts for his employer.

The prerequisite for securing a Haitian relief contract depended more on political connections than experience. For instance, Dalberg Global Development Advisors, a New York-based consulting firm whose team "never lived overseas, [had no French speakers], didn't have any disaster experience or background in urban planning...never carried out any program activities on the ground," was awarded a $1.5 million contract to assess land areas the U.S. was considering for the creation of new communities outside of Port-au-Prince. After reviewing its work, the USAID determined "One of the sites they said was habitable was actually a small mountain...It had an open-mined pit on one side of it, a severe 100 foot vertical cliff, and ravines…it became clear that these people may not even have gotten out of their SUVs." [21]

Like a ravenous pack of jackals, other private groups fought for a share of the disaster bounty, irrespective of whether it was deserved or had the capabilities to perform the assignment. The Orlando Sandford Airport is a prime example of the level of greed. It demanded and received $583,000 for accepting 9,500 evacuees, which did not include additional "reimbursements of $32,000 for new carpets, $160,000 in landing and ramp fees, more than $23,000 for the CEO's time on the scene, and $223,000 in other staff time." [22] In contrast, the Miami International Airport didn't request reimbursement even though it handled four times the traffic.

The Clinton Bush Haiti Fund claimed it collected $54 million in donations as of 2011. The legitimacy of how the money was spent is in question. Clinton gave actor Sean Penn's foundation $500,000 to build a bridge. [22] Its donation of $2 million for an *equity interest* in a luxury hotel raised eyebrows. "[T]he gargantuan Oasis Hotel, partially funded by Bill Clinton [is in] stark contrast between the gleaming orange towers and the grey desolation surrounding paints a clear picture of the current social stratification in Haiti. It also perfectly exemplifies the misappropriation of funds and the skewed prioritization in regards to development." [23] The fund was subsequently dissolved, but it has not been publically disclosed who now owns its equity share in the $29 million hotel.

Clinton's showcase reconstruction project in Haiti is the Caracol Industrial Park located in a rural area in Haiti that was undamaged by the earthquake. Taking $224 million of relief subsides, he promised to create jobs and housing. Other promoters tout that the park will make Haiti globally competitive, but disregarded labor issues and environmental concerns. Caracol's principal investor, Korean-based SAE-A, has a bad labor relations history in the sweat shops it operates around the world. One labor organization called SAE-A "one of the major labor violators."[24] An acrimonious dispute with its workers' labor union in Guatemala, for instance, threatened to shut down its factory. Allegations of unfair anti-union activities, including acts of violence and intimidation prompted the A.F.L.-C.I.O. to urge American and international investors to reconsider their commitments to the Caracol project. That did not slow-Clinton's push to get it operational. He was determined to exploit Haitian workers to enrich himself and investors with no regard for SAE-A's workplace history of socially unacceptable working conditions, long hours, and low wages not commensurate with the work performed.

Economic development in Haiti is, of course, desirable, but does not override the critical need for housing. Polls showed that the Haitian people have no trust in the government and aid groups' reconstruction efforts. Their fears are justified. Those in charge of rebuilding are corrupt, wasteful, and projects are more beneficial to foreigners instead of the Haitian people. A month before the fourth anniversary of the earthquake, roughly one out of every six people in Port-au-Prince still slept in a tent camp.[25] The country remains the poorest nation in the Western Hemisphere. Its place on the UN development index has fallen by 16 countries since the earthquake.

William E. Cloud

Despite Bill Clinton's call to "build Haiti back better," America's failure to follow though shows its lack of commitment to relieve the country's huddled masses.

Whenever Haiti is mentioned, the words *troubled* and *corrupt* are most often used to describe this seemingly forsaken nation. Haiti, throughout its history, has been constantly raped by the West, which the corporate media conveniently avoids reporting. The people continue to cry out for help, but there is no one to rescue them. The mis-rulers in position to help relieve their agony have abandoned them for counterfeit wealth. The one who fervently tried to serve the people was demonized, and then forcibly removed by the U.S. government.

Will there ever be hope for Haiti? If there is, it could never come from the unscrupulous, immoral, and deceitful West. When and wherever there are resources to be had, labor to exploit, and riches to be gained, we are all for it seems to be the foreign policy of the West towards developing, non-militarized nations. Haiti has been specifically targeted for retaliation because it was the only nation to challenge and beat the system of slavery and colonial rule. Always stolen from, but never altruistically given anything.

Damn, damn, damn…we weep for Haiti.

William E. Cloud

CHAPTER 13

Long Live the Spirit of Hugo Rafael Chávez Frias, aka Hugo Chávez

Venezuela is a free country, and we will not be blackmailed by anyone. We will not accept being told what to do over Iran; we will not accept being anyone's colony.

~ Hugo Chavez

Venezuelan President Hugo Chávez was on George W. Bush's hit-list well before he stole the election with the help of his father's U.S. Supreme. His administration demonized Chávez for privatizing Venezuela's oil industry and nationalizing other strategic resources, including electricity and telecommunications, eschewing U.S. corporate and political interests. Venezuela's National Assembly passed laws to compel foreign corporations to pay back taxes and royalties. Chávez spearheaded the creation of organizations that promoted Latin American integration and cooperation, and was at the vanguard and a driving force behind Latin American independence and sovereignty for the 21st century. The U.S. government was deeply vexed by Venezuela's dramatically diminished acquiescence to the U.S. agenda and its loss of influence in the region.

The international banking cartel also resented Chávez because Venezuela was one of only a handful of countries that refused to privatize its central bank or become a member of the BIS.

Predictably, media opinion mirrored the administration's foreign policy dictated by the power elite. The thrust of its propaganda campaign was to accuse Chávez of using despicable means to achieve his objectives. He was painted as a ruthless dictator with profoundly anti-democratic leanings who repeatedly stole elections with cleverly engineered gerrymandering schemes. They said he disqualified formidable opponents from running for office for bogus reasons. And when that didn't work, the spread rumors that Chávez used fear and intimidation to suppress the vote. The Bush administration also asserted that Chávez' mismanagement of the economy was bringing long-term negative consequences for the Venezuelan people despite clear evidence that the poor substantially benefitted from his social and development programs. Finally, they said that he was a socialist closely allied with Cuba and supported the Revolutionary Armed Forces of Columbia (FARC), a peasant-based guerrilla group that fought the Colombian government for a half-century.

For those of who believed the corporatocracy that Chávez was a bad man...a very bad man, were hoodwinked. It's all false propaganda. Elected in 1999, Chávez was the first president Venezuelan of African and Indigenous ancestry from a poor background. He proudly embraced his heritage and was not ashamed he was born into poverty. "Hate against me has a lot to do with racism," he once said. "Because of my mouth, because of my curly hair. And I'm so proud to have this mouth and this hair, because it's African."[1]

Venezuelan society is quite diverse. There are forty-four native communities, including Africans brought over as slaves, mainly Spanish European colonizers, and more recently Asians and Middle Easterners. Before Chávez, the power and wealth in Venezuela was in the hands of the minority white elite who made no attempt to conceal their racial hatred of Chávez, and throughout his presidency openly referred to him as a *monkey*. "Venezuela's simian prince and second coming of the 'Monkey of the Andes,' Hugo Chávez, has triumphantly returned to Venezuela to take his rightful place on the throne," wrote Alberto de la Cruz. "After receiving medical treatment in Castro's Cuba, the cancerous cancer of Latin America will return to the important work of destroying the economy and enslaving the Venezuelan people...Any monkey that does less, would be less than a monkey."[2]

Privately-owned Venezuelan television stations, dominated by the white elite or very light complexioned individuals, consigned blacks and dark skinned people to an inferior social class or criminals. The leading stations, Venevision, Globovision, RCTV, and Eleven played a major role in the attempted April, 2002 coup, backed the neo-liberal right-wing candidate Henriques Capriles Radonski's unsuccessful run against Chávez for president in 2012. It is noteworthy that Mr. Radonski is Jewish and promised to reestablish diplomatic relations with Israel and sever ties with Cuba and Iran. More important, the majority of Venezuelans objected to his connections with big business and his pledge to reverse Chávez's land reform program that redistributed Venezuelan land from wealthy foreign owners to poor Venezuelan farmers. "The expropriations were a big mistake, the whole policy has been a fiasco," he claimed. "Nothing works now. Venezuela has 30 million hectares of fertile land but we only use less than 10 percent of it and we now import 80 percent of our food, including rice from the so-called U.S. 'imperialists'."[3] Aside from being a lie, commonsense dictates Venezuelan farmers would not vote him into office because he wanted to take their land and give it back to the wealthy. Radonski lost by a landslide.

Although Venezuela has the fifth largest oil reserves in the world it was a U.S. oil colony. The profits derived from the sale of its most important export did not fairly transfer for the peoples' benefit. When oil was discovered in the early 1900's the country was raided by foreign oil companies that struck deals with corrupt politicians. For many decades afterwards, foreign investors immensely profited from the exploitation of its oil, leaving the country undeveloped and its people mired in grinding poverty. Conflicts between the Venezuelan workers and their foreign bosses fermented for decades over who should control the oil.

One famous Venezuelan novelist wrote about the antagonism in 1927. "The workers asked for a miserable salary increase and those blond, blue-eyed men who own millions of dollars, pounds and gulden in European and U.S. banks refused."[4] Fed up with the inequitable distribution of oil profits, in 1976 the discontented populous pressured the government to take more control over the oil industries. The government's halting steps toward modifying its relationship with the oil companies accelerated when Chávez was elected president in 1999.

Upon taking office, Chávez began to implement a leftist social movement he referred to as the Bolivian Revolution. Strikingly similar to Franklin Roosevelt's New Deal, Chávez instituted a progressive income tax, extensive public works and social security, and provided cheap electricity. This elevated him to hero status with most poor Venezuelans. His white elite critics who had been in power for four centuries rejected sharing the oil wealth with the indigenous people. Chávez ignored them and began executing an ambitious land reform program that by decree confiscated large estates and farms from wealthy landowners, broke them up into small parcels, and redistributed it to the rural poor. The minimum wage was increased, and a constitutional amendment was ratified to recognize housework as an economic activity for which the government paid wages to 200,000 indigent homemakers. As part of creating a new Venezuelan national healthcare system, Chávez invested nearly a half billion dollars to upgrade hospitals that among other things for the first time provided free medical care to children and made free education compulsory. Local production initiatives were put into place. State-run production companies in critical industries were created.

Peter Bohman of *Counterpunch* stated, "This is a key part of overcoming Venezuela's underdevelopment and achieving genuine sovereignty. The new economic model is oriented towards human need rather than private profits."[5] To better public policy, elected community planning councils were created to encourage greater participation by Venezuelans. According to the United Nations Human Development Report in 2009, life expectancy, access to education, and income dramatically rose after he took office.[6]

"Thanks to Mr. Chávez's social programs, poorer Venezuelans have certainly benefited from the country's oil wealth more than they did under what he has called the rotten elites that used to be in charge. The country now boasts the fairest income distribution in Latin America," wrote BBC News Business reporter Robert Plummer. "To the majority indigenous poor, Chávez was looked upon as neither a 'firebrand' nor an 'autocrat' but a humanitarian and a democrat who commands almost two thirds of the popular vote, accredited by victories in no less than nine elections."[7] Venezuelan society, like other Latin American countries, was deeply affected by Spanish colonialism. And while it "is an incredibly diverse society, three quarters of its population are mixed heritage, of African origin or Indigenous origin. However as its wealth and power have always been dominated by a small, white elite, the struggle for equality in Venezuela has had to place tackling racism and discrimination at its center."[8]

According to an internal report by the U.S. Department of Energy, Venezuela is estimated to have five times the oil reserves than Saudi Arabia. In 2000, Chávez began consolidating power over the state oil monopoly, Petróleos de Venezuela, S.A. (Citgo), and appointed a new board of directors; a move that was strenuously opposed by the country's white minority elite, American oil companies, and the U.S. government. In April, 2002, he replaced Petroleos' executives. In retaliation and in support of company dissidents, the trade unions backed by the Chamber of Commerce declared a strike. A mutinous military high command demanded Chávez resignation and staged a coup when he refused. He was taken into custody although and the nation was told he resigned.

The Bush administration denied any complicity in the coup. America and the Caribbean officials were told that Chávez's removal was not a rupture of democratic rule, as he had resigned and was "responsible for his fate." The administration said the U.S. would support the illegal government. The editorial boards of several major newspapers followed the government's lead and greeted Chávez' ouster with giddy enthusiasm. In an April 13, 2002 editorial the *New York Times* triumphantly declared Chávez's "resignation" meant that "Venezuelan democracy is no longer threatened by a would-be dictator."[9] Conspicuously avoiding the word "coup," the *Times* explained that Chávez "stepped down after the military intervened and handed power to a respected business leader."…"Three days later, Chávez had returned to power and the *Times* ran a second editorial (4/16/02) half-apologizing for having gotten carried away."[10]

As it turned out, based on confident assurances by the plotters that the coup would be successful, the U.S. funneled $2 million to opposition groups. Its denial of any involvement in the coup was a lie.

The coup participants and the U.S. terribly underestimated Chávez's popularity with the vast majority of Venezuelans. Fearful of the return of repression and misery, hundreds of thousands of people from the shantytown barrios and countryside streamed onto the streets of the capitol Caracas the morning after the coup and converged on the Palacio de Miraflores to demand his release and restoration to the presidency. When the police were unable to suppress the protests, key elements of the military and even parts of the anti-Chávez movement re-swore their allegiance to him. They seized the presidential palace without a shot being fired. Within 48 hours after the coup, the interim government collapsed, and the Chávez was restored to power. The conspirators escaped to Miami, Florida.

The Venezuela media suppressed its coverage of the overthrow and aftermath because they favored the failed coup. The opposition continued to agitate for his removal. Later that year, Chávez's adversaries orchestrated a second Petroleos strike that crippled the nation's oil industry for months. Chávez ended the strike by removing the company's officials and firing 18,000 workers. With the Venezuelan state oil company firmly in his control, he nationalized and seized the crude oil fields owned by American companies including Chevron, Exxon, Mobile, British Petroleum, and ConocoPhillips. He also negated contracts with European and British oil companies.

William E. Cloud

A regional oil company was created to supply 13 Caribbean countries with cheap fuel, primarily produced by Venezuela, was launched in 2002.

As a supplier of 15% of America's imported oil, the U.S. government was seriously concerned about the distinct possibility the Chávez's government might cut off shipments especially since it was involved in the coup. Meanwhile, Venezuela's mega-hoard of oil gave it increased clout in the Organization of the Petroleum Exporting Countries (OPEC) while decreasing the power of the royal Saudi Arabian family. Indeed, Chávez lobbied OPEC to officially recognize Venezuela as the cartel's reserve leader; a development that could potentially have negative consequences for the *openly-secret* 40-year relationship between the Caveats are always included, chiefly austerity programs which gives the organization leverage to dictate the nation's economic affairs or risk financial destruction. Every nation it has given monies found itself in a worst position and beholden to its detriment for decades thereafter. Craig Unger claimed in his book *House of Bush House of Saud: The Secret Relationship between the World's Two Most Powerful Dynasties* that as of 2004, the Saudis had invested $1.4 billion with friends and business organizations closely tied to the Bush family. "[T]today's terrorist movements and the modern wars that have sprung up," he asserts are the result of "a series of business deals between the ruling Saudis and the powerful Bush family.[11] It's important to understand that Saudis have historically sold the country's petroleum for petro-dollars and then recycled the enormous profits back to the United States to buy

U.S. Treasury bills and other U.S. assets. In exchange for their considerable investments in the U.S. economy, the Saudis received military protection.

Chávez's idea was to keep the petro-dollars Venezuela earned in Latin America instead of spending it in the United States, as did the Saudi's. He withdrew $20 billion from the U.S. Federal Reserve and advanced it to other Latin American nations. He subsequently transferred billions of dollars in cash reserves deposited in U.S. banks and the BIS to banks in Russia, China, and Brazil. In August, 2011, Chávez pulled out 160 tons of gold from U.S., European, and Canadian banks. "It's coming to the place it never should have left...The vaults of the central bank of Venezuela, not the bank of London or the bank of the United States. It's our gold," he said on national television.[12]

The IMF's despotic lending procedures is destructive to developing countries although it espouses that its foremost role is to fund economic development with loans meant to help with payment issues, steady financial markets, and promote sustainable growth for its member countries. Caveats are always included, chiefly austerity programs which gives the organization leverage to dictate the nation's economic affairs or risk financial destruction. Every nation it has given monies found itself in a worst position and beholden to its detriment for decades thereafter. Chávez knew the truth of the matter, however. and urged Latin American nations to withdraw from the U.S.-based IMF and create their own International Humanitarian Fund (IHF).

William E. Cloud

According to the IMF, the U.S. has less than 5% of the world's population, holds the highest percent of total voting shares. The next highest is Japan with 6.23% voting shares. Thirty-six percent of the world's population lives in China, yet it's voting shares are only 4% of total voting quota.[13]

Chávez counseled Latin American nations to create an International Humanitarian Fund (IHF) based on cooperation with fair trade and exchange. He envisioned the fund would directly aid the people instead of propping–up corrupt leaders who for personal gain are willing to give their country's natural resources to western imperialist nations.

In 2009, with a pledge of $4 billion, Venezuela was at the forefront of Latin American nations that established the Bank of the South, a competing *tropical* monetary fund and lending organization to finance southern hemisphere construction, infrastructure projects, and social programs. Under Chávez' leadership Venezuela was also instrumental in the formation of the Union of South American Nations (UNASUR), the Bolivarian Alliance for the Peoples of Our Americas (ALBA), the Community of Latin American and Caribbean States (CELAC), PetroCaribe, the Petrocaribe Energy Cooperation Agreement, and the region's first television network, TeleSUR.

The Bush administration reacted to Chávez' perceived insolence with open hostility. Top officials denounced him as a demagogue who used oil money to undermine democracy and destabilize the region. These allegations couldn't be further from the truth. Television charlatan evangelist and Bush alter ego, Pat Robertson,

William E. Cloud

suggested to his viewer that the U.S. should kill him for trying to undermine Western economic interests. "If he thinks we're trying to assassinate him. I think that we really ought to go ahead and do it. It's a whole lot cheaper than starting a war...and I don't think any oil shipments will stop."[14]

Chávez had no love for Bush either. He showed his disdain when he called Bush an illegitimate president, a drunkard, and a donkey. In a globally televised speech at the United Nations in 2006, he fearlessly called Bush Satan. "The devil was here yesterday. Yesterday, the devil came here, exactly here," as he made the sign of the cross to protect himself from a curse. "This stand still smells of sulfur still today..."[15] It's hard to imagine a worst insult to Bush's stature as the leader of the free world, but most leaders of the developing world probably concurred with Chávez.

In 2006, Chávez's compassion for the poor was demonstrated to Americans when he offered humanitarian aid to victims of hurricane Katrina. Despite the Bush administration's delayed and deplorable response to one of the worst natural disasters in American history, and the overwhelmingly Black disaster victims' desperate need for humanitarian relief, Bush turned down Chávez' offer based on nothing more than the U.S.'s strained relationship with Venezuela. A senior State Department official said that any unsolicited offer by Venezuela could be "counterproductive."[16] How? That was a disgraceful disregard for the welfare of the people suffering in New Orleans.

William E. Cloud

Hurricanes Katrina and later Rita caused heating oil prices in the U.S. to skyrocket. In response, a group of U.S. Senators asked subsidy receiving oil companies and oil producing nations to donate heating oil to Americans who could not afford the high costs. Not one American oil company stepped up. Venezuela's Citgo was the *only* oil company that offered to help, and true to form, instead of expressing gratitude, the Bush administration criticized the program as being politically motivated. The media likewise spun the benevolent humanitarian gesture as a public relations stunt to embarrass the U.S. The recipients of the Venezuelan oil, on the other hand, expressed gratitude for the assistance.

Venezuela's Low Home Income Assistance Program (LIHEAP) took on greater significance in 2012 at the time Obama was requesting Congress to slash $2.5 billion or more than 70% from the budget for energy assistance that would hit hardest women with families and the elderly, the most vulnerable in our society struggling to pay heating bills during the winter months. Fortunately, Congress only cut 25% of the budget. Attributable to sequestration cut of $155 billion in Fiscal Year 2013, over 300,000 families were dropped from the energy assistance program. Those who still receive assistance are getting even less support than in the past.

In spite of U.S. criticism, Venezuela continued its heating oil program that helped more than 1.7 million Americans stay warm during the coldest months of winter. By the close of 2013, it delivered 200 million gallons of heating oil worth more than $400 million. The program qualifies as, "One of the most important energy assistant

William E. Cloud

efforts in the United States...a humanitarian symbol of unity between the people of Venezuela and those in need in the United States."[17]

Staying on script, Obama still declined to recognize Venezuela's crucial contribution to America's needy during economic hard times. Instead, he lamely tried to deflect criticism by chastising Chávez for maintaining relationships with Cuba and Iran and imaginary human rights abuses. "It is up to the Venezuelan people to determine what they gain from a relationship with a country that violates universal human rights and is isolated from much of the rest of the world," he said.[18] Casting aspersions on Chávez with phony claims of human rights abuses are ludicrous coming from Obama who has intensified Bush's militaristic foreign policy whereas Cuba and Iran are not engaged in any wars.

In 2013, Chávez revealed that he had brain cancer. Maybe coincidently, several other the Latin American leaders were beset by cancer around the same time. As can be attested by Fidel Castro, it is not beneath the U.S. to assassinate foreign leaders it does not like. Accordingly, it is within the realm of possibility that Chávez and other Latin American leaders, all who blasted U.S. imperialism and wanted self-determination for their nations, may have been victims of an unseen force. Even Russian Communist Party head Gennady Zyuganov was suspicious, "I don't know but...it is very odd that we have seen [Paraguay's] Lugo affected by cancer, [Brazilian President] Dilma when she was a candidate, me, going into an election year, not long ago [Brazilian President] Lula and now [Argentine President] Cristina...It is very hard to explain, even with the law of probabilities, what has been happening to some leaders in Latin America. It's at the very least strange, very strange.".[19] Pat Robertson's suggestion that Chávez should be murdered may have been followed!

As Chávez's impending death drew near, the U.S. and Venezuela opposition propaganda campaigns went into overdrive to sway the vote against Chávez' heir apparent, Nicolas Maduro, in the election after Chávez was no longer around. They published story after story about how his purported dictatorial government had been bad for the country. Maduro won by a slim margin.

Chávez led the vanguard of the movement in Latin American to cast off United States' economic domination. He seized control of his nation's oil production and used the profits to raise the standard of living for the Venezuelan people and others. His death was a tremendous loss to Venezuela and the developing world.

William E. Cloud

CHAPTER 14

Mali: France's Recolonization of Africa

A little country [France], with a small amount of strength, we can move a planet because [of our]...relations with 15 or 20 African countries.

~ Jacques Godfrain, former French foreign minister

France invaded Mali in 1892, and colonized the once-glorious African country up until 1960 when it *approved* independence. It was not yet done with Mali or its other former African territories, however. It launched military operations in the poverty-stricken Central African Republic (CAR) in December, 2013. French President Francois Hollande justified the invasion of the CAR with the same feeble excuse he used to attack Mali less than a year earlier, to wit, "France is not here in the Central African Republic out of any self-interest...France has come to defend human dignity."[1] If true, this would be a departure from its history as a brutal colonialist power. Given its previous invasions of the Ivory Coast and Somalia, French neo-colonialism in Africa is now an official reality.

France launched a military invasion of Mali in January, 2013 code-named Operation Serval. Hollande explained that France was intervening on behalf of the Malian government in its conflict with Islamist rebels for strictly humanitarian reasons and to fight the war on terror. "France is a liberating force, living up to its ethics, its values," he said with a straight face. "It has no material interests in Mali. There are no economic or political calculations involved. It is acting uniquely in the service of peace."[2] The truth is to the contrary. France is not known for its humanitarianism, especially when it involves its former colonies. The French invasion of Mali was motivated by economic greed and political domination.

The fact that France called the incursion Operation Serval, it ironically named after an African cat of prey, who the Portuguese call a wolf-deer, suggests its true motives. The serval has the peculiar traits of urinating thirty times an hour to mark its territory and eating so quickly that it sometimes gags and regurgitates when food clogs its throat. Like the serval, France's invasion of Mali smacked of the excessive actions of a greedy predator which may have bit off more than it could chew.

France has been an oppressive force in Africa since the 1500's, and has always put its self-interests for the continent's vast natural resources before any humanitarian consideration. It has no reservation about resorting to violence to take what it wants. Since 9-11, France has used the illusory war on terrorism as cover for its imperialist ambitions to reassert its domination and control of Africa's strategic resources and markets. Hollande's denial that France was acting out of self-interest in Mali was therefore preposterous.

William E. Cloud

Mali is the third poorest country in the world. Farming and agricultural activity, never producing enough food for its people, has been severely disrupted by war. Widespread food insecurity reached endemic proportions in many parts of the country. More than a million, including an estimated 660,000 children faced the risk of severe malnutrition in 2014, especially in areas inhabited by displaced Malians. France's definition of humanitarian aid apparently does not encompass reliving famine or pervasive poverty.

The French ruling elite is keen on expanding their imperialist quest for Mali's natural resources. The Malian peoples' misery and suffering to them is unavoidable collateral damage. France, of course, is not alone. All the Western powers are intensifying their efforts to exploit the continent's vast reserves of oil, diamonds, and precious metals. Competition for control and access to these raw materials is fierce, not just among themselves, but also with China which has invested nearly $100 billion in African projects over the last decade. Brazil is enhancing its relationship with Africa, and Russia is intent on establishing full-scale cooperation with African countries. France's international prestige, already diminished by the deepening economic crisis in Europe, would erode even further without Africa's raw materials, strategic resources, and increasing markets. France's continued relevance as an international power depends on continued access to these resources.

Mali's survival is dependent on Western aid. Its government has been perpetually plagued by corruption, instability, violence, and war, with the involvement of French and Western citizens in many of

William E. Cloud

the criminal enterprises. For instance, Malian children are sold into slavery in France, and its women end up in Moroccan brothels and other places. The brigands held sway over the vast desert and the criminal element flourished until the pesky Muslim Tauregs, a nomadic pastoral people who inhabit northern Mali, decided to put a stop to it. To end the criminality and debauchery, the Tauregs started executing bandits who committed desert robberies, stopped drug smuggling and human trafficking. The Taureg's institution of Shari'ah law to protect its citizen's disrupted trade making it more difficult for French and Western corporations to plunder Mali's natural resources. To ensure a continued flow of raw material, France, as do other Western countries, installed and propped-up despotic bufferclass puppets willing to protect the interests of their European benefactors instead of the wellbeing of the people.

French propaganda, repeated by the corporate media echo-chamber, that the Tuareg was waging an unprovoked war against the Malian government was just as ridiculous as the assertion that its military assault was strictly motivated by humanitarian concerns. France's declaration that it simply wanted to restore the legitimate government and bring back peace and stability to the country is raw propaganda. In reality, it intervened in the conflict to create a controlled atmosphere of turmoil and instability to provide the justification that indefinite military occupation was necessary to maintain peace. In a question to Holland at the start of the war in January, 2013 as to when he expected troop withdrawal to begin, he responded that they would be withdrawn by the end of March, 2013.

William E. Cloud

In November, 2014, nearly two years later, French troops continued to occupy the country.[3] The military contingent had been drawn down from 4,000 to 1,600 soldiers, but complete withdrawn is unlikely given the French's inability to strengthen the Malian Army sufficient to protect its strategic interests.

The conflict originated with the ouster of Mali's president, Amadou Toure, in a March, 2012 coup. To prevent the Tuareg separatists and their so-called Islamist, al-Qaeda allied militants who control the north from moving south, France claimed that it was urgently necessary to intervene to restore to power the government it was confidence it could continue enjoying a good relationship with.

Again, the real reason behind France's brutal invasion of Mali, which has killed hundreds and displaced an estimated 800,000, was to gain and assure continued control of its vast uranium reserves as well as its substantial deposits of gold, diamonds, and oil. This is a new crusade of aggression to economically re-enslave this resource rich, but otherwise impoverished nation.

France's civilian nuclear energy program has 59 reactors that produce more than 80 percent of its electricity. It is the world's largest net exporter of electricity, generating more than $2.25 billion in revenue annually. Its sole nuclear energy producer, Areva, is heavily involved in the development and export of nuclear-reactor technology. France is greatly dependent, therefore, on a secure source of uranium to fuel its reactors. Its energy security was threatened when Areva ran into difficulty in Niger after protests erupted over the discovery that local drinking water had been contaminated with high levels of radioactive waste. Consequently, Areva lost its nearly exclusive right to Niger's uranium. Malians later began their own protests over environmental degradation, but also complained that foreign investor beneficiaries were stealing the nation's resources. Virtually shut out of Niger, the loss of French access to Mali's estimated 5,200 tons of untapped uranium sources would have been catastrophic. Thus, France found it urgent to install a friendly government and repress the Malian population.

Leery of world condemnation if it seized control of Mali's uranium without some sort of plausible justification, France trotted out the always reliable war on terrorism bugaboo as another justification for declaring war on a group of desert nomads. It persuaded Mali President Toure to provoke the Tuareg into actions which could be portrayed by the West as former rebels turning to terrorism. Toure dutifully complied by arresting and imprisoning Rhissa ag Boula, the former leader of the rebel Front de Libération de l'Azawak et de l'Aïr (FLAA) and subsequently a government minister on trumped up suspicion of murder allegations. According to Dr. Jeremy Keenan, of SOAS, University of London, "He was released without charge after 13 months, but not until a number of Tuareg had been provoked into taking up arms. That enabled the government to send some 150 of its newly US-trained troops into the Tuareg stronghold of the Aïr Mountains."[4] France successfully manipulated the Tuareg into a war, thereby creating its flimsy justification for intervention.

William E. Cloud

France took its manufactured terrorist threat to democracy in Mali to the U.N. Security Council to seek authorization for military intervention. British Prime Minister David Cameron encouraged European support for France because control of Mali's natural resources was in Europe's interest as well. Then U.S. Secretary of State Hillary Clinton vigorously lobbied to secure authorization for France to intervene because, as asserted in the *Washington Post*, the separatists and foreign militants in Mali "are an enemy that appears determined to broaden the conflict into a wider struggle against the West."[5] The *Post* elaborated in a subsequent article that, "Western governments see the intervention as vital to rooting out an insurgency that could threaten African governments and Western interests from Mauritania to oil-producing Nigeria, and pose a terrorist threat to Europe."[6] This is patently untrue. No evidence remotely suggests the separatist struggle in Mali posed a terrorist threat to its African neighbors, France or the West. Again, there was no mention of Mali's resources or French neo-colonialism.

Although the Security Council was surely aware of France's ulterior motives, in December, 2012 it "authorized a military peacekeeping mission in Mali to help retake its vast northern region from Islamist rebels...The mission aims to help rebuild the capacity of Mali's security and defense forces and to help the Malian authorities recover the areas in the north."[7] To give the appearance of legitimacy, the council approved the use of African-led troops to support the mission. Not surprisingly, the U.S. and other Western

William E. Cloud

countries pledged to financially back the operation as well as provide airlift and intelligence logistical support.

France ignored the fact that the U.N. resolution authorizing intervention in Mali stressed the importance of negotiations before any intervention, and pursued the separatist without even a pretense of trying to negotiate a peaceful solution. The resolution also specified the intervention force would be African-led, and precluded Western forces from direct involvement in the conflict. France violated this prohibition when it attacked Mali without African Union forces. More than that, the African Union peacekeeping operation was replaced with a U.N.-led operation. This is yet another instance of the West impeding African nations' right to conduct peacekeeping operations with their own forces to solve their own problems. The reason for this is simple. The international community has no intention of leaving it to Africa to solve its own security issues because that would threaten its control of their resources.

Not coincidentally, France's order to launch air strikes coincided with Hollande's visit to Abu Dhabi, the oil-rich economic powerhouse of the United Arab Emirates. The assault was going to be spearheaded by France's premiere Rafale fighter jets it had been trying to land a multi-billion dollar contract to sell to Abu Dhabi since 2008. The Rafale fighters' good performance under combat conditions would give "a hefty diplomatic boost to the French effort to win the $10 billion contract."[8]

French and Malian government forces initially encountered unexpectedly fierce resistance from the rebels. Mali soldiers weren't

William E. Cloud

much help because they were divided, demoralized, and poorly equipped, whereas the separatist forces were better equipped than anticipated and highly motivated. It was only with superior firepower, France pushed them out of the major towns and into hiding in the desert and mountains terrains they are thoroughly familiar with.

It's important to dismiss as an out-and-out lie pumped by mainstream media that the U.S. has remained on the sidelines of the fray in Mali. The U.S. government is "preliminarily…planning a new drone base in Africa that would expand its surveillance of al Qaeda fighters and other militants in northern Mali, a development that would escalate American involvement in a fast-spreading conflict."[9]

France continues to claim, a year after the invasion, that it will withdraw its forces as soon as possible to allow the U.N. peacekeepers to hunt down the rebel remnants. Some observers believe that like the U.S.'s disastrous military ventures in Iraq and Afghanistan, France may be in for a long slog because its invasion plans were also not well thought out and it has no exit strategy. There are signs that the French invasion is already turning into a quagmire from which it might take longer for its military to extricate itself than anticipated. As long as the Tuaregs' genuine grievances against the Malian state, in terms of self-determination and economic justice, remains unresolved, the country will continue to be unstable and not conducive to France's imperialist's strategy.

Like the serval, France has marked the territory it's after, but greed may cause it to disgorge it.

William E. Cloud

CHAPTER 15

Obama's Warning Shot to the Government Dissenters

Those who have dared to speak out against the injustices in this country, both Black and white, have paid dearly for their courage, sometimes with their lives. "

~ Assata Shakur, *Assata: An Autobiography*

They don't just want my death, they want my silence.

~ Mumia Abu-Jamal

The FBI's announcement in May, 2013, that it added Assata Shakur, formerly known as Joanne Chesimard, to its 10 Most Wanted Terrorist list brought to mind the U.S. government's assassination and harassment of personal friends who were victims of the FBI's illegal COINTELPRO covert counterintelligence program. The program was designed to eradicate dissent to U.S. government's policies and thwart the rise of Black self-determination that many in white society deem undesirable.

One afternoon in 1967, my mother called me and in a calm voice told me that she was lying on the kitchen floor because a gun battle was raging in the front of the house between one of my high school buddies and Cleveland police. I was living in Queens, New York at the time. I heard muffled gunfire in the background. My friend, whose name I can't recall, was a small-framed, mild-mannered guy who was radicalized by the civil rights movement and joined a Black Nationalist organization. He was visiting my mother when unmarked police cars suddenly drove up in front of the house. Several plainclothes cops jumped out with guns drawn and ordered him to raise his hands. Before giving him an opportunity to comply, however, they opened fire. He returned fire. I later learned that he started carrying a gun because he believed his life was in danger after receiving threats in connection with his political activities.

After a short gun battle, he was shot multiple times and critically wounded. He was alive and writhing in pain when emergency medical technicians arrived, but police refused to permit them to treat him. Despite pleas from neighbors to take him to a hospital, the cops stood by and stepped over him for more than an hour while life drained from his body. The police let him die like a dog in the street. The authorities never offered an explanation as to what crime he was accused of committing that warranted deadly force. The local news media likewise did not deem the murder of a Black man, much less a Black nationalist, worth mentioning.

I met Rick E.R. Reed in New York City a few months later. We became instant friends even though we were politically polar opposites. Rick was radical, and I was comparatively politically naive. He encouraged me to get involved in the civil rights movement. To be candid, I was afraid to join him because he was a serious revolutionary. For example, he was involved with the radical Weathermen Underground and participated in their protests on the campus of Columbia University. He later participation in the protest of the construction of a proposed New York State office building on 125th street in Harlem. He lived in a tent on the construction site for several weeks until the police brutally evicted the protestors from the property.

In 1969, he joined a furtive Black revolutionary group. He declined to give any specifics about its activities, but later confided that he suspected the organization had been infiltrated by undercover FBI agents and police informants who were fermenting dissention within the group. He was convinced his telephone was tapped and under constant surveillance. As he left a meeting one evening, he was ambushed and shot by an unknown assailant. In fear for his life, he went underground. I learned two years later that he went to Cuba to volunteer to harvest sugar cane. He later went to China during the cold war when it was frowned upon by the U.S. government.

In July, 1972, Rick invited me to go Atlanta where he lived to check out the *New South*. Although my impression of the South was that it was Klu Klux Klan territory, I reluctantly agreed to go. I was unemployed at the time. I lost my job after I punched the supervisor in the mouth for disrespectfully speaking to me. In hindsight, getting fired was a blessing in disguise. Anyway, I loaded my wife and two young children into Rick's rented car the next morning and we headed south. Within two hours after we arrived in Atlanta, I decided

William E. Cloud

to relocate there. I enrolled in Morris Brown College, and a month and a half later moved into an apartment in the four-unit building where Rick lived.

Predictably, Rick was in another a secret organization. He wanted me to join the group without knowing its agenda. I declined. I was focused on graduating from college so that I could go to law school. During the year I lived there, I can honestly say that I never had an inkling of the organization's purpose. I can say without reservation, though, that they were definitely serious about their business. They met every day for hours on end. Members disappeared for days from time to time without explanation. Like the Underground Railroad, strangers arrived in the middle of the night for meetings and left the next night. There were more women than men in the organization. For security reasons, four of them asked my wife for permission to have a *principled* sexual relationship with me to avoid dealing with outsiders who might be government informants. My wife rejected their intriguing offer and threatened me with deadly consequences should I decide to do my part for the cause.

My apartment was burglarized. Within minutes after calling the police to report it, two police cars screeched to a stop in the building's parking lot with emergency lights flashing. The officers cautiously approached me. I asked them why they were treating a simple burglary as if an armed robbery was in progress. They told me that the building was considered to be occupied by dangerous individuals and standing orders required at least two patrol cars respond to any request for service, and to approach with caution. Strangely, they left without taking a report.

A few hours later, two detectives showed up to allegedly investigate the break-in. They initially seemed more interested in learning who lived in the building than investigating the burglary. They conducted a search of the property instead of a burglary investigation. They even asked for permission to search the other units. Needless to say, Rick was furious I called the police that brought unwanted attention to the building.

Prior to moving to Atlanta, I owed federal taxes. Shortly after moving there, I informed the Internal Revenue Service (IRS) of my new address. Within a month or so, the IRS notified me that an appointment was scheduled for me to meet with a Special Revenue Agent. I found it odd that I would be meeting with a special agent who performed criminal investigations instead of a revenue officer who dealt with debt collection. When we met, it was clear that he was more interested in the apartment building I lived in than the taxes I owed. He already knew who owned it, but wanted to know who lived there, how much rent tenants paid, and what was the purpose of the organization operating out of it. I played dumb. He told me that the IRS would forgive my debt if I agreed to cooperate in its investigation. I was shocked! This fool was asking me to be a confidential informant to help the IRS prosecute my friends in exchange for writing off a small tax debt. In my mind I was yelling, "Kiss my ass," but promised him I'd to think about it.

William E. Cloud

When I told Rick what happened, he reminded me about the burglary. He warned that the group was under heavy surveillance and had been infiltrated. I assume Rick informed his organization of the incident, and the embedded informant reported it back to his handlers. Rick's group suddenly disbanded under unexplained circumstances, and its members moved to different states around the country. I later received an IRS notice that my tax obligation had been forgiven. The IRS never contacted me again. The encounter with the IRS gave me more confidence that the government was somehow involved in the political assassination of my friend and the attempted assassination of Rick. It's crystal clear now, however, that both had been targeted by the FBI's illegal counterintelligence program.

The news media learned of the COINTEPRO program in 1971, but did not report on its existence for more than a year in compliance with the FBI's request to delay revealing its activities. The program was organized by then FBI Director J. Edgar Hoover to undermine the upward swing in radical politics in the 1960's. Its mission was to eliminate radical political opposition inside the U.S. by targeting individuals and groups the government considered subversive, particularly those in the Black liberation movement. FBI field operatives were instructed to create a negative public image for targetted individuals and groups; release negative personal information to the public; create internal havoc within organizations and dissension between groups; and restrict their ability to organize protests. The traditional methods of repression failed to sufficiently stem the growing tide of insurgency. Instead curtailing, the liberation

William E. Cloud

movements gained momentum. The Bureau then secretly resorted to using fraud, criminal prosecution on trumped-up charges, and murder to disrupt constitutionally protected political activity. Scores of Black liberation, civil rights, anti-Viet Nam, women liberation and many other progressive groups were targeted for their political activities. Like them, Shakur's sin was to get actively involved in the struggle for Black liberation. She wrote in her autobiography that:

"Nobody back then had ever heard of the counter-intelligence program (COINTELPRO) set up by the FBI. Nobody could possibly have known that the FBI had sent a phony letter to Eldridge Cleaver in Algiers, 'signed' by the Panther 21, criticizing Huey Newton's leadership. No one could have known that the FBI had sent a letter to Huey's brother saying the New York Panthers were plotting to kill him. No one could have known that the FBI's COINTELPRO was attempting to destroy the Black Panther Party in particular and the Black Liberation Movement in general, using divide-and-conquer tactics. The FBI's COINTEL program consisted of turning members of organizations against each other, pitting one Black organization against another. Huey ended up suspending Cet and Dhoruba from the Party, branded them as 'enemies of the people,' and caused them to go into hiding, in fear for their very lives. No one had the slightest idea that this whole scenario was carefully manipulated and orchestrated by the FBI."[1]

William E. Cloud

When the program was exposed, Hoover declared that it already had been shut down and that all future counter-intelligence operations would be handled on a case-by-case basis. No one in the government was ever held accountable for the crimes committed. Edward Snowden's recent revelations, though, demonstrate that rather than stop illegal governmental surveillance, particularly of dissident groups, it has been expanded to include every American.

Shakur was a member of the Black Panther Party before joining the Black Liberation Army (BLA), a revolutionary organization that's stated goal was to take up arms to fight for the liberation and self-determination of Black people in the United States. Her association with the BLA placed her squarely within Hoover's case-by-case criteria, and was made the poster child for the still operational COINTELPRO program. Just about every time someone was shot or a bank was robbed in New York between 1973 and 1977, the government tried to frame Shakur for committing the crime even with a solid alibi that she was in another state at the time.

The rightwing *Washington Times* reported, "From February 15, 1977 to March 25, 1977, Ms. Chesimard was tried and convicted of first-degree murder, second-degree murder, atrocious assault and battery, assault and battery against a police officer, assault with a dangerous weapon, assault with intent to kill, illegal possession of a weapon, and armed robbery. She was also tried between 1971 and 1973 for two separate instances of bank robbery, and one count of kidnapping, but was acquitted of those charges."[2] All lies! She was acquitted three times, a hung jury ended another trial, and the government was forced to dismiss the charges in the other three cases for lack of evidence. She was never accused of terrorism.

In 1973, Shakur was a rear seat passenger in a car that was stopped by State Troopers Werner Foerster and James Harper on the New Jersey Turnpike. A gun battle between the driver and the troopers resulted in the deaths of the driver, a passenger and Trooper Foerster. Trooper Harper was wounded and Shakur was shot multiple times. She was charged with killing and wounding the troopers.

Her defense that she didn't fire a weapon was supported by forensic evidence. No gunpowder residue was found on her fingers at the scene nor were her fingerprints found on any weapon. A bullet severed her median nerve which instantaneously paralyzed her right arm making it anatomically impossible for her to have shot a gun. Indeed, expert medical witnesses testified at her trial that the trajectory of the bullet proved her arm was in the air when she was shot. The judge improperly barred the introduction of additional expert testimony that would have further buttress her claim of innocence.

The 15 jurors selected for the trial were all white – five of whom had personal connections with state troopers. Not one was a peer of Assata Shakur. A New Jersey State Assembly member met with jurors in the hotel where they were sequestered and urged them to convict her. Juror composition, conflicts of interest, and misconduct virtually assured her conviction, even though the state's star witness Trooper Harper wrote three different versions of the events in his

William E. Cloud

reports. Indeed, under cross-examination he admitted committing perjury when he falsely testified before the grand jury about the discrepancies in the reports. Despite the fact that the prosecution presented no credible evidence that Shakur shot the trooper in the trial fraught with irregularities she was convicted and sentenced to life in prison.

The truth is Shakur was an innocent victim of a racist legal system. Had the judicial system been fair and just, the trial irregularities, intentional misrepresentations, and lack of forensic evidence would have resulted in the case being dismissed or an she acquittal. As fate would have it, in November, 1979 she escaped from prison and surfaced five years later in Cuba where she was granted political asylum.

The addition of Shakur's name to the FBI's 10 Most Wanted Terrorist list was announced 40-years to the day after her kangaroo court conviction. Nothing in her case changed since her conviction and she had not engaged in any terroristic activities while in Cuba. Despite this, she was the first woman to be placed on the most-wanted terrorist list with the reward for her capture doubled to $2 million.

Shakur, now a grandmother in her sixties, has lived in exile in Cuba for over 29 years and maintains a low profile. She does not pose a threat, much less an imminent threat to the U.S. What motivated the government's renewed interest in her capture and branding her a terrorist? Aaron Ford, a Black Special Agent in charge of the Newark, New Jersey, field office failed to specify what new developments in her case justified her reclassification as a terrorist

William E. Cloud

other than to say, "While living openly and freely in Cuba she [Joanne Chesimard] continues to maintain and promote her terrorist ideology. She provides anti-US Government speeches espousing the Black Liberation Army message of revolution and terrorism. No person, no matter what his or her politics or moral convictions are, is above the law."[3] If Shakur's message of revolution and terrorism posed a grave enough threat to warrant placing her on the premier terrorist list and doubling of the bounty on her head, Special Agent Ford should have been able cite specific examples of the terroristic rhetoric she is accused of espousing, instead of speaking in vague generalities of how her words constitute a clear and present danger to U.S. national security. None were given, and most likely none exists unless he considers her a terrorist because she said: "I have declared war on the rich who prosper on our poverty, the politicians who lie to us with smiling faces, and all the mindless, heartless, robots who protect them and their property."[4]

The Obama administration apparently does not recognize American citizens' right to freedom of speech. Even if Ford had concrete evidence that she spoke against the actions of the U.S. government, criticism of the government does not make someone a terrorist. Ford correctly stated that Shakur was convicted of murder but it didn't seem to matter to him that the charges were bogus, the criminal proceedings were stacked against her, and that illegal tampering with the jury occurred. The elephant in the room is the Obama Justice Department's failure to mention the substantial role its illegal COINTELPRO program played in her legal saga. Surely,

William E. Cloud

the administration knows she was a victim of the illegal program, but Obama, Holder, and Ford were obliged to account to their masters, saying, "Yalsa Boss, I is goin to lie on my Black sista just liken you don told me to."

In today's war on terrorism atmosphere, anyone, including American citizens, especially those living in a foreign country who proselytizes views contrary to American policies, risk being branded terrorists. Shakur foresaw that, "The first thing the enemy tries to do is isolate revolutionaries from the masses of people, making us horrible and hideous monsters so that our people will hate us."[5]

Attorney Lennox Hinds, one of Shakur's murder trial lawyers, said putting her on the terrorist list was purely political to "pressure on the Cuban government and to inflame public sentiment."[6] He is still convinced that "there is no evidence that she in fact either caused the death or was involved in the shooting of the state trooper...The allegation that Ms. Shakur is a terrorist is unfounded. The attempt at this point by the New Jersey State Police to characterize her as a terrorist is designed to inflame the public who may be unfamiliar with the facts."[7]

One must also consider whether the government sought to heighten the American public's antiterrorism sentiment in the wake of the Boston Marathon bombing just two weeks before. If so, Shakur is another government created boogeyman, like Osama bin Laden, to keep Americans in perpetual fear and a state of blind obedience to a police state government.

William E. Cloud

A commentary by Glen Ford on *Black Radio Agenda* summed it up nicely when he said, "President Obama and Attorney General Eric Holder, the two Black men who are most responsible for making Assata Shakur the face of domestic terror in the United States, are fully conversant in the language of symbolism. They are publicly defining the Black liberation movement – or what's left of it, or those who might attempt to revive it – as a priority domestic target for repression."[8] What's most ironic is, but for Black liberation luminaries likes of Shakur, Malcolm X, and others on the militant end of the civil rights movement, that the Black administration lackeys who made the decision to designate her a terrorist would not be in the positions of power they occupy.

The FBI appealed to Pope John Paul II to push for her extradition while visiting Cuba in 1988. Shakur wrote him an open letter. "As a result of being targeted by [the FBI program] COINTELPRO, I was faced with the threat of prison, underground, exile or death…I am not the first, nor the last, person to be victimized by the New Jersey system of 'justice'. The New Jersey State Police are infamous for their racism and brutality."[9]

There must be a clear definition of what makes someone a terrorist especially if that someone is an American citizen. With no well-defined designation, the authorities have too much latitude to entrap and inculpate anyone it legitimately or illegitimately deems an undesirable troublemaker regardless whether he or she has not broken the law. This precisely describes the *terrorist* trick bag the Obama administration put Shakur into, and is yet another bowshot over the

William E. Cloud

heads of any government dissenter who dare challenges the status quo. Their message is to toe the line or face dire consequences.

William E. Cloud

NOTES

CHAPTER 1 Mainstream Media Mind Control

1. Arthur Schlesinger, Jr., *Foreign Affairs*, July/August 1995. http://www.globalistagenda.org/quotes.htm. Accessed August 23, 2014.
2. Bagdikian, Ben, "The Media Monopoly," *Wikipedia,* 1983. http://en.wikipedia.org/wiki/Ben_Bagdikian. Accessed May 20, 2014. Accessed June 12, 2014.
3. Lutz, Ashley, "These 6 Corporations Control 90% of The Media In America," *Business News Insider*, June 14, 2012. http://www.businessinsider.com/these-6-corporations-control-90-of-the-media-in-america-2012-6. Accessed July 1, 2014.
4. "The Modern Suppression of African American Psyche," *The African Executive*, May 20, 2009. http://www.africanexecutive.com/modules/magazine/sections.php?magazine=229&sections=42. Accessed August 23, 2014.
5. "Propaganda (Book)," *Wikipedia*. http://en.wikipedia.org/wiki/Propaganda_(book). Accessed August 14, 2014.
6. "A Brief History of Propaganda," *Changing Minds*. http://*changingminds*.org/techniques/propaganda/propaganda_history.htm. Accessed August 1, 2014.
7. "Woodrow Wilson," *Uncyclopedia*. http://uncyclopedia.wikia.com/wiki/Woodrow_Wilson. Accessed August 9, 2014.
8. "Woodrow Wilson," *Wikiquote*, http://en.wikiquote.org/wiki/Woodrow_Wilson. Accessed August 14, 2014.
9. Tye, Larry, "Watch Out for the Top Banana," *Cabinet Magazine*, Issue 23 Fruits Fall 2006. http://cabinetmagazine.org/issues/23/tye.php. Accessed May 20, 2014.
10. Fischer, Brendan, "A Banana Republic Once Again?" *PR Watch*, December 27, 2010. http://www.prwatch.org/news/2010/12/9834/banana-republic-once-again. Accessed August 8, 2014.
11. Center for Media and Democracy, *Source Watch*. http://www.sourcewatch.org/index.php/Center_for_Media_and_Democracy. Accessed August 4, 2014.
12. "Fake TV News," *Source Watch*, 2006. http://www.sourcewatch.org/index.php/Fake_TV_news. Accessed August 3, 2014.
13. Miller, Laura, "U.S. House Says No Government-Funded Fake News," *PR Watch*, July 1, 2005. http://www.prwatch.org/spin/2005/07/3812/us-house-says-no-government-funded fake-news. Accessed August 31, 2014.
14. "Fraud, Sigmund", "Is Everything in the Mainstream Media Fake? – 6 Examples of Media Manipulation," *Waking Times*, February 27, 2014. http://www.wakingtimes.com/2014/02/27/everything-mainstream-media-fake-6-examples-media-manipulation/. Accessed August 3, 2014.

15. Id.
16. Id.
17. "Media distraction and bias," *Rootstrike*. http://rootstrike.com/2. Accessed August 3,
18. "Facebook mind control experiments linked to DoD research on civil unrest," *RT.com*, July 02, 2014 http://rt.com/usa/169848-pentagon-facebook-study-minerva/. Accessed August 12, 2014.
19. Id.
20. Id.
21. "About Us," *CBS*, June 24, 2014. http://www.cbsnews.com/60-minutes/about-us/. Accessed September 13, 2014.
22. Greenberg, Andy, "Watch Top U.S. Intelligence Officials Repeatedly Deny NSA Spying on Americans Over the Last Year," *Forbes*, June 6, 2013. http://www.forbes.com/sites/andygreenberg/2013/06/06/watch-top-u-s-intelligence-officials-repeatedly-deny-nsa-spying-on-americans-over-the-last-year-videos/ Accessed July, 18, 2014.
23. Id.
24. Queally, Jon, Latest NSA Revelations Debunk Obama's 'No Spying on Americans' claim," *Common Dreams*, August 9, 2013. http://www.commondreams.org/news/2013/08/09/latest-nsa-revelations-debunk-obamas-no-spying-americans-claim. Accessed August 9, 2014.
25. "NSA Speaks out on Snowden Spying," Bloomberg News, December 15, 2013. http://www.cbsnews.com/news/nsa-speaks-out-on-snowden-spying/. Accessed August 31, 2014.
26. Greenwald, Glenn, "The crux of the NSA story in one phrase: 'collect it all." *The Guardian*, July 15, 2013. http://www.theguardian.com/commentisfree/2013/jul/15/crux-nsa-collect-it-all. Accessed August 9, 2014.
27. Zornick, George, "'60 Minutes' Gets Disability Insurance All Wrong," *The Nation*, October 7, 2013. http://www.thenation.com/blog/176532/60-minutes-gets-disability insurance-all-wrong. Accessed August 1, 2014.
28. Greszler, Rachel, "Social Security Disability Insurance Trust Fund Will Be Exhausted in Just Two Years: Beneficiaries Facing Nearly 20 Percent Cut in Benefits," The Heritage Foundation, August 1, 2014. http://www.heritage.org/research/reports/2014/08/social-security-disability-insurance-trust-fund-will-be-exhausted-in-just-two-years-beneficiaries-facing-nearly-20-percent-cut-in-benefits. Accessed August 12, 2014.
29. Id.
30. "Media Matters for America," *Wikipedia*. http://en.wikipedia.org/wiki/Media_Matters_for_America#Analysis_of_weekend_television_commentary. Accessed August 26, 2014.
31. Webb, Stew, "John McCain's Wife Hiding War Profits Untaxed in Off-shore Accounts," Veterans Today, August 15, 2013. http://www.stewwebb.com/2013/08/15/john-mccains-wife-hiding-war-profits-untaxed-off-shore-accounts/. Accessed September 13, 2014.

32. "Nancy Grace Bids Farewell to Johnnie Cochran," *Knight-Ridder Newspapers*, April 23, 1997.
http://news.google.com/newspapers?nid=1914&dat=19970423&id=J9kgAAA
AIBAJ&sjid=HWsFAAAAIBAJ&pg=5298,3700773.   Accessed August 4,
2014].

33. Barrett, Kevin, "Mainstream Journalist Expose 9/11 Hoax, *PressTV*. October 19, 2013.
http://www.presstv.com/detail/2013/10/19/330112/mainstream-journalists-expose-911-hoax/. Accessed August 26, 2014.

34. "Transcript of President Bush's Speech," *CNN.com*, September 20, 2001.
http://edition.cnn.com/2001/US/09/20/gen.bush.transcript/.
Accessed August 31, 2014.

35. "War on Terror's financial cost: Trillions," *OC Register*, September 12, 20111, updated August 21, 2013.
http://www.ocregister.com/taxdollars/strong-478268-war-http.html.   Accessed
September 13, 2014.

36. Theobald, Ben, "After 9/11: Sacrificing liberty for security," *Iowa State Daily*, September 11, 2011.
http://www.iowastatedaily.com/911/article_91e8f1f0-da31-11e0-9e25-
001cc4c002e0.html. Accessed August 26, 2014.

37. Majority Says the Federal Government Threatens Their Personal Rights," *Pew Research Center*, January 31, 2013.
http://www.people-press.org/2013/01/31/majority-says-the-federal-
government-threatens-their-personal-rights/. Accessed August 29, 2014.

38. Zahn, Drew, "Americans Fear Government More than Ever," *WND*, April 28, 2013.   http://www.wnd.com/2013/04/americans-fear-government-more-than-terror/. Accessed August 27, 2014.

39. "Cynthia McKinney exposes Zionist stranglehold on U.S.A.," *The Realist Report*, May 23, 2011.
http://www.therealistreport.com/2011/05/cynthia-mckinney-exposes-
zionist.html. Accessed September 13, 2014.

40. Hajjar, Lisa, "Is Gaza Still Occupied and Why does it Matter," *Jadaliyya*, July 14, 2014.
http://www.jadaliyya.com/pages/index/8807/is-gaza-still-occupied-and-why-
does-it-matter. Accessed August 31, 2014.

41. Darcy, Shane and Reynolds, John, "'Otherwise Occupied': The Status of the Gaza Strip from the Perspective of International Humanitarian Law," *Journal of Conflict   and   Security   Law*,   August   13,   2011.
http://jcsl.oxfordjournals.org/content/early/2010/08/11/jcsl.krq011.   Accessed
August 28, 2014.

42. "Collateral Damage," Wikipedia.
http://en.wikipedia.org/wiki/Collateral_damage. Accessed September 13, 2014.

43. Geneva Convention, (II) "War Crimes: Violations of the law or Customs of War (Article 3), *Human Rights Watch*.
http://www.hrw.org/reports/2004/ij/icty/3.htm. Accessed August 29, 2014.

44. Wempel, Erik, "Rula Jebreal deplores *MSNBC's* Palestinian Journalist' label," *Washington Post*, July 24, 2014.

http://www.washingtonpost.com/blogs/erik-wemple/wp/2014/07/24/rula-jebreal-deplores-msnbcs-palestinian-journalist-label/. Accessed August 3, 2014.

45. Goodman, Amy, "MSNBC's Sole Palestinian Voice Rula Jebreal Takes on Pro-Israeli Gov't Bias at Network & in US Media," *Democracy Now*, July 23, 2014. http://www.democracynow.org/2014/7/23/msnbcs_sole_palestinian_voice_rula_jebreal. Accessed August 3, 2014.

46. Alexis, Jonas, "The U.S. Trained Terrorist Group ISIS in 2012," *Veterans Today*, June 20, 2014. http://www.veteranstoday.com/2014/06/20/the-u-s-trained-terrorist-group-isis-in-2012/comment-page-1/. Accessed August 9, 2014.

47. Fisher, Max, "The US bombing its own guns perfectly sums up America's total failure in Iraq," *Vox*, August 8, 2014. http://www.vox.com/2014/8/8/5982501/the-us-is-now-bombing-its-own-military-equipment-in-iraq. Accessed August 12, 2014.

48. "Hagel: ISIS 'beyond anything that we've seen,' US must 'get ready'," *Foxnews.com*, August 22, 2014. http://www.foxnews.com/politics/2014/08/22/isis-beyond-anything-that-weve-ever-seen-hagel-says/. Accessed August 30, 2014.

49. Id.

50. Ford, Glen, "The Superpower and the Caliphate," *Black Agenda Report*, July 2, 2014. http://blackagendareport.com/content/superpower-and-caliphate. Accessed August 30, 2014.

51. Ford, Glen, "Obama Schemes to Attack Syria, Under the Guise of Fighting ISIS," *Black Agenda Report*, August 27, 2014. http://www.blackagendareport.com/node/14383. Accessed August 20, 2014.

52. Swhartz, Peter, "The geopolitical dimensions of the coup in Ukraine," *International Committee of the Fourth International (ICFI)*, February 27, 2014. http://www.wsws.org/en/articles/2014/02/27/geop-f27.html. Accessed July 20, 2014.

53. "Assistant Secretary of State Victoria Nuland Travel to Germany, Greece, Cyprus, Czech Republic, and Ukraine, January 31 - February 6," *U.S Dept. of State*, January 30, 2014. http://www.state.gov/r/pa/prs/ps/2014/01/221059.htm. Accessed September 14, 2014.

54. Jackson, David, "U.S. pledges $1 billion aid to Ukraine, condemns Russia," *USA TODAY*, March 4, 2014. http://www.usatoday.com/story/news/politics/2014/03/04/obama-russia-ukraine-1-billion-putin-crimea/6006759/. Accessed July, 30, 2014.

CHAPTER 2 Military Propaganda Tells Americans That War is Good

1. *HLN News*. http://www.hlntv.com/. Accessed August 11, 2014.

2. Jeep's Operation Safe Return Hero at Home Program. http://www.jeep.com/en/operation_safe_return/. Accessed August 11, 2013.

3. Operation Gratitude. https://www.operationgratitude.com/. Accessed August 11, 2013.

4. Chomsky, Noam," On Propaganda Noam Chomsky interviewed by unidentified interviewer,"

WBAI, January, 1992. http://www.chomsky.info/interviews/199201--.htm. Accessed August 11, 2013.

5. Dumitru, Liliana,"Pentagon to Spend More on PR," *EverythingPR*, February 6, 2009. http://everything-pr.com/pentagon-to-spend-more-on-pr/2629/. Accessed August 13, 2013.

6. "Pentagon Spending Billions on PR to Sway World Opinion," *Fox News*, February 5, 2009. http://www.foxnews.com/politics/2009/02/05/pentagon-spending-billions-pr-sway-world-opinion/. Accessed August 12, 2013.

7. Id.

8. Id.

9. Hudson, John. "U.S. Repeals Propaganda Ban, Spreads Government-Made News to Americans," *The Cable-Foreign Policy*, July 14, 2013. http://thecable.foreignpolicy.com/posts/2013/07/12/us_backs_off_propaganda_ban_spreads_government_made_news_to_americans. August 12, 2013.

10. "Pentagon Spending Billions on PR to Sway World Opinion," *Fox News*, February 5, 2009. http://www.foxnews.com/politics/2009/02/05/pentagon-spending-billions-pr-sway-world-opinion/. Accessed August 11, 2013.

11. Baker, Ralph O. (Brigadier General U.S. Army) Information Operations From Good to Great," *Military Review*, August 31, 2011. www.usacac.army.mil/CAC2/MilitaryReview/Archieves/English/MilitaryReview_20110831_art004.pdf. August 11, 2013.

12. Jessica Lynch, *Wikipedia*. http://en.wikipedia.org/wiki/Jessica_Lynch Accessed August 11, 2013

13. Kampfner, John, "The Truth About Jessica," *The Guardian*, May 15, 2003. http://www.theguardian.com/world/2003/may/15/iraq.usa2 Accessed August 11, 2013.

CHAPTER 3 The Defense Authorization Act of 2012 Is a Grave Threat to Freedom Speech

1. Seaman, David, "The New National Defense Authorization Act Is Ridiculously Scary," *Business Insider*, December 2, 2011. http://www.businessinsider.com/the-new-national-defense-authorization-act-is-ridiculously-scary-2011-11. Accessed August 20, 2014.

2. National Defense Authorization Act for Fiscal Year 2012, *Wikipedia*. http://en.wikipedia.org/wiki/National_Defense_Authorization_Act_for_Fiscal_Year_2012. Accessed August 20, 2014.

3. Slavo, Mac, "Paul to Congress: 'Someone Who Has Guns, Ammunition, 7 Days of Food' Can Be Considered a Potential Terrorist," *SHFT Plan.com*. December 5, 2011. http://www.shtfplan.com/headline-news/paul-to-congress-someone-who-has-guns-ammunition-7-days-of-food-can-be-considered-a-potential-terrorist_12052011. Accessed August 20, 2014.

4. "CAIR Troubled By New Detention Law, Despite President's 'Reservations'," CAIR Iowa, December 31, 2014. http://www.cair-iowa.org/president-s-reservations-on-ndaa, Accessed August 21, 2014.

5. Bell, Zachary, "NDAA's indefinite detention without trial returns," Salon.com, December 19, 2012. http://www.salon.com/2012/12/19/ndaas_indefinite_detention_
6. Id.
7. "EXECUTIVE ORDER -- REVIEW AND DISPOSITION OF INDIVIDUALS DETAINED AT THE GUANTÁNAMO BAY NAVAL BASE AND CLOSURE OF DETENTION FACILITIES," The White House, January 2, 2009. http://www.whitehouse.gov/the-press-office/closure-guantanamo-detention-facilities. Accessed August 21, 2014.
8. Cloud, William, "You May be Considered a Terrorist by Reading this Blog," Blacknewsexaminer.com, January 7, 2013. http://blacknewsexaminer.com/564/. Accessed August 21, 2014. .Congress quote about releasing prisoners
9. Goodman, Amy, "Journalist, Plaintiff Chris Hedges Hails 'Monumental' Ruling Blocking NDAA Indefinite Detention," Democracy Now, May 17, 2012. http://www.democracynow.org/2012/5/17/journalist_plaintiff_chris_hedges_ha ils_monumental. Accessed August 21, 2014.
10. Hedges, Chris, "The Last Chance to Stop the NDAA," *Truthdog*, September 2, 2013. http://www.truthdig.com/report/item/the_last_chance_to_sp_thendaa_2013090 2. Accessed August 21, 2014.
11. Ackerman, Spencer. "How to beat terrorism: refuse to be terrorized," *Wired.Co.UK*, September 12, 2011. http://www.wired.com/2011/09/end-911-era/ Accessed August 21, 2014.
12. Ford, Glen, "Why Barack Obama is the More Effective Evil," *Black Agenda Report*, March 21, 2012. https://www.google.com/#q=Why+Barack+Obama+is+the+More+Effective+E vil. Accessed August 21, 2014.

CHAPTER 4 Bank of International Settlements is at the Apex of the International Banking Cartel

1. Garner, William Dean, "Bank For International Settlements (BIS): How The Rothschilds Control And Dictate To The World," *Bushstole*. http://www.bushstole04.com/monetarysystem/bis.htm. Accessed June 8, 203,
2. Snyder,Michael, "Controls The Money? An Unelected, Unaccountable Central Bank Of The World Secretly Does," *Economic Collapse*, February 5, 2013. http://theeconomiccollapseblog.com/archives/who-controls-the-money-an-unelected-unaccountable-central-bank-of-the-world-secretly-does. Accessed June 8, 2013.
3. Brown, Ellen, "The Tower of Basel: Secretive Plans for the Issuing of a Global Currency," *Global Research*, April 17, 2003. http://www.globalresearch.ca/the-tower-of-basel-secretive-plans-for-the-issuing-of-a-global-currency/13239 April 17, 2003. Accessed June 8, 2013.

CHAPTER 5 Federal Reserve – Gonifs *(Yiddish for crooks or thieves)* *Extraordinaire*

1. Ford, Henry. Brainy Quotes.
   http://www.brainyquote.com/quotes/quotes/h/henryford136294.html. Accessed August 21, 2014.
2. "Private Banks (Jefferson Quotes), Thomas Jefferson Monticello."
   http://www.monticello.org/site/jefferson/private-banks-quotation.   Accessed August 21, 2014.
3. "Corrupt Central Banks Bleeding World Dry," *United Nations of Film*, May 14, 2010
   http://unitednationsoffilm.com/?p=1166. Accessed February 26, 2013.
4. Liberty Tree. http://quotes.liberty-tree.ca/quotes_by/barry+goldwater. Accessed February 24, 2013.
5. Kurtz, Annalyn, "This could be the largest Fed stimulus yet," *CNN Money*, October 28, 2013.
   http://money.cnn.com/2013/10/28/news/economy/federal-reserve-qe-stimulus/.
   Accessed March 1, 2014.
6. Irvy, Bob, Keoun, Bradley and Kuntz, Phil, "Secret Fed Loans Gave Banks $13 Billion Undisclosed to Congress," *Bloomberg*, Nov 27, 2011.
   http://www.bloomberg.com/news/2011-11-28/secret-fed-loans-undisclosed-to-congress-gave-banks-13-billion-in-income.html. Accessed March 1, 2013.
7. Grim, Ryan, "Fed Inspector General Knows Roughly Nothing About The Fed (VIDEO)," *Huffington Post*, June 6, 2009: Updated: 05/25/11. Accessed March 2, 2013.
   http://www.huffingtonpost.com/2009/05/06/fed-inspector-general-kno_n_197934.html.
8. Inspector General Act of 1978, (Current through Pub. L. 112-239, enacted January 2, 2013).
   http://www.ignet.gov/pande/leg/igact_1978_asof_0413.pdf. Accessed August 21, 2014.
9. Dr. Eowyn, "Federal Reserve's Secret Taxpayer-Funded $12 Trillion Bailout of Global Banks," *Fellowship of Minds*, December 15, 2010.
   http://fellowshipofminds.wordpress.com/2010/12/15/federal-reserves-secret-taxpayer-funded-12-8-trillion-bailout-of-global-banks/ Accessed February 23, 2013.
10. "U.S. Bailout funds saved European banks – without much transatlantic reciprocity," *European Institute*, August, 2010. http://www.europeaninstitute.org/August-2010/us-bailout-funds-saved-european-banks-without-much-transatlantic-reciprocity.html.   Accessed February 24, 2013.
11. Irvy, Bob, Keoun, Bradley and Kuntz, Phil, "Secret Fed Loans Gave Banks $13 Billion Undisclosed to Congress," *Bloomberg*, Nov 27, 2011. http://www.bloomberg.com/news/2011-11-28/secret-fed-loans-undisclosed-to-congress-gave-banks-13-billion-in-income.html. Accessed March 4, 2013.
12. Dodd Frank Act of 2010,
   https://www.sec.gov/about/laws/wallstreetreform-cpa.pdf.
   Accessed August 21, 2014.
13. H.R. 459 (112th): Federal Reserve Transparency Act of 2012. Introduced: January 26, 2011 (112th Congress, 2011-2013).

14. Hopkins, Cheyenne, "Congressman Stymied in Promise to Undo Dodd-Frank Rules," *Bloomberg*, May 22, 2014. http://www.bloomberg.com/news/2014-05-22/congressman-stymied-in-promise-to-undo-dodd-frank-rules.html. Accessed June 10, 2014.

15. "Democrats Oppose Fed Audit, Don't Want to Give the Impression That They Meddle in Financial Affairs," *Town Hall*, July 26, 2012. http://townhall.com/tipsheet/townhallcomstaff/2012/07/26/democrats_oppose_fed_audit_dont_want_to_give_the_impression_that_they_meddle_in_financial_affairs. Accessed August 21, 2014

16. "Lincoln's Private War: The Trail of Blood," Excerpt from Out of Print Article from *Koinoinia House*, 1995. http://www.servelec.net/lincoln.htm. Accessed October 20, 2013.

17. Cedric X, "President Kennedy, the Fed and Executive Order 11110," *Rense.com*, November 20, 2003. https://www.google.com/#q=President+Kennedy%2C+the+Fed+and+Executive+Order+11110. Accessed August 21, 2014.

18. "Executive order 11110 - President Kennedy - Conspiracy- Assassination?" *Yahoo Answers*. https://answers.yahoo.com/question/index?qid=20130129172029AAWgJGf. Accessed October 20, 2013.

19. Durden, Tyler, "Ukraine Capital Control Crunch: Largest Bank Limits Cash Withdrawals To $100 Daily," *Zero Hedge*, March 2, 2014. https://www.google.com/#q=Ukraine+Capital+Control+Crunch%3A+Largest+Bank+Limits+Cash+Withdrawals+To+%24100+Daily. Accessed June 2, 2014.

CHAPTER 6 Ariel Sharon: A Western Revered War Criminal

1. Ariel Sharon Died at 85: The World Reacts," *ABC News*, January 11, 2014. http://abcnews.go.com/blogs/headlines/2014/01/ariel-sharon-dead-at-85-the-world-reacts/. Accessed August 23, 2014. Accessed August 23, 2014.

2. Siemaszko, Corky, "Ariel Sharon dies at 85: Joe Biden attends memorial ceremony to honor former Israeli prime minister," *NY Daily News*, January 13, 2014. http://www.nydailynews.com/news/politics/joe-biden-attends-sharon-memorial-ceremony-article-1.1577696#ixzz3BFZtight. Accessed August 23, 2014.

3. Frankel, Glenn, "Ariel Sharon dies at 85: Former Israeli prime minister epitomized country's 'Warrior' past," *Washington Post*, January 11, 2014. http://www.washingtonpost.com/local/obituaries/ariel-sharon-dies-at-85-former-israeli-prime-minister-epitomized-countrys-warrior-past/2014/01/11/8da0ce6c-ffd3-11df-b0ed-379d1148ca53_story.html. Accessed August 23, 2014.

4. Sniegoski, Stephen, "The Alleged Transformation of Ariel Sharon: Mostly Myth, Little Reality," *Comcast.net*. Accessed August 23, 2014.

5. Cole, Juan, "The Jailer," *Salon*, January 12, 2005. http://www.salon.com/2006/01/12/sharon_25/. Accessed September 3, 2014.
6. Kharel, Gopi, "Ariel Sharon a Friend or Enemy of Peace? Latest Reactions to Controversial Former Israel PM's Death," *International Business Times*, January 12, 2014. http://www.ibtimes.co.in/ariel-sharon-a-friend-or-enemy-of-peace-latest-reactions-to-controversial-former-israel-pms-death-533936. Accessed August 23, 2014.
7. Goodman, Amy, Noam Chomsky on the Legacy of Ariel Sharon: Not Speaking Ill of the Dead "Imposes a Vow of Silence" *Democracy Now*, January 13, 2014. http://www.democracynow.org/2014/1/13/noam_chomsky_on_the_legacy_of. Accessed August 23, 2014.
8. "Ariel Sharon eulogized as Israel's 'military legend,' 'warrior'." *FoxNews.com, January 13, 2014.*

CHAPTER 7 Susan Rice's Sordid Foreign Policy Record

1. Cloud, William, "U.N. Susan Rice – Warmonger Extraordinaire," *Black News Examiner*, Apr 12, 2013. http://blacknewsexaminer.com/category/susan-rice-nomination-secretary-of-state/. Accessed August 21, 2014.
2. Ford, Glen, "The Shameless Vacuity of Susan Rice's Black Boosters," *Blackagendareport*, January 5, 2012. http://www.blackagendareport.com/content/shameless-vacuity-susan-rices-black-boosters. Accessed August 21, 2014.
3. United Nations Convention on the Prevention and Punishment of the Crime of Genocide; http://www.hrweb.org/legal/genocide.html.
4. Groll, Elias, "5 Highlights from Susan Rice's Diplomatic Career," *Blog Foreign Policy.com*, June 5, 2013. http://blog.foreignpolicy.com/posts/2013/06/05/5_highlights_from_susan_rice_s_diplomatic_career_national_security_advisor. Accessed April 7, 2014.
5. Hatzfeld, Jean, *Machete Season: The Killers in Rwanda Speak* and *Laid Bare: The Survivors in Rwanda Speak*, reviewed by Lee Ann Fujii, *African Studies Review*, Volume 50, Number 1, April,2005. http://www.amazon.com/Life-Laid-Bare-Survivors-Rwanda/dp/1590512731; http://www.rwandanstories.org/genocide/marshes.html6.
6. "Genocide and Recovery in Rwanda." *Rwandan Stories*. Accessed April 3, 2013. http://www.rwandanstories.org/index.html.
7. Id.
8. "SHATTERED LIVES: Sexual Violence during the Rwandan Genocide and its Aftermath," *Human Rights Watch*, September, 1996. Accessed April12, 2013. http://www.hrw.org/reports/1996/Rwanda.htm
9. United Nations Convention on the Prevention and Punishment of the Crime of Genocide. http://www.hrweb.org/legal/genocide.html.
10. Hirsh, Michael, "Susan Rice: Benghazi May Be Least of Her Problems," *National Journal*, November 16, 2012. April 12, 2013. http://www.nationaljournal.com/nationalsecurity/susan-rice-benghazi-may-be-least-of-her-problems-20121116. Accessed August 21, 2014.

11. Spector, James,"US: The boiling of Susan Rice," *Daily Maverick*, November 20, 2012. http://www.dailymaverick.co.za/article/2012-11-20-us-the-boiling-of-susan-rice/#.U6t_GvldVfA. Accessed April 13, 2013.

12. Stearns, Jason K., "Rwandan Ghosts Benghazi isn't the biggest blight on Susan Rice's record." *Foreign Policy*, November 29, 2012. Accessed April 14, 2013.

13. Biedemariam, Amanuel, "Stop Ambassador Susan Rice from Triggering Rwanda-Like Genocide in Africa," *Ertra*, October 18, 2011. http://www.tesfanews.net/archives/4513.

14. Damu, Jean, "Did Susan Rice Give Osama bin Laden a Get Out of Jail Free Pass?," *Black Agenda Report*, December 18, 2012. http://www.blackagendareport.com/content/did-susan-rice-give-osama-bin-laden-get-out-jail-free-pass. Accessed April 14, 2013.

15. Cooper, Helen, "U.N. Ambassador Questioned on U.S. Role in Congo Violence," *N.Y. Times*, December 9, 2012. http://www.nytimes.com/2012/12/10/world/un-envoy-rice-faulted-for-rwanda-tie-in-congo-conflict.html?pagewanted=all&_r=0. Accessed April 15, 2013.

16. Id.

17. Id.

18. Id.

19. Id.

20. Wallance, Gregory J., "The Real Reason Susan Rice Didn't Deserve to Be Secretary of State," *Forbes,* December 14, 2012. http://www.forbes.com/sites/forbesleadershipforum/2012/12/14/the-real-reason-susan-rice-didnt-deserve-to-be-secretary-of-state/. Accessed April13, 2013.

21. Id.

22. Id.

23. "The U.S./ NATO gold heist of Libya," *Charleston Voice*, October 20, 2011; http://chasvoice.blogspot.com/2012/11/the-us-nato-gold-heist-of-libya.html. Accessed August 21, 2014.

24. "US intel: No evidence of Viagra as weapon in Libya," *The Guardian*. http://www.nbcnews.com/id/42824884/ns/world_news-mideastn_africa#.U4In5PldVfA. Accessed April 13, 2013.

25. Garris, Eric, "Susan Rice's Viagra Hoax: The New Incubator Babies," *Antiwar.com*, April 30, 2011 http://antiwar.com/blog/2011/04/30/susan-rices-viagra-hoax-the-new-incubator-babies/. Accessed April 13, 2013.

26. MacAskill, Ewen, Authorize Libya air strikes, US urges UN, *The Guardian*, March 17, 2011. http://www.theguardian.com/world/2011/mar/17/libya-air-strikes-urged-us-un. Accessed April 13, 2013.

27. Holden, Michael, "NATO failed to probe Libya civilian deaths: Amnesty International," *al Arabia News*, 19 March 2012. http://english.alarabiya.net/articles/2012/03/19/201739.html. Accessed April 11, 2013.

28 "Casualties of the Libyan War," *Wikipedia*. http://en.wikipedia.org/wiki/Casualties_of_the_Libyan_Civil_War. Accessed June 9, 2013.

29. Black, Ian, Libyan revolution casualties lower than expected, says new government, *The Guardian*, January 8, 2013.
http://www.theguardian.com/world/2013/jan/08/libyan-revolution-casualties-lower-expected-government. Accessed September 9, 2013.

30. Holden, Michael, NATO failed to probe Libya civilian deaths: Amnesty International, *al Arabia News*, 19 March 2012;
http://english.alarabiya.net/articles/2012/03/19/201739.html. Accessed April 12, 2013.

31. Id.

32. Gosztola, Kevin, "Obama's National Security Advisor Delivers a Myth-Addled Speech on Waging War on Syria," *The Dissenter*, September 9, 2013.
http://dissenter.firedoglake.com/2013/09/09/susan-rice-delivers-myth-addled-speech-on-waging-war-on-syria/. Accessed August 21, 2014.

33. Karam, Zeina and Dozier, Kimberly, "Doubts linger over Syria gas attack responsibility," *Associated Press*, September 8, 2013.
http://bigstory.ap.org/article/lingering-doubts-over-syria-gas-attack-evidence. Accessed September 9, 2013.

34. Id.

35. Ford, Glen, "The Shameless Vacuity of Susan Rice's Black Boosters," *Black Agenda Report*, December 4, 2012. Accessed December 3, 2014.
http://www.blackagendareport.com/content/shameless-vacuity-susan-rices-black-boosters.

36. "Assassination of Junebal Habyarimana and Cyprien Ntaryamira," Wikipedia.
http://en.wikipedia.org/wiki/Assassination_of_Juv%C3%A9nal_Habyarimana_and_Cyprien_Ntaryamira.
Accessed December 3, 2014.

37. "Rwanda's Untold Story," *BBC2*, October 3, 2014.
http://www.bbc.co.uk/programmes/b04kk03t. Accessed December 3, 2014.

38. Garrison, Ann, "BBC Asks 'What Really Happened in Rwanda? History of the Genocide. Role of the US," Global Research, October 11, 2014.
http://www.anngarrison.com/audio/2014/10/11/530/bbc-asks-what-really-happened-in-rwanda. Accessed December 3, 2014.

39. Id.

40. "Rwandan Genocide Denial," Wikipedia."
http://military.wikia.com/wiki/Rwandan_Genocide. Accessed December 3, 2014.

CHAPTER 8 War Criminal Bush's Illegal Iraq War

1. Stump, Scott, "George W. Bush tells Jenna: I hope world leaders see 'spirit' of my portraits," *Today*, April 3, 2014.
http://www.today.com/news/george-w-bush-tells-jenna-i-hope-world-leaders-see-2D79476677. Accessed April 5, 2014.

2. Blumenthal, Sydney, "Bush knew Saddam had no weapons of mass destruction," Salon, September 6, 2007.
   http://www.salon.com/2007/09/06/bush_wmd/. Accessed April 3, 2014.
3. Pilger, John, "Breaking the Silence. In Two Special Events, John Pilger Examines 'Unofficial Truths' and the Last taboo of World War," April 5, 2002. http://johnpilger.com/articles/breaking-the-silence-in-two-special-events-john-pilger-examines-unofficial-truths-and-the-last-taboo-of-world-war. Accessed April 3. 2014.
4. Hedges, Chris, "The Press and the Myths of War," *The Nation*, April 3, 2003. http://www.thenation.com/article/press-and-myths-war.
   Accessed August 15, 2014.
5. Pincus,Walter, "Ex-CIA Official Faults Use of Data on Iraq", *Washington Post*, February 10, 2006.
6. Id.
7. Paine, Katie Delahaye, "The Measurement Standard," Katie Paine's Measurement blog. http://painepublishing.com/blog/. Accessed April 3, 2014.
8. Rosenberg, "Rumsfeld Memo to National Security Council: How to Win the Spin War," World Magazine, March 27, 2003.
   http://www.freerepublic.com/focus/f-news/877282/posts.
   Accessed April 3, 2014.
9. Tyler, Patrick, "After the War; Powell Says U.S. Will Stay in Iraq for some Months," *NY Times*, March 23, 1991.
   http://www.nytimes.com/1991/03/23/world/after-the-war-powell-says-us-will-stay-in-iraq-for-some-months.html, Accessed August 14, 2014.
10. Iraq Body Count https://www.iraqbodycount.org/. Accessed August 15, 2014.
11. Yigal Carmon, *Wikispooks*,
    https://wikispooks.com/wiki/Yigal_Carmon. Accessed August 14, 2014.
12. MEMRI.
    http://www.memri.org/middle-east-media-research-institute.html Accessed August 14, 2014.
13. Brian Whitaker, "Selective Memri," The Guardian, August 12, 2002.
    http://www.theguardian.com/world/2002/aug/12/worlddispatch.brianwhitaker.
    Accessed August 14, 2014.
14. Id.
15. Tutu, Desmond, "Why I had no Choice but to Spurn Tony Blair, *"The Guardian*, September 1, 2012. www.theguardian.com/commetsisfree. Accessed August 14, 2014.
16. Id.

CHAPTER 9 Israel: Palestinians are Never Going to Get a State

1. "Full Transcript: Prime Minister Netanyahu's Speech to AIPAC Policy Conference, 2014.
   http://www.algemeiner.com/2014/03/04/full-transcript-prime-minister-netanyahu%E2%80%99s-speech-at-2014-aipac-policy-conference/. Accessed August23, 2014.
2. Eldar, Akiva. "Perfect English or not, Netanyahu shares no common language with Obama. *Haaretz* Feb 10, 2009
   www.haraetz.com/opnions/ get link

3. Id.
4. Toameh, Khaled Abu, "Abbas reaffirms refusal to recognize Israel a Jewish state," Jewish Post, January 11, 2014. Accessed July 16, 2014. http://www.jpost.com/Diplomacy-and-Politics/Abbas-reaffirms-refusal-to-recognize-Israel-as-a-Jewish-state-337854
5. "Arab League refuses recognizing Israel as 'Jewish state'," *RT*, March 10, 2014. http://rt.com/news/arab-league-israel-state-834/. Accessed August 23, 2014.
6. "Netanyahu: We are committed to the 'unity of Jerusalem' with US support," *Middle East Monitor*, May 30, 2011. https://www.middleeastmonitor.com/news/middle-east/2410-netanyahu-we-are-committed-to-the-qunity-of-jerusalemq-with-us-support. Accessed August 23, 2014.
7. Ronen, Gil, "Secretary of State suggests to Abbas that 80, 000 Palestinian 'refugees' will 'return' to Israel in peace deal," *Israel National News*, January 8, 2014. http://www.israelnationalnews.com/News/News.aspx/176058#.U_jbo_nIZRY. Accessed August 23, 2014.
8. "Jon Kerry: Peace between Israel and Palestinians not 'Mission Impossible," *CBS News*, January 2, 2014. http://www.cbsnews.com/news/john-kerry-peace-between-israel-palestinians-not-mission-impossible/. Accessed August 23, 2014.
9. Marcus, Itamar and Zilberdik Nan Jacques, "Hamas leader Haniyeh: Goal is destruction of Israel" *Palestinian Media Watch* December 27, 2011 www.ptalwatch.org/main.aspx?fi=157&doc1_id=6024. Accessed August 23, 2014.
10. David Ben-Gurion, quote Ben-Gurion's Declaration on the exclusive and inalienable Jewish Right to the whole of the Land Of Israel at the Basle Session of the 20th Zionist Congress at Zurich (1937).
11. Id.
12. Nathanael, Brother, "Are Jews the Chosen People," Real Jew News, August 24, 2012. http://www.realjewnews.com/?p=748. Accessed September 17, 2014.
13. Lennard, Natasha, "Max Blumenthal: I knew Alterman would freak out", *Salon*, December 4, 2013; http://www.salon.com/2013/12/04/max_blumenthal_i_knew_alterman_would_freak_out/. Accessed August 23, 2014.
14. Id.
15. Khoury, Jack, "*Haaretz* paper Prawer Plan quote Shelving of Prawer Plan paves way for new government approach to Bedouin," *Haaretz*, December 14, 2013. http://www.haaretz.com/news/national/1.563497. Accessed August 23, 2014.
16. Silverstein, Richard, Ben Gurion Foresaw Palestinian Expulsion in 1937, Tikum Olam, December 28, 2013. http://www.richardsilverstein.com/2013/12/28/ben-gurion-foresaw-palestinian-expulsion-in-1937/. Accessed August 23, 2014.
17. Id.

18. Lendman, Stephen, "Israel's Genocidal Killing Machine," *Rense*, August 24, 2014. http://www.rense.com/general96/isgenokillmach.html. Accessed August 30, 2014.

19. Ben Gurion quote, Councillor Terry Kelly, Sept, 26, 2009, http://councillorterrykelly.blogspot.com/2009/09/westole-arabs-country-david-ben-gurion.html. Accessed August 23, 2014.

20. Ramachandran, Jaya, "Israel starving off Palestine's economy," *Arab News,* September 15, 2013. http://www.arabnews.com/news/464649. Accessed August 23, 2014.

21. Editor *Redress Information and Analysis* "Twenty years of Israeli-Palestinian talks – of shattered hopes, unfulfilled obligations, betrayed promises" September 13, 2013. http://www.redressonline.com/2013/09/twenty-years-of-israeli-palestinian-talks-of-shattered-hopes-unfulfilled-obligations-betrayed-promises/. Accessed August 23, 2014.

22. Sherman, Martin "The Politics of Water in the Middle East: An Israeli Perspective on the Hydro-Political Aspects of the Conflict", Saint Martins Press (New York: 1999) p. 130.

23. International Criminal Court (ICC) http://www.icccpi.int/en_menus/icc/about%20the%20court/Pages/about%20the%20court.aspx. Accessed August 23, 2014.

24. Lynch, Colum and Greenburg, Joel, "U.N. votes to recognize Palestine as 'non-member observer state'" *Washington Post* http://www.washingtonpost.com/world/national-security/united-nations-upgrades-palestines-status/2012/11/29/5ff5ff7e-3a72-11e2-8a97-363b0f9a0ab3_story.html November 29, 2012

25. "Clinton: U.N. Vote on Palestine Hurts Peace Hopes," *San Jose Mercury News*, November 29, 2012. http://www.mercurynews.com/ci_22095600/clinton-un-vote-palestine-hurts-peace-hopes. Accessed August 23, 2014.

26. Ezzat, Dina, "Two decades after the Oslo Accords, few prospects for peace" *Ahramonline,* September 12, 2013. http://english.ahram.org.eg/News/81464.aspx. Accessed August 23, 2014.

27. "UN's Ban Ki-moon warns Israel of 'fatal blow' to peace," *BBC.com*, December 2012. http://www.bbc.com/news/world-middle-east-20576201. Accessed August 23, 2014.

28. Rudoren, Jodi, U.S. and Israel Said to Be Near Agreement on Release of Spy, *NY Times*, April 1, 2014; http://www.nytimes.com/2014/04/02/world/middleeast/jonathan-pollard.html?hpw&rref=world&_r=. Accessed August 23, 2014.

29. "Golda Meir," *Wikipedia*, http://en.wikiquote.org/wiki/Golda_Meir. Accessed August 23, 2014.

30. Geneva Convention, Part III. Status and Treatment of Protected Persons, 3.1 Section I. Provisions common to the territories of the parties to the conflict and to occupied territories, 3.1.1 Collective punishments, 3.2 Section III. Occupied territories. Accessed August 23, 2014.

31. "Israel keeps Palestinians a centimeter above the line of starvation," *RT*, June 06, 2010. http://rt.com/news/israel-gaza-aid-conflict/. Accessed August 23, 2014.

32. Cole, Juan, Creepy Israeli planning for Palestinian food insecurity in Gaza revealed," *Informed Consent*, http://www.juancole.com/ 2012/10/creepy-israeli-planning-for-palestinian-food-insecurity-in-gaza-revealed.html.   Accessed August 23, 2014.

33. Id.

34. Abunimah, Ali, "Israeli lawmaker's call for genocide of Palestinians gets thousands of Facebook likes," July 7, 2014.
http://electronicintifada.net/blogs/ali-abunimah/israeli-lawmakers-call-genocide-palestinians-gets-thousands-facebook-likes.
Accessed August 23, 2014.

35. Balmer, Crispian, "EU warns Israel, Palestinians of the cost of peace failure," *Reuters.*   http://www.reuters.com/article/2014/01/22/us-israel-palestinians-eu-idUSBREA0L1PT20140122. Accessed August 23, 2014.

37. "Libya says Gaza 'worst' than Nazi Concentration Camps, *USA Today*, April 24, 2018.
http://usatoday30.usatoday.com/news/world/2008=01-24-1405682050_x.htm.
Accessed August 23, 2014.

38. Weingarten, Benjamin, "An in-depth interview with Jerusalem Post editor and former Netanyahu staffer Caroline Glick on her controversial one-state plan for peace in the Middle East," *The Blaze*, March. 11, 2014.
 http://www.theblaze.com/blog/2014/03/11/an-in-depth-interview-with-jerusalem-post-editor-and-former-netanyahu-staffer-caroline-glick-on-her-controversial-one-state-plan-for-peace-in-the-middle-east/. Accessed August 23, 2014.

39. "Vatican cardinal – Gaza Like a Nazi Death Camp, *Rense*, January 8, 2009. http://www.rense.com/general84/card.htm. Accessed August 23, 2014.

40. Buchannan, Pat, Gaza Concentration Camp – the most horribly abused and largest concentration camp in the world today," January 9, 2009. https://sites.google.com/site/palestiniangenocide/gaza-concentration. Accessed August 23, 2014.

41. Benhorin, Yitzhak, "Ron Paul in 2009: Gaza a concentration camp," *YNetNews.com*, January 9, 2012.
http://www.ynetnews.com/articles/0,7340,L-4172992,00.html.   Accessed August 23, 2014.

42. Zaeley, Kermit, "I Agree with Helen Thomas–"Jews Should Get the Hell Out of Palestine" Kermit Zaeley Blog.
http://www.patheos.com/blogs/kermitzarleyblog/2013/07/i-agree-with-helen-thomas-jews-should-get-the-hell-out-of-palestine/#ixzz3BEikiLUm.   Accessed August 23, 2014.

43. Id.

44. Siun, "Gaza Update: Cluster Bombs," *Firedoglake Blog*, January 4, 2009. http://firedoglake.com/2009/01/04/gaza-update-cluster-bombs/.   Accessed August 23, 2014.

45. Sharon, Gilad, "A decisive conclusion is necessary," *Jerusalem Post*, November 18, 2012.
http://www.jpost.com/Opinion/Op-Ed-Contributors/A-decisive-conclusion-is-necessary. Accessed August 23, 2014.
46. Caldwell, LEIGH ANN, "OBAMA: ISRAEL HAS RIGHT TO DEFEND ITSELF," *CBS NEWS. November 19, 2012.*
http://www.cbsnews.com/news/obama-israel-has-right-to-defend-itself/. Accessed August 23, 2014.
47. Henshaw, Mitchell, "Israel's Grand Design – Zionism Plans in 1967," *Rense*, March 5, 2003. http://www.rense.com/general35/si.htm. Accessed August 23, 2014.
48. Israel's Grand Design: Leaders Crave Area from Egypt to Iraq," *Media Monitors*, April 14, 2002.
http://www.mediamonitors.net/johnhenshaw1.html. Accessed August 23, 2014.
49. BDS in Egypt, August 28, 2012.
https://road2tahrir.wordpress.com/2012/08/. Accessed August 23, 2014.
50. Ezzat, Dina, "Two decades after the Oslo Accords, few prospects for peace," *Ahram.org*, September 12, 2013.
http://english.ahram.org.eg/NewsContentPrint/2/0/81464/World/0/Two-decades-after-the-Oslo-Accords,-few-prospects-.aspx.
Accessed August 23, 2014.

References

Booth, William and Eglash, Ruth, Palestinians, worried that peace talks will fail, plan for 'day after," *Washington Post*, March 30, 2014. http://www.washingtonpost.com/world/palestinians-plan-for-day-after-talks/2014/03/30/233c40ba-b830-11e3-80de-2ff8801f27af_story.html. Accessed August 23, 2014
Geneva Convention
http://www.icrc.org/ihl.nsf/385ec082b509e76c41256739003e636d/6756482d86146898c125641e004aa3c5. Accessed August 23, 2014.
Andrew Flibbert, "The Gaza War: Instrumental Civilian Suffering?," *Middle East Policy Council*," Journal Essay, Volume XVIII, Number 1 Spring 2011, http://mepc.org/journal/middle-east-policy-archives/gaza-war-instrumental-civilian-suffering?print. Accessed August 23, 2014.
Smile, Livni's, "The Boss Has Gone Mad," *Counterpunch*, January 19, 2009. http://www.counterpunch.org/2009/01/19/the-boss-has-gone-mad/.   Accessed February 7, 2013

CHAPTER 10 The United States of Israel's Constructive Chaos in the Middle East

1. 22 U.S. Code Section 8422- Authorization of Assistance
2. Sink, Justin, "Kerry: There is no justification for Thai military coup," The Hill, May 22, 2014.
http://thehill.com/policy/international/206979-kerry-no-justification-for-thai-military-coup. Accessed October 3, 2014.

3. Rudoren, Jodi, "Region Boiling, Israel Takes Up Castle Strategy," January 18, 2014.
   http://www.nytimes.com/2014/01/19/world/middleeast/region-boiling-israel-takes-up-castle-strategy.html. Accessed May 10, 2014.
4. Stein, Jeff, "Israeli Spymaster Efraim Halevy Sizes Up Middle East Threats," Newsweek, February 13, 2014.
   http://www.newsweek.com/2014/02/14/israeli-spymaster-efraim-halevy-sizes-middle-east-threats-245522.html. Accessed May 10, 2014.
5. "Interview | Noam Chomsky: While Syria descends into suicide, Israel and the US are enjoying the spectacle," *Ceasefire*, September 7, 2013.
   http://ceasefiremagazine.co.uk/noam-chomsky-syria-descends-suicide-israel-enjoying-spectacle/.Accessed May 10, 2014.

CHAPTER 11 Gadaffi's Sin: African Economic Independence

1. Laub, Karen, "Libya: Estimated 30,000 Died In War; 4,000 Still Missing", *Huffington Post*, September 8, 2011.
   http://www.huffingtonpost.com/2011/09/08/libya-war-died_n_953456.html. Accessed March 17, 2014.
2. Whitehouse.http://www.whitehouse.gov/photos-and-video/video/2011/10/20/president-obama-death-muammar-qaddafi#transcript. Accessed March 17, 2014
3. Watson, Steve, "Stratfor Emails: US Government Contractor was Involved in Gaddafi Killing," March 20, 2012.
   http://www.infowars.com/stratfor-emails-us-government-contractor-was-involved-in-gaddafi-killing-now-aiding-syrian-regime-change/. Accessed March 17, 2014.
4. "The facts About Libya," *Geocities*.
   http://www.geocities.com/Athens/8744/libfacts.htm.
   Accessed August 22, 2014.
5. Wile, Anthony, Gadaffi Planned Gold Dinar, Now Under Attack, *Silver Bear Share*.
   http://www.silverbearcafe.com/private/05.11/dinar.html.
   Accessed March 17, 2014.
6. Muhammad, Brian, "Gold, Oil, Africa and Why the West Wants Gadhafi Dead," *Final Call*, June 7, 2011.
   http://www.finalcall.com/artman/publish/World_News_3/article_7886.shtml.
   Accessed March 17, 2014
7. "Was Muammar Gaddafi Killed because of his plans to Introduce a Gold Dinar Currency Threatened the US Dollar," This is Fifty, October 22, 2011.
   http://www.thisis50.com/profiles/blogs/was-muammar-gaddafi-killed-because-his-plans-to-introduce-a-gold?xg_source=activity. Accessed March 17, 2014.
8. Goodman, Amy, "Confessions of an Economic Hit Man: How the U.S. Uses Globalization to Cheat Poor Countries Out of Trillions," *Democracy Now*, November 9, 2004.

http://www.democracynow.org/2004/11/9/confessions_of_an_economic_hit_m
an. Accessed March 18, 2014.

9. Daly, Corbett. "Clinton on Quaddafi: 'We came, we saw, he died.'" *CBS News,* October 20, 2011. www.cbsnews.com/news/Clinton-on-qaddafi-we-came-we-saw-he-died/. Accessed March 18, 2014.

10. McKinney, Cynthia, "The Illegal War on Libya, edited by Cynthia McKinney," *The Dignity Project,* 2012. http://www.claritypress.com/McKinney.html. Accessed March 18, 2014.

11. Dehghapisheh, Babak, "Libya's Hysteria Over African Mercenaries," *The Daily Beast,* March 11, 2011. http://www.thedailybeast.com/articles/2011/03/06/libyas-hysteria-over-african-mercenaries.html#url=/articles/2011/03/06/libyas-hysteria-over-african-mercenaries.html. Accessed March18,2014.

12. Wenzel, Robert, "Libyan Rebels Form central Bank, *Economic Policy Journal,* March 28, 2011. http://www.economicpolicyjournal.com/2011/03/libyan-rebels-form-central-bank.html.Accessed March 17, 2014.

13. Snyder, Michael, "Wow That Was Fast! Libyan Rebels Have Already Established a New Central Bank of Libya," *The Economic Collapse,* March 29, 2011. Accessed March 18, 2014.

14. Brown, Ellen," Libya all about oil, or central bankers?," *Asia Times,* April 14, 2011. http://www.atimes.com/atimes/Middle_East/MD14Ak02.html.   Accessed October 9, 2014.

15. Jones, Owen, "Libya is a disaster we helped create. The west must take responsibility," *The Guardian,* March 24, 2014. http://www.theguardian.com/commentisfree/2014/mar/24/libya-disaster-shames-western-interventionistshttp://www.theguardian.com/commentisfree/2014/mar/24/libya-disaster-shames-western-interventionists. Accessed June 4, 2014.

16. Laessing, Ulf, "U.S. forces hand over seized oil tanker to Libya," *Reuters,* March 22, 2014. http://www.reuters.com/article/2014/03/22/us-libya-oil-fighting-idUSBREA2L06020140322. Accessed March 17, 2014.

17. Hauslohner, Abigail, "Khalifa Hiftar, the ex-general leading a revolt in Libya, spent years in exile in Northern Virginia," *Washington Post,* May 20, 2014http://www.washingtonpost.com/world/africa/rival-militias-prepare-for-showdown-in-tripoli-after-takeover-of-parliament/2014/05/19/cb36acc2-df6f-11e3-810f-764fe508b82d_story.html. Accessed June 11, 2014.

18. Retsos, Nikos, "Khalifa Hiftar: The CIA's aspiring dictator for Libya," *My Telegraph,* May 20, 2014. http://my.telegraph.co.uk/retsos_nikos/nikos_retsos/16011797/khalifa-hiftar-the-cias-aspiring-dictator-for-libya/. Accessed October 10, 2014.

19. Nada, Aya, "U.S. Pulls Diplomates in Libya Following Fresh Clashes," *Daily News Egypt,* July 26, 2014. http://www.dailynewsegypt.com/2014/07/26/us-pulls-diplomats-libya-following-fresh-clashes/. Accessed September 8, 2014.

20. "Libyan Government institutions risk collapse," *Human Rights Watch*, March 7, 2014.
http://www.hrw.org/news/2014/03/07/libya-government-institutions-risk-collapse. Accessed October 5, 2014.

CHAPTER 12 The Never Ending Rape of Haiti

1. "Remarks by the President on Rescue Efforts in Haiti," *The White House*, January 13, 2010. http://www.whitehouse.gov/the-press-office/remarks-president-rescue-efforts-haiti. Accessed August 28, 2014.
2. Id.
3. "Haitian Revolution," *Wikipedia*.
http://en.wikipedia.org/wiki/Haitian_Revolution. Accessed August 28, 2014.
4. Kessler, Glenn, "Quake may provide chance for fresh start in U.S.-Haiti relations," *Washington Post*, January 15, 2010.
http://www.washingtonpost.com/wp-dyn/content/article/2010/01/14/AR2010011404747.html.
Accessed August 28, 2014.
5. Mont-Reynard, Marie, "The failure of American Occupation of Haiti," *Windows on Haiti*, March, 2002.
http://windowsonhaiti.com/windowsonhaiti/am-occup.htm. Accessed October 4, 2014.
6. Eid, Linda, 'Haiti: Beyond Relief," *The Vienna Review*, February 1, 2010.
http://www.viennareview.net/commentary/commentary-commentary/haiti-beyond-relief. Accessed August 28, 2014.
7. Robinson, Randall, "An Unbroken Agony: Haiti, from Revolution to the Kidnapping of a President".
http://www.randallrobinson.com/agony.html. Accessed August 28, 2014.
8. Lendman, Stephen, "Baby Doc Duvalier In Haiti," *Rense.com*, January 18, 2011.
http://rense.com/general92/baby.htm. Accessed August 28, 2014.
9. "Haiti Appeals Court Reinstates Crimes Against Humanity Charges Against Baby Doc Duvalier," *Center for Justice & Accountability*, February 21, 2014.
http://www.ijdh.org/2014/02/topics/law-justice/haiti-appeals-court-reinstates-crimes-against-humanity-charges-against-baby-doc-duvalier/#.U4Z6AfldVfA.
Accessed August 28, 2014.
10. Pierre, Jemina, The Puppet, the Dictator, and the President: Haiti Today and Tomorrow, *Black Agenda Report*, January 17, 2012.
http://blackagendareport.com/content/puppet-dictator-and-president-haiti-today-and-tomorrow. Accessed August 28, 2014.
11. "We Made a Devil's Bargain": Fmr. President Clinton Apologizes for Trade Policies that Destroyed Haitian Rice Farming," *Democracy Now*, April, 1, 2010.
http://www.democracynow.org/2010/4/1/clinton_rice.
Accessed August 28, 2014.
12. "Haiti: Forced evictions worsen the already dire lot of earthquake homeless," *Amnesty International*, 23 April 2013.
http://www.amnesty.org/en/news/haiti-forced-evictions-worsen-already-dire-lot-earthquake-homeless-2013-04-23. Accessed August 28, 2014.

13. Daniel, Trenton, "USAID focusing on housing finance in Haiti," *Associated Press*, December 9, 2013.
http://bigstory.ap.org/article/usaid-now-focusing-housing-finance-haiti. Accessed August 28, 2014.

14. Kelley, Michael, "The Air Force Announced It's Upgrading The One Plane It Needs To Bomb Iran," *Business Insider*, March 28, 2012. Accessed August 28, 2014.

15. Quigley, Bill, "Amber, Haiti: Where is the Money," *University of Arkansas at Little Rock*, February 26, 2012.
http://ualr.edu/socialchange/2012/02/26/haiti-where-is-the-money/. Accessed August 11, 2014.

16. Porter, Catherine, "Why Richard Morse left Haiti's government," *The Star*, April 5, 2013.
http://www.thestar.com/news/world/2013/04/15/i_left_because_of_corruption_in_the_palace_and_infrastructure_sabotage_why_richard_morse_left_haitis_government.html. Accessed September 30, 2013.

17. Id.

18. Mendoza, Martha, "And yet more debt as Martelly's government steals Haiti's future," *Associated Press*, July 22, 2012. http://www.haitian-truth.org/and-yet-more-debt-as-martelly-government-steals-haiti%E2%80%99s-future/. Accessed September 13, 2013.

19. Quigley, Bill and Ramanauskas, Amber, "Haiti: Where is the Money," *University of Arkansas at Little Rock*, February 26, 2012. http://ualr.edu/socialchange/2012/02/26/haiti-where-is-the-money/. Accessed October 5, 2013.

20. Id.

21. Id.

22. Id.

23. Serpef, Gina, "Bill Clinton Penns in $500,000 Donation for Haiti," *E online*, Oct. 8, 2010. http://www.eonline.com/news/204640/bill-clinton-penns-in-500-000-donation-for-haiti. Accessed October 5, 2013.

24. Id.

25. Haiti "Reconstruction": Luxury Hotels, Sweat Shops and Deregulation for the Foreign Corporate Elite *Global Research* August 16, 2013
www.glabarresearch.ca/haiti-reconstruction-luxury-hotels-sweat-shops-and-deregulation-for-the-foreign-coporate-elite/5344546. Accessed August 8, 2014.

26. "Haiti marks third anniversary of earthquake that may have taken more than 300,000 lives with simple ceremony," *Associated Press*, January 12, 2013. http://www.nydailynews.com/news/world/haiti-marks-anniversary-devastating-earthquake-article-1.1239021#ixzz2JBq77IbK. Accessed October 8, 2013.

CHAPTER 13 Long Live the Spirit of Hugo Rafael Chavez Frias a.k.a, Hugo Chavez

1. "Afro-Venezuelans and the Struggle Against Racism," *Embassy of the Bolivarian Republic of Venezuela to the United States*, April 29, 2011. http://venezuelanalysis.com/analysis/6159. Accessed March 24, 2014

2. de la Cruz, Alberto, Behold: "The monkey of the Andies Chavez reruens to Venezuela," *Babalublogn*, July 5, 2011
   http://babalublog.com/2011/07/05/behold-the-monkey-of-the-andes-chavez-returns-to-venezuela/. Accessed October 5, 2014.

3. Sherwell, Phillip,"Henrique Capriles Radonski: Israel's Man in Venezuela," *nsnbc*, January 26, 2013.
   https://nsnbc.wordpress.com/page/16/ Accessed March 24, 2014.

3. Sherwell, Phillip, "Venezuela's marathon man looks to run down Chavez," *The Telegraph*, 29 September 29, 2012.
   http://www.telegraph.co.uk/news/worldnews/9576153/Venezuelas-marathon-man-looks-to-run-down-Chavez.html. Accessed March 14, 2014.

4. "History of the Venezuelan oil industry," *Wikipedia*.
   http://en.wikipedia.org/wiki/History_of_the_Venezuelan_oil_industy

5. Bohmer, Peter, In Venezuela the Revolution Continues," CounterPunch.org, June 6, 2012.

6. Human Development Report 2009: Overcoming barriers: Human mobility and development.
   http://hdr.undp.org/sites/default/files/reports/269/hdr_2009_en_complete.pdf. March 14, 2014.

7. Chavez Lives BBC News Business reporter Robert Plummer http://blacknewsexaminer.com/chavez/. Accessed March 14, 2014.

8. Kiely, Aaron, "The fight against racism in Venezuela Left Futures," Left Futures, September 10, 2012.
   http://www.leftfutures.org/2012/10/the-fight-against-racism-in-venezuela/. Accessed March 11, 2014.

9. Vulliamy, Ed, "Venezuela coup linked to Bush team Specialists in the 'dirty wars' of the Eighties encouraged the plotters who tried to topple President Chavez," *The Guardian*, April 21, 2002.
   http://www.theguardian.com/worldhttp://fair.org/extra-online-articles/u-s-papers-hail-venezuelan-coup-as-pro-democracy-move//2002/apr/21/usa.venezuela. Accessed March 15, 2014.

10. Coen, Rachel, "U.S. Papers Hail Venezuelan Coup as Pro-Democracy Move," Fair, June 1, 2002. Accessed June 15, 2014.
    http://fair.org/extra-online-articles/u-s-papers-hail-venezuelan-coup-as-pro-democracy-move/

11. Unger, Craig "House of Bush House of Saud: The Secret Relationship Between the World's Two Most Powerful Dynasties." (2007), *Square Books*

12. Hall, Peter Christian, "What will become of Chávez's gold hoard?," *Reuters*, March 13, 2013.
    http://blogs.reuters.com/great-debate/2013/03/13/what-will-become-of-chavezs-gold-hoard/. Accessed November 1, 2013.

13. IMF Members' Quotas and Voting Power, and IMF Board of Governors last updated February 7, 2014.
    www.imf.org/external/np/sec/memdir/members.aspx.
    Accessed February 9, 2014.

14. "Pat Robertson calls for assassination of Hugo Chavez," *USA Today*, August 22, 2005.

www.usatoday30.usatoday.com/news/nation/2005-08-22-robertson-_x.htm. Accessed November 1, 2013.

15. Stout, David, "Chavez Calls Bush 'the Devil' in U.N. Speech," *New York Times*, September 20, 2006. www.nytimes.com/2006/09/20/world/americas/20cnd-chavez.html?_r=0. Accessed September 11, 2013.

16. How are America's medias presenting Hugo Chavez?," HockeyFutures.com, August 29, 2005.
http://hfboards.hockeysfuture.com/showthread.php?t=165345&page=3. Accessed September 11, 2013.

17. Citgo, "Eighth Annual Citgo-Venezuela Heating Oil Program Launched," *Venezuelanalysis.com*, February 4, 2013.
http://venezuelanalysis.com/news/7670. Accessed September 21, 2013.

18. "Obama offers Cuba 'new beginning,'" *BBC*, April 18, 2009. http://news.bbc.co.uk/2/hi/americas/8004798.stm'\. Accessed September 21, 2013.

19. Barrett, Dr. Kevin, "Hugo Chavez: Another CIA Assassination Victim?," *Final Call*, march 16, 2013.
www.finalcall.com/artman/publish/Perspectives_1/article_9861.shtmlAccessed September 13, 2013.

CHAPTER 14 Mali: France's Recolonization of Africa

1. Kumaran, Ira, "French war in Central African Republic intensifies humanitarian crisis," World Socialist Website, December 16, 2013.

2. Prince, Rob, "In Mali, Conflict Continues a Year After the French-led Invasion," Foreign Policy in Focus, December 17, 2013. http://fpif.org/mali-conflict-continues-year-french-led-invasion/

3. "France to leave Mali 'next month'," Express, February 6, 2013.
http://www.express.co.uk/news/world/375970/France-to-leave-Mali-next-month. Accessed August 22, 2014.

4. Elliott-Cooper, Adam, "Blood for Uranium: France's Mali intervention has little to do with terrorism," *Ceasefire*, January 17, 2013. http://ceasefiremagazine.co.uk/blood-uranium-frances-mali-intervention-terrorism/. Accessed August 22, 2014.

5. Raghavan, Sudarsan, In northern Mali's war, al-Qaeda affiliate is directing the fight." *Washington Post*, January 28, 2013.
http://www.washingtonpost.com/world/middle_east/in-northern-malis-war-al-qaeda-affiliate-is-directing-the-fight/2013/01/28/212a909c-68a4-11e2-9a0b-db931670f35d_story.html. Accessed August 22, 2014.

6. "Islamic extremist destroy bridge near Niger border in Mali" *JNews Portal*, January 25, 2013.
http://jnews.cs.um.edu.mt/news/Islamic_extremists_destroy_bridge_near_Niger_border_in_Mali.html. Accessed August 22, 2014.

7. Roth, Richard, "U.N. Security Council authorizes military mission in Mali," CNN World, December 21, 2012. http://www.cnn.com/2012/12/20/world/africa/u-n--mali/. Accessed August 22, 2014.
8. "France uses Mali war to boost Rafale jet," R DefPense, January 19, 2013. http://rpdefense.over-blog.com/article-france-uses-mali-war-to-boost-rafale-jet-114515334.html. Accessed August 22, 2014.
9. *Washington Post*, Jan. 30, 2012, p.A-7

CHAPTER 15 Obama's Warning Shot to the Black Liberation Movement

1. Martinez, Carlos, "Assata: A bibliography – Review and Quotes," BlackAgendaReport, September 10, 2014. http://www.blackagendareport.com/node/14406. Accessed September 20, 2014.
2. Crockett, Derek "Is designating Joanne Chesimard a terrorist a threat to us all?" *The Washington Times* May 3, 2013 http://www.communities.washingtontimes.com/neighborhood/political-potpurri/2013/may/3/designating-joanne-chesimard-terrorist-threat-us-a/
3. Jones, David, "New Jersey Trooper's Killer is first Woman on FBI's Ten Most Wanted Terrorist List http://www.reuters.com/article/2013/05/02/us-usa-crime-wanted-idUSBRE94114020130502
4. Shakur, Assata, "Assata Shakur – An Autobiography," *Goodreads*. https://www.goodreads.com/quotes/1117284-i-have-declared-war-on-the-rich-who-prosper-on. Accessed August 2, 2014.
5. Id.
6. Thompson, Krissah, "Assata Shakur was convicted of Murder, is she a terrorist," *Washington Post*, May 8, 2013. http://www.washingtonpost.com/lifestyle/style/assata-shakur-was-convicted-of-murder-is-she-a-terrorist/2013/05/08/69acb602-b7e5-11e2-aa9e-a02b765ff0ea_story.html. Accessed July 23, 2013.
7. Maag, Christopher, "New push to capture woman in '73 Killing of state trooper," *NY Times*, May 2, 2013. http://www.nytimes.com/2013/05/03/nyregion/chesimard-sought-in-new-jersey-turnpike-killing-is-put-on-fbis-most-wanted-list.html?_r=0. Accessed March 12, 2014.
8. Ford, Glenn, "Defend Assata, Defend Ourselves the Black Is Black Coalition," *Black Agenda Report,* May 3, 2013. http://www.blackagendareport.com/content/defend-assata-defend-ourselves-black-black-coalition-rallies-harlem. Accessed May 30, 2013.
9. Assata Shakur in Her Own Words: Rare Recording of Activist Named to FBI Most Wanted Terrorist List, *Democracy Now,* May 2, 2013. http://www.democracynow.org/blog/2013/5/2/ex_black_panther_assata_shakur_added_to_fbis_most_wanted_terrorist_list

Index

38920709R00166

Made in the USA
Middletown, DE
30 December 2016